Nation, Empire, Decline

CLASSICAL INTER/FACES

Series editors: Susanna Braund and Paul Cartledge

Celebrity in the Ancient World:
From Media Tarts to Tabloid Queens
Robert Garland

Gender and the Interpretation of Classical Myth
Lillian E. Doherty

The Delusions of Invulnerability:
Wisdom and Morality in Ancient Greece, China and Today
G.E.R. Lloyd

Lucretius and the Modern World
W.R. Johnson

Nation, Empire, Decline:
Studies in Rhetorical Continuity from the Romans
to the Modern Era
Nancy Shumate

Pity Transformed
David Konstan

Plato's Progeny
Melissa Lane

Radical Theatre
Rush Rehm

Rome and the Literature of Gardens
Victoria Emma Pagán

Translating Words, Translating Cultures
Lorna Hardwick

The Tragic Idea
Vassilis Lambropoulos

NATION, EMPIRE, DECLINE

Studies in Rhetorical Continuity from the Romans to the Modern Era

Nancy Shumate

Duckworth

First published in 2006 by
Gerald Duckworth & Co. Ltd.
90-93 Cowcross Street, London EC1M 6BF
Tel: 020 7490 7300
Fax: 020 7490 0080
inquiries@duckworth-publishers.co.uk
www.ducknet.co.uk

A catalogue record for this book is available
from the British Library

ISBN-10: 0 7156 3551 4
ISBN-13: 978 0 7156 3551 3

Typeset by e-type, Liverpool
Printed and bound in Great Britain by
CPI Bath

Contents

Acknowledgements 6

Introduction 7

1. Them and Us: Constructing Romanness in the *Satires*
   of Juvenal 19

2. Augustan Nation-Building and Horace's 'Roman'
   Odes (3.2, 3.5, 3.6) 55

3. Tacitus and the Rhetoric of Empire 81

4. 'Crazy Egypt' and Colonial Discourse in Juvenal's
   Fifteenth Satire 129

Notes 159

Works Cited 177

Index 187

Acknowledgements

I would like to express my thanks to the series editors and especially to Susanna Braund, who provided continuous support and advice from the time the draft first crossed her desk. At Duckworth, Deborah Blake was a model of editorial efficiency and good sense.

I am grateful to Smith College for granting me sabbatical time for work on the book, especially during the academic year of 2002-3. As always, the project could not have been completed without the daily support of the staff of Neilson Library, especially the Interlibrary Loan department headed by Christina Ryan. Mary Bellino compiled the index and offered copyediting help above and beyond the call of duty.

These essays have taken shape over a number of years, during which they were presented in various forms to audiences at a number of institutions and conferences. These include Dartmouth College, Stanford University, and the University of Hamburg, as well as annual meetings of the Classical Association of the United Kingdom (at the Universities of Manchester and Warwick), the Classical Association of the Atlantic States (in New York City), and the American Philological Association (in Chicago). I am indebted to those in attendance at these events who provided useful comments and criticism. Special thanks are due to Tamar Mayer for her guidance in the literature of modern nationalism.

A version of Chapter 2 originally appeared in *Helios* (32.1 [2005] 81-107) under the title 'Gender and Nationalism in Horace's "Roman" Odes'. I am grateful to the editors of that journal for permission to print a revised version of that article here.

N.S.

Introduction

The often overlapping discourses of nationalism and imperialism, along with ideas of social decline that are frequently bound up with them, have been central in nineteenth- and twentieth-century Anglo-European world construction. Indeed, they are often regarded as the signature discourses of the era, whose social, political, and economic realities alone (it is thought) could have given rise to them at all. This book offers four close readings of Latin literary texts to show that in fact the templates for these 'modern' discourses were forged in their essentials by the early Roman Imperial period. Each chapter follows the relevant rhetorical thread in works of Horace, Tacitus, or Juvenal, comparing their strategies with the defining features of modern rhetorics of nationalism or imperialism and its secondary formation, colonialism.[1] What can be discerned in each case are interlocking sets of general rhetorical principles which are remarkably persistent from antiquity to our era in spite of radical differences in the historical circumstances under which particular articulations of them were produced.

To many this claim will no doubt appear uncontroversial, yet it flies in the face of views now widely established as axiomatic among scholars of modern Europe. In this sector the birth of the European nation-state and the development of nationalist ideology are regarded as inseparable and unique features of modernity, necessarily linked to the growth of industrial capitalism, the rise of the bourgeoisie, the spread of democracy, and the ascendancy of mass media and mass culture. Anthony Smith, the prominent scholar of modern nationalism, has called the insistence on these connections 'the modernist orthodoxy'. From its various strains he extracts two basic premises: that nation-states, nationalist ideologies, and ideas of national identity are all modern, 'both recent in date and novel in character'; and that furthermore 'nations and nationalisms are the

7

product of modernization and modernity' (2000: 27-8, emphasis mine). Surveying the main proponents of this view, Smith notes that they reject 'any form of "retrospective nationalism" ' on the grounds that it '[imports] ideas and concepts from the modern into earlier epochs' (51). Adherents to the 'modernist orthodoxy' are in some fairly distinguished company, which includes Ernest Gellner, Eric Hobsbawm, and Benedict Anderson. While there is some variation in their orientation, emphases, and precise cause-and-effect proposi-tions, they are united in the view that 'it is the modern, professionalized state, powered by capitalism and industrialism, that has been responsible for the rise and spread of nations and nation-alism' (Smith 2000: 30).

A similar conflation of its modern incarnations with the generic phenomenon has characterized definitions of imperialism formulated by those who study its later forms. Webster summarizes the current conventional wisdom in the following way:

> [F]or many historians, 'imperialism' is a modern phenomenon, the rise of Europe to world hegemony ..., which began *c.* 1400 ... . Furthermore, for some theorists, particularly those on the left who understand imperialism to be the globalization of the capitalist mode of production, imperialism has only properly existed for the last one hundred and fifty years.
>
> 1996a: 2

This 'leftist' understanding of imperialism as an advanced (and espe-cially decadent) form of capitalism originated with the writings of the British anti-imperialist economist J.A. Hobson (*Imperialism*, 1902) and V.I. Lenin's *Imperialism, the Highest Stage of Capitalism* (1916). In this view the force that drives imperialistic expansion, properly defined, is capitalism's modes of production and its unquenchable thirst for new markets, new fields for investment and new sources of raw materials. Under this definition the policies of the Roman state were not imperialistic, strictly speaking, even in the period of its greatest acquisition of provinces and client states in the middle and late Republic, because the Roman economy was pre-capitalist, agrarian, and lacking in excess production. Even scholars who lean less heavily on Marxist criteria insist that systematic domination and exploitation, chiefly in an economic sense, are central to any definition of true imperialism, which then can only be dated to the late nineteenth century. As Ashcroft et al. put it, 'there is general agreement that ... "imperialism", as a conscious and openly advocated policy of acquiring colonies for economic, strategic, and political advantage, did not emerge until around 1880' (2000: 122).

Many classicists and Roman historians have reproduced and perpetuated the modernists' stress on a qualitative difference between more recent forms of nationalism and imperialism and anything that has gone before. Thus Katharine Toll, for example, in a fine article on the role of the *Aeneid* in forging a new Roman national identity to unite Romans and Italians after the Social Wars, feels obliged to issue the following disclaimer: 'I use "nation" and "nationalism" here aware that the Roman entities differ from modern ones both in the mechanics of their formation and in the nature of their coherence, and without meaning to assimilate the two' (1997: 34 n. 1). She then directs readers to Anderson's *Imagined Communities* for theoretical background on modern nation-formation, while steering those interested in 'first-century Roman notions of "nationalism"' to the studies of Bonjour and Miles. Of course the distinction she makes is not wrong, but the fact that it seems necessary indicates the extent to which this particular discourse of difference has established itself among scholars of antiquity and modernity alike as an orthodoxy from which any deviation must be explained. (It should be noted that Toll, having made her disclaimer, proceeds in the rest of the article to apply 'nation', 'national identity', and related terms to Rome as if they were self-evidently appropriate.)

Likewise many historians of Rome have sought, in Webster's words, to 'place clear water between the Roman Empire and "imperialism"' (1996a: 2). These historians are influenced at least in part by an awareness that 'the concept of imperialism as systematic domination, and the Marxist conflation of imperialism with the development of monopoly capitalism in the nineteenth century'

(Webster 1996a: 2) have come to be widely accepted as what is meant by the categorical term 'imperialism'. Hence their sense that it is important for them to intervene in any easy assumptions that the *imperium Romanum* conformed to these patterns.[2] Webster (2-4) goes on to discuss the various shades of resistance on the part of Roman historians to the drawing of parallels between modern empires and Rome's, touching on the work of Freeman (1996), Millett (1990), and Woolf (1990), among others. The recent volume of Hurst and Owen, whose essays interrogate the validity of analogies between ancient and modern patterns of colonization, represents a variation on this position.

To be sure, the idea of the singularity of modern nations and empires has had its detractors. Smith discusses the work of scholars whose responses together comprise a 'perennialist critique' of the dominant view of nations and nationalism (2000: 34-50). As usual this school has several branches, but the proponents of the one that is most relevant here, 'recurrent perennialism', insist that the nation is 'a transhistorical phenomenon, recurring in many periods and continents, irrespective of economic, political, or cultural conditions'; Armstrong's *Nations Before Nationalism* is a notable example of scholarship based on this premise. According to perennialist critics, as Smith explains, '[p]articular nations, national identities and even nationalisms may come and go, but the phenomenon itself is universal and, as a form of association and collective identity, disembedded'. Regardless of variations in their understanding of details, perennialists are united in attacking

> ... modernist historiography, which is generally the preserve of modern historians, for its historical shallowness; its narrowly modernist definitions of the nation and nationalism; [and] its preoccupation with citizenship, capitalism, and other facets of modernization ...
>
> 2000: 34-5

Similarly, some scholars have pushed back against narrow definitions of imperialism that codify conditions unique to modernity, especially the economic exploitation associated with unfettered capitalism, as the *sine qua non*. William Harris, for example, in his magisterial study of Roman expansion during the Republic, makes this point:

> Writers who artificially redefine imperialism as such-and-such, prove to their own satisfaction that Rome's expansion was not a case of such-and-such, and therefore was not imperialism, have proved only what all Roman historians have long known: that Roman imperialism was not identical with any imperialism of the nineteenth or twentieth century.
>
> 1979: 4

Earlier, in the immediate aftermath of the First World War, the economist J.A. Schumpeter had famously disputed arguments like those of Hobson and Lenin that imperialism proper could only be a function of industrial capitalism. For Schumpeter it was the opposite, a vestige of the primitive aggression of highly militarized pre-industrial societies; imperialism was thus in fact anti-modern and an obstacle to modern progress, economic and otherwise. His definition of imperialism is simple, and general enough to include many historically contingent variations: it is 'the objectless disposition on the part of a state to unlimited forcible expansion' (1951: 7). For their part, and for what their claims are worth, generations of British imperialists themselves certainly saw continuities between the Roman imperial project and their own as they invoked Rome as a paradigm and enlisted classical literature in the rationalization of their own empire-building.[3]

No one would argue that 'Rome' was a nation-state of the kind that began to develop in Europe in the eighteenth century, or that the motivations behind its territorial expansion and the methods it used to spread its influence, if not establish its control, were identical in every particular to those of the later European imperial powers. Still, to be a Roman and specifically to be a Roman citizen anywhere in the empire involved sharing a cohesive political and cultural identity with other 'Romans', even if that identity was inflected by local

11

colouring. This common sense of identity was moreover bound up with an allegiance to the Roman state, regardless of one's geographical or ethnic origins; in this respect it is true that it was perhaps more akin to the American experience of national identity than to traditional European senses of the same. Furthermore, from the fourth century BC onward, the Romans clearly practised imperialism as defined by Schumpeter, or by Harris ('the behaviour by which a state or people takes and retains supreme power over other states or peoples or lands'), not to say by common sense.[4] No one would argue that the ancient and modern worlds are not radically different places and that in studying antiquity we should not be very cautious about assimilating the former to the latter, always conscious of the anachronism that can result from casting ancient cultures in familiar terms and not taking them on their own. But this caution should not blind us to common threads where they do exist. Harris's observation captures the determination of historians of the modern to deny common ground by simply describing modern articulations of nationalism or imperialism and then arbitrarily equating these descriptions with general definitions, rather than understanding them as variations on a theme.

The persistence of the themes is especially evident if we turn our attention away from the particular social, political, and economic institutions of actual 'nations' and 'empires' in different periods (that is, the variations), and instead direct it to the rhetorical systems that have constructed national identities and represented and justified imperial projects, broadly defined, from Greco-Roman antiquity to the present day. From this perspective it becomes clear that these systems rely on generic rhetorical principles, which over time have adapted themselves to a wide range of historically specific enactments of nationalism and imperialism. Webster makes this distinction when she is careful to note that in the papers included in *Roman Imperialism: Post-Colonial Perspectives*, 'what are compared are not "colonialisms" but the discourses which enable colonialism ...' (1996a: 9); likewise Ashcroft et al. distinguish between 'imperial rhetoric' and 'imperial representation' on the one hand and specific imperial practices on the other (2000: 126).[5] A similar distinction can be made between the discourses that construct national identities and the nation as an abstraction, and the concrete features of individual nations and nation-states as specific kinds of political, social, and economic units. It is the rhetorical constants more than any practices that are the subject of this book, and indeed one of its points is that *in spite of* the many and profound differences between Roman and modern ways of enacting national and imperial projects, certain key strains in the ideological and discursive infrastructures are remarkably durable. A book that asks the reader to consider how deeply rooted these ways of thinking are in the Western, if not the human, imagination may be especially timely in view of the resurgence of divisive nationalist impulses and the pursuit of neo-colonial enterprises in our world today.

There has been a great deal of work in recent years on Roman national identity and imperial ideology, a good sampling of which will be cited in what follows. Among the authors of these studies will be a large number who, unlike most modern historians, will need no persuading that Roman and later incarnations of 'nationalism' and 'imperialism' are different points on the same genealogy. This is evident in the fact that classicists routinely speak of 'Roman national identity' as if it were an unproblematic concept – even, in the end, Toll with her dutiful disclaimer, as we have seen (see also, for example, Toll 1991; Gruen 1995; Syed 2004). It is evident especially in the work of critics who apply elements of post-colonial theory developed from and for modern texts to Greek and Latin 'colonial' literature and thus implicitly posit the generic character of colonial discourse, wherever it may appear.[6] What will be new here for classicists is the systematic rhetorical analysis of several important Latin 'nationalist' and 'colonialist' texts as such, along with an explicit concern with tracing the lines of continuity between Roman and later European articulations of these discourses. Other studies of ideas of Romanness and the Roman rhetoric of empire, even those informed by an awareness of modern theory, tend to read backwards and sideways, so to speak: their primary interest is in establishing the background and contemporary context of these discourses as they appear in given Latin texts. This one, on the other hand, reads forward, shifting the focus away from the sources of the tropes and conventions that feed into the Roman versions of these discourses and directing it toward where they seem to be going. In this respect the book should serve as a useful complement to existing related work.

In addition, by concentrating mainly on what might be called the dominant discourses in the texts examined here, I am consciously putting aside the 'reading against the grain' approach now established in Latin literary studies, which focuses on subtexts that seem to complicate and undermine the overt signification of the text. Such readings have their place, but they also have a depoliticizing effect that lets classical antiquity off the hook for some of its more pernicious inventions. Charles Martindale makes this point about the 'two voices' tradition of reading the *Aeneid* going back to Adam Parry, which foregrounds the note of melancholy and loss that accompanies Aeneas' fulfilment of his mission. Far from interrogating the imperial project, Martindale argues, such an element could be read as amounting to a 'subtle *apologia* for Empire', more effective in some ways than cruder propaganda. 'Such accounts,' he continues, 'trivialize the *Aeneid* by refusing to take it seriously as a massively influential ideological vehicle' (1993: 42). By almost any measure the *Aeneid* is in a class by itself, and as it happens there will be ample occasion in the chapters below for consideration of ambiguity, internal critiques, self-deconstructing texts and related matters. The general point, however, still stands.

Finally, I would like to clarify some of the limitations of this study. First, it makes no claim to original scholarship on colonial or nationalist discourses per se. For its conception of the shapes that these have assumed in their modern articulations, it relies primarily on some of the more important and/or synoptic studies out of the many produced in these fields in recent years. The rhetorical strategies of nineteenth- and twentieth-century nationalism and imperialism/colonialism are already well understood. The book's contribution is in writing Rome into these studies in a way that lengthens their perspective and invites reformulation of some of their basic assumptions. This is also a good place to acknowledge that since its birth

14

with Said's *Orientalism* in 1978, colonial discourse analysis has undergone a series of shifts away from his conception of a monolithic and inflexible binary system of representation that exercises a tyrannical power over colonizer and (especially) colonized alike; in other words, away from Said's 'static model of colonial relations', in Loomba's words (1998: 49). Such a model, goes the critique, robs the colonized of agency and perpetuates rather than dismantles the power structures of colonialism. 'Colonial discourse studies today,' observes Loomba, 'are not restricted to delineating the workings of power – they have tried to locate ... oppositions, resistances, and revolts ...' (51).[7] Cannadine begins his book in the same vein with an overview of the backlash against *Orientalism* and derivative studies, noting how they have been criticized for 'ignoring the extent to which empire was about collaboration and consensus as well as about conflict and coercion' (2001: xvi).

Correctives have alternately stressed the gap between rhetoric and reality; manipulation of and resistance to the system on the part of the colonized; and the complexity and dynamism of actual interactions in colonial situations. Attention has also been drawn to the contradictions, fissures, and weaknesses in the discourse of the colonizer itself. In a sense Roman social historians participate in this revision when they interpret Romanization as creative cultural exchange (for example, Woolf 1998; MacMullen 2000), or analyse the processes through which Roman imperial ideology came to be accepted and internalized by provincial subjects all over the empire – how provincials, in other words, actively consented in their own subordination (Ando). But my aim here is not to reconstruct social history or to examine how the gap between cultural discourse and social reality was negotiated. Once again, I want to go back to the discourses themselves, in the belief that their Roman articulations have never been fully appreciated as such or systematically unpacked as a first step in following how they played out on the ground, so to speak. But in the end, in spite of the academic distinction being made here, I recognize that rhetoric and reality are inextricably bound up with one another, as Alcock and Morrison contend in their discussion of imperial ideologies:

15

> Much previous scholarship ... tended to treat the ideological
> realm as epiphenomenal to the 'real' facts behind processes of
> empire-building and social domination .... What we suggest ...
> is that there can be no simple divide between mental and
> material ...
>
> 2001: 279-80

Ultimately, there is no such thing as 'mere' rhetoric: it means something, it has consequences in the real world.

A final word on the selection of texts. This book is in no way intended to be an exhaustive or comprehensive treatment of the subject. Furthermore, the particular texts chosen for analysis are seen as more representative than unique; they comprise a subset of a larger pool of texts that could have been enlisted to demonstrate the same or related continuities (including Greek predecessors, with their inscription of the discourses of Athenian imperialism and ethnic identity). Such a selection is inevitably subjective, and there are some obvious omissions: Cicero, Caesar, and Virgil come immediately to mind as potentially rich repositories of these themes, and in fact they have received attention in this connection, though without the parallel reading of modern texts.[8] The satires of Juvenal will strike some as an idiosyncratic choice for such a project, with their complicating necessity of sorting out author from satiric *persona*.[9] In fact they are unusually instructive, inasmuch as we get in one text both nationalist or colonialist discourse and its critique; moreover the discourse, which is my focus, is both crystalline in its reductiveness and otherwise unrecoverable, representing as it does a voice not heard elsewhere in extant Latin literature. The nationalism of the Juvenalian speaker also serves as a complement to that of the 'Roman' Odes, the former apparently visceral and spontaneous, the latter a case study in Hobsbawm's idea of nationalism as social engineering by elites involved in the conscious formulation and marketing of a nationalist programme. Likewise, turning to colonial discourse, Juvenal's speaker, who is constructed as marginal by the poet, balances the 'establishment' voice of Tacitus, and the relatively short poem into which his colonialist assumptions are packed stands against the sweep of the Tacitean corpus. In short, the selection represents variety and range on a number of levels in spite of its modest scale. I hope that my observations will encourage others to add to it.

1

Them and Us: Constructing Romanness
in the *Satires* of Juvenal

The true Roman and his bête(s) noire(s)

Recent Juvenal criticism has tended to focus on the relationship
between poet and dramatic *persona*, and the extent to which the
views of the author and the speakers he creates correspond or
diverge. In this chapter I would like to revisit the rhetoric on the
surface of the texts, that is, the words and ideas assigned to Juvenal's
speakers. At this level the poems preserve, albeit in an indirect way,
the otherwise lost voice of a Roman 'silent majority' that had its own
ideas about what constituted Romanness, ideas at variance with official discourses of assimilation and 'naturalized' citizenship. Here,
the construction of national identity is an almost entirely negative
project, organized around the fabrication of an enemy, or enemies, of
Romanness against whom the beleaguered male native – usually the
main speaker of the poem – can define and stabilize his own precarious sense of self. 'True' Romanness, in other words, is articulated
less as a positive assertion of who 'we' are and what 'we' stand for
than as a defensive declaration of who 'we' are not, and what 'we'
stand against. These poems plunge the reader into a Manichean
world where the 'real' Roman finds himself beset on all sides by
upstart foreigners disrupting his once secure place in the social hierarchy and greedily claiming his traditional entitlements. The native
experiences the world very much in terms of 'us' and 'them'; for him,
the human race consists of two hostile camps: people like him, and
everyone else.

It is how this latter group is imagined that will concern us, in
particular how the array of actually distinct 'Others' against whom

the native situates himself is (to use a term of Mosse to which we will return) 'homogenized' in the speaker's rhetoric in such a way that differences among them are blurred and they are all imagined as embodying the same essential complex of threats. The details of this process demonstrate how anxieties about gender and sexuality can drive nationalist discourses: feminization is the glue that holds together the composite Other looming so large in the speaker's fevered imagination. The construction of an enemy of Romanness that he so desperately needs to rationalize his own failures hinges on an articulation of the categories of ethnicity, gender, and class that renders all 'outsiders' essentially the same and functionally inter-changeable. Standing against the alien threat that they collectively represent is the normative male native, the 'true' Roman who cham-pions lost traditional values (when they benefit him) and imagines himself a model of reason, moderation, and good sense in a world gone mad.

In a general sense, the rhetorical interchangeability of the figures opposing and thus defining community identities and cultural ideals was established and ubiquitous in classical antiquity, going back to the binarism of woman/barbarian/slave/*cinaedus* (sexually deviant man) versus free male citizen that structured so much of Athenian thinking. In recent years classicists have profitably mined the vein of 'othering' studies first opened by Said with his *Orientalism* in 1978, and their work often exposes the operation of some variation of this 'homogenizing' principle and its misogynistic underpinnings in Greek and Latin texts of various orders.[1] What we see in Juvenal, who has not figured prominently in these studies, is a pivotal junc-ture in the development of the discourse, when it begins to split off into one of its characteristically modern uses as the blunt instrument in the hammering out of a particular kind of national identity. Moreover when we read Juvenal we experience that hammering first-hand by virtue of being forced to share subject positions with the sort of man who processes the claims of the rhetoric not as abstract truths or cultural givens but as visceral emotional responses. But in general, whether the texts are ancient or modern, the focus of 'othering' studies has increasingly shifted from identifying how ideology controls representation to looking for signs of resistance on the part of those who bear the burden of negative representation, or in texts whose apparent endorsement of the dominant discourse can be read as being undercut by irony.[2] Much recent scholarship on Juvenal mirrors this larger trend in assuming a gap between the poet and the speaking character that he creates and in foregrounding the critique of the speaker's discourse that materializes in that gap. My focus is on the structures of the discourse itself, and on the ways in which the words of Juvenal's speakers forcefully articulate a rhetorical scheme usually associated with modern nationalist ideology of a certain stripe, and in particular how they anticipate with remarkable closeness some of the modern era's more pernicious forms of nationalist othering.

Critics have often noted that Juvenal's speaker, at least in the earlier satires, is a reactionary, a 'redneck' in a toga.[3] None, however, has followed up by analyzing the speaker's reactionary rhetoric systematically or by demonstrating how well worked out its strategies of exclusion and self-definition are. I have chosen four poems especially suited to this purpose: 1 and 3, both panoramic overviews of the causes of the speaker's alienation in the increasingly foreign city of Rome; 2, which deals with male gender and sex deviants; and 6, the famous broadside against women. Each of these screeds is delivered by a variation of what Braund (1996a) calls the 'angry satirist': 1, 2, and 6 by an unnamed speaker usually identified in the past with the poet himself; and 3, for the most part, by this speaker's friend, there called Umbricius. Together these poems 'star' the three groups – foreigners, women, and (in modern terms) 'homosexuals' – that the speaker shakes up and blends into the composite Other, the national enemy who threatens to overwhelm the dwindling ranks of 'real' Roman men.[4] While it is only in 1 and 3 that the collapse of Romanness and the marginalization of its true vessels are articulated as explicit issues, these poems (along with the other two of Book 1) can be read as a continuous text unfurling a continuous, incremental characterization of the generic 'angry' speaker who unifies them all. Each poem reveals a different corner of his store of prejudices and grievances, and together they comprise a complete characterization of the type – a complete psychology, one might say – so that attitudes expressed in one poem may be imported as subtext into another. The misogyny that courses through his attack on women (6), for example, is the same misogyny that shapes his representation of male sex deviants and foreigners in 1, 2, and 3. I will begin by examining the salient features in the speaker's representation of each of the three groups in turn, noting in particular how these features are shared from group to group: whichever of the three demonized Others he is explicitly targeting at any given moment, in the speaker's world, they are always the same person.

In antiquity as in the modern world, feminization is the baseline from which any refinements of national enemy construction proceed. For that reason it makes sense to begin with women and with traits perceived as female. Misogyny did not begin with Juvenal, of course; the stereotypes of feminine vice catalogued in Satire 6 have a long history in Greek and Roman culture and go back in literature to Hesiod's portrait of the first woman (*Works and Days* 60-105; *Theogony* 570-612). But here, Juvenal embeds the old stereotypes in a larger discourse of the Roman and the not-Roman in a way that prefigures more closely later uses to which they have been put in gendered constructions of ideal national types and anti-types. The charges that his speaker lobs against women in this poem establish the main terms upon which his characterization of foreigners in the more overtly nationalist satires (1 and 3) is also built. These charges can be gathered under the general heading of absence of self-control, traditionally the fundamental flaw in women and the one from which their other deficiencies stem. The speaker claims that women are by nature slaves to the senses, helpless to control their lust and given to drunkenness, materialism, and all manner of irrational impulses. The poem opens with several memorable *exempla* of female sexual excess: the 'groupies' at the theatre who live for glimpses, and more, of their favourite actors and dancers and who respond to every performance with public and audible sexual arousal (60-81); the aristocratic lady Eppia whose addiction to her gladiator lover leads her to abandon her husband and children (82-113); and the empress Messalina, the royal whore (*meretrix Augusta*) driven by lust to slum as a working girl in the brothels of Rome (114-32).[5]

The speaker uses the crudest and most graphic terms to pin on women a primal sexual insatiability and an utter lack of control over animal urges: 'Is one man enough for Hiberina?' (*unus Hiberinae vir sufficit?*, 53); Messalina 'goes home worn out by men but still not satisfied' (*lassata viris necdum satiata recessit*, 130); Tuccia is unable to control her bladder whenever the effeminate dancer Bathyllus appears on stage (*molli saltante Bathyllo | Tuccia vesicae non imperat*, 63-4). Especially significant for our purposes is the consistent characterization of the men toward whom these aristocratic ladies gravitate as lower-class, foreign, and/or effeminate; the women's primary transgressions of promiscuity and adultery are thus compounded by the inappropriateness of their objects of desire. Furthermore, in linking Roman women to effeminate foreign habitués of the urban demimonde, the speaker bundles together in one stroke all the imagined enemies of normative male Romanness. Also noteworthy (throughout, but especially at 60-81) is the coding of the theatre (*spectacula*, 61) not only as the quintessential transgressive space, a site that invites the flouting of sexual and class conventions (the farm girl Thymele begins her education in depravity there, 66), but also as an emblem of female artifice in general.[6] But even sacred rites – those of the Bona Dea, for example (314-51) – are only a pretext for the unleashing of alcohol-fuelled female lust, described again in the coarsest terms: their 'itch' (*prurigo*) goads the 'worshippers' to shriek 'bring in the men!' and they will settle for anything male they can get their hands on.

The speaker's indictment expands to include charges of material extravagance (149-57, the wife who impoverishes her husband with her demands for luxuries; 352-65, the woman whose expensive tastes drive her to spend beyond her means); superstition (511-91, women's devotion to astrology and foreign cults, often orgiastic); and gratuitous cruelty, especially toward slaves (219-23; 475-95). These tendencies exemplify the speaker's larger claim that women are strangers to reason in all its forms. At their worst they are driven by greed and lust to be murderers: the *mater familias* could be slipping poison to unsuspecting family members (133-5; 610-61). The suggestion here and elsewhere that the face presented by a woman in public is not to be trusted surfaces explicitly at 268-78, where the speaker accuses women of resorting to manipulation and melodrama to get what they want: they are, in a word, born performers to whom duplicity and deception are as natural as breathing. Thus a wife feigning jealousy to hide her own affairs pretends (*simulat*, 271) to weep, invents a mistress (*ficta paelice*, 272) to throw in her husband's face, and has an uncanny ability to keep her ever-ready supply of tears in check or to allow them to flow according to the needs of the situation (*uberibus semper lacrimis semperque paratis /in statione sua atque expectantibus illam / quo iubeat manare modo*, 273-5). For her, acting is a way of life.

The speaker's rage in the sixth satire is inexhaustible and extreme. Its verisimilitude deepens when we read it, with Johnson 1996, as panic about a perceived crisis in Roman masculinity displaced onto women, which would further connect it to the core issues of the first three satires as well as to the driving force behind much reactionary nationalist posturing in the modern world. Satire 6 is by far the most sustained attack on any of the three out-groups in Juvenal's corpus.[7] As such it offers a degree of detail and elaboration that the reader is left to supply in the case of the other two groups, cued by a system of associations that bind all three together. With the template so clearly laid out in connection with 'real' women, the reading of male gender outlaws and foreigners as virtual women – the worst thing a speaker like this could call other men – is an easy step. In Satire 2 his indignation is directed at men who present themselves in public as paragons of the manly virtue of the ancients, while in private carrying on like the drag queens and pathics that they really are. Duplicity – coded as 'female' both traditionally and in Satire 6 – thus figures prominently among the vices imputed to this out-group as well. The speaker even makes a lame attempt (15-19) to claim that he feels something like compassion for the honest, open *cinaedus*, implying that the real issue for him is the hypocrisy of the 'stern-faced perverts' (*tristes obsceni*, 8), but this gesture does nothing to mitigate the palpable horror at their

24

assumed sexual practices and at male effeminacy in general that he
betrays throughout the poem. The allegation of lack of transparency,
of lack, in a sense, of reality, is an important move in the assimilation
of male 'homosexuals' and women, as Winkler (169-70) recognizes
when he notes, '[t]he *frontis nulla fides*' (there's no trusting appearances, 2.8) '... of Satire 2, might as well be applied to women'. The
charge appears again in Juvenal's other satire with a 'homosexual'
theme (9) in connection with the poser Virro who masquerades as a
respectable family man but hires Naevolus to service him on the side.

The speaker's discourse implicates this group in 'female' sexual
excess *ipso facto*; their sexual proclivities – playing the 'girl', relinquishing agency – would in themselves constitute in his mind a
rejection of the male prerogatives of control (of self and others) and
bodily integrity. To strengthen the link, he imagines in the 'homo-
phobic' Satire 2 a scene of orgiastic excess that is parallel to the
women's bacchanal at 6.314-51. Both events involve the abuse of a
legitimate religious rite as a cover for depravity; both, in other words,
are pointedly presented as travesties of a 'real' thing. The men's bash
(2.83-116) features mincing drag queens, much fussing over extravagant hair-dos, costumes, and make-up, free-flowing wine, and more
than a hint of sexual hanky-panky. The foregrounding of exaggerated
'female' behaviour in this scene reduces to the level of stylized
gesture the comprehensive embrace of role reversal that is at the
heart of this group's offences against the proper sex and gender order
(likewise Creticus and his swishy comportment in court, complete
with see-through frock, 65-78). As if to confirm his angry speaker's
suspicions of collusion between these two groups and their identification with one another in his mind, Juvenal brings them together at
6.O1-34, where the lady of the house is in cahoots with the phalanx
of effeminate live-in retainers (*turpes similesque cinaedis*, O3).
Together they conspire to conceal the wife's affairs from her duped
husband, all the while polluting his household with their unclean
habits. But appearances cannot be trusted here either: these men
make their way in life by playing roles, wearing a mask (*persona*,
O26), and the more effeminate (*mollior*) they appear, the more virile
they will prove in bed (O23-5). Thus we have the paradox of the

'adulterer in a hair-net' (*reticulatus adulter*, O22), the effeminate womanizer whose apparently contradictory halves are unified in the logic of this discourse through the trope of 'female' excess. This figure is reconstituted in the feminized Jewish man of modern European anti-Semitism, who is simultaneously imagined as effeminate and as a sexual threat to Gentile women.[8]

Ultimately the feminizing rhetorical net pulls in foreigners, or at least some of them, as the traditional gendered opposition between the rationally ordered male subject and 'female' excess is projected onto cultural encounters. It is no surprise that the 'feminized colonial Others' of Juvenal's *Satires* are all from the East, which had been identified in the Greek cultural imagination with 'feminine' luxury, lack of self-restraint, and sexual ambiguity as early as 472 BC with the production of Aeschylus' *Persians*. Perhaps the most schematic Roman appropriation of the terms of this Orientalizing rhetoric is in Augustus' propaganda against Cleopatra, which itself was engaged in the project of constructing a national enemy, though in that instance on the level of governmental 'party line' (see Chapter 4, p. 145). In Satires 1 and 3, Juvenal's edgy panoramas of life in the dog-eat-dog world of the multicultural metropolis, foreigners take the brunt of the speaker's wrath, and he naturally relies on inherited stereotypes in his characterization of immigrants from the East, though his voice and his perspective are distinctive. Egyptians, Syrians, Greeks – they are all the same to him, upstarts and parvenus encroaching on his rightful territory: the Egyptian-born nouveau riche freedman Crispinus with his effeminate gestures and conspicuous consumption (on a hot summer day he hitches up his purple mantle and ventilates his fingers, sweaty with gold rings, exclaiming ostentatiously that he can't bear to wear his larger gems in such weather, 1.26-30); another freedman, another budding capitalist, this one born on the banks of the Euphrates, marked out by his unmanly earrings (*molles ... in aure fenestrae*, 1.104) and flaunting new money, elbowing poor deserving natives like the speaker out of the dole line (1.102-9); and especially the 'hungry little Greek' (*Graeculus esuriens*, 3. 78) of Satire 3 (69-125). Whereas the salient traits of the first two are their effeminate comportment and

26

crass materialism, which would imply their guilt of other 'female' vices such as lasciviousness as well, the Greek is feminized through the stress on his lechery and the speaker's insistence that duplicity is instinctive to his mode of operation. The *Graeculus* is a scheming, shameless, smooth-talking flatterer, a calculating chameleon who will say anything and play any part to achieve his ends, a master of artifice from a nation of natural actors (*natio comoeda est*, 3.100).

The principle of substitution that governs the conceptualization of these groups becomes very clear if we imagine them classified in three adjacent columns, whose constituent terms can be moved around with no damage to the system's basic structure. Thus, women are, in several senses, sex and gender deviants, as well as xenophiles and class traitors; male sex and gender deviants are 'female', as well as xenophiles and class traitors; and foreigners are also 'female', as well as sex and gender deviants and class transgressors. Apart from their alleged sexual excess, the very fact of being female marks women as gender outlaws, in the reading of the female as deficient male that goes back to Aristotle and seems to lurk pervasively in Satire 6.[9] So does their practice of brazenly intruding into male realms: the lawcourts (6.242-4, the litigious woman); intellectual circles (6.434-56); politics and public affairs (6.398-412); and athletics (6.246-67). The transgressive women in the last two passages are explicitly coded as 'unnatural', the quintessential exclusionary move that links them further with male 'homosexuals' (see below): the mannish political woman's breasts are dry and milkless (*siccis mamillis*, 401), and her attitude is *audax* (399), 'bold', an epithet which, when applied to women, would cue thoughts of a dangerous violation of the natural and social orders; the athletic woman is a 'fugitive from her sex' (*fugit a sexu*, 253).[10] In their efforts to avoid pregnancy (6.366-78, 592-7), women are guilty of this same reckless and deluded resistance to the destiny that nature has assigned them. Their affinity with the foreign is manifested in their attraction to non-native favourites and paramours, as mentioned above; in their superstition and interest in exotic cults (6.511-91, with eunuchs – *semiviri* – as priests, 513); and in their penchant for conversation in Greek, the language of the theatrical counter-culture

27

(6.185-96). These tendencies involve them in mixing at lower levels of the social hierarchy than is seemly for Roman women of a certain class, in the speaker's prim view.

The mix-and-match interchangeability of the three out-groups in the reactionary speaker's mind is further reproduced when he in turn constructs male sex and gender deviants as female in the ways outlined above and relegates them to the extra-normal class of 'freaks' (*monstra*, 2.122; cf. 9.38), thus eliding them further with 'unnatural' women (in both cases the speaker gloats when nature intervenes to impose her limitations and expose the pretence of men playing women and women playing men: 2.137-42; 6.264). Like women, deviant men are also xenophiles (their association with frenzied foreign cult practices, 2.110-16; cf. 9.60-2), and class traitors (the trashy comportment of Creticus in court is entirely inappropriate to his rank, 2.65-78; the downward mobility of the nobly-born Gracchus who, playing the bride, 'marries' a trumpeter, and fights as a gladiator in the arena, 2.117-48 – a display that is also branded 'monstrous', at 143).[11] By the same token, the speaker's calculus feminizes foreigners (see above), which in itself carries the suggestion of the sort of unconventional sexual practices that would simultaneously class them as sex and gender deviants, an identification further confirmed by their sexual omnivorousness (3.109-12), their association with prostitution (3.65), and their freakish ability to impersonate women characters onstage (3.93-7, where the tropes of artifice and gender transgression fuse). Finally, immigrants are the worst class transgressors and the greatest beneficiaries of the social mobility that so distresses the speaker. They have the ambition and the energy to 'make it' in the urban jungle, throwing the traditional social and economic order into confusion and leaving passive and resentful natives like the speaker behind as they pass him on the social ladder (Satires 1 and 3 in toto).

There are several additional features in the characterization of these groups that will be relevant when we come to consider how the structures and tropes of this discourse are recycled in modern projects of national enemy construction. First, the speaker comes close to asserting the essential viciousness of Greeks as a 'race', so to speak, when he says that their despicable behaviour flows from a flaw common to them as a people (*gentis vitio*, 3.121), and that the poison they disseminate has its font in their *natura* (3.123). Second, all three out-groups are consistently linked with criminality. This is sometimes explicit, as it is with the foreigner/Greek, who is implicated in all sorts of shady enterprises in Satire 3, and with women, whose pursuit of material and sexual gratification drives them to commit murders, among other things (6.133-5, 610-61). But the link is always implied by the association of all of them with the city, and by the speaker's habit of indiscriminately mixing them in with 'real' criminals (thieves, forgers, arsonists, assassins, et al.) in his ubiquitous catalogues of anti-types to Roman tradition in Satires 1 and 3. Finally, the imagery of disease and contagion abounds. The physical presence in the body politic of perverts and foreigners in particular is imagined as presenting a threat of contamination to respectable Romans; social difference is conflated with moral disorder and physical disease. The idea of outsiders as carriers of disease is explicitly articulated in Satire 2, where *morbus* (disease) and *contagio* are used to designate transgressive male sexual practices and their potential to infect the general population if not contained (2.17; 78-80: 'infection has brought this disaster and will bring it to more, just as the whole herd dies from contact with the mange of one', *dedit hanc contagio labem / et dabit in plures, sicut grex totus in agris / unius scabie cadit*; cf. 9.49).[12] But the same idea is surely implied in the famous image of immigration from the East as a tide of raw sewage polluting native Roman *mores* (3.61-6).

In his 'angry' satires, then, Juvenal characterizes his speaker as a static figure in a dynamic world, a relic of an old order whom rapid social and economic changes have left behind. His response to these changes is not to adapt himself to them, but rather to claim the high moral ground in a last-ditch effort to stake out his territory against the march of 'modernity'. His aggressive tone and moral righteousness are masks for anxieties about his own identity as a Roman, as a man, and as a client (a non-productive dependent on the largesse of the aristocratic better-off), in a world where the stability of these very categories has begun to slip. This character is a brilliant study of 'othering' as a self-centreed project, as a means of stabilizing one's own self-definition, and of aggressive self-assertion as a cover for deep insecurities: the speaker recognizes at some visceral level that any fluidity in the social, economic, and gender order represents a threat to his own precarious place in it.

The incoherence, not to say hysteria, that is barely hidden behind his superior self-representation illustrates the principle that the affirmation of any authority tends to become shriller the more seriously that authority is contested. Spurr (1993: 121-4) observes this syndrome in colonial discourse when he analyses an editorial published in *Le Monde* during the Algerian crisis, where repeated confident assertions of French authority as self-evidently right correlate directly with the rejection of that authority on the ground. As he writes:

> In theory, a clear and fully present authority ... would never find itself in the position of having to defend itself ... . Once authority begins to be asserted, however, there opens up a split between assertion and authority itself, in which the latter is revealed as conditional and contingent on its representation. Affirmations of authority can now be seen as strategic devices necessary for the maintenance of that authority, rather than as simple manifestations of an unquestioned presence.
>
> 1993: 124

The Juvenalian speaker resorts intuitively to this strategy as he struggles in vain to reassert his traditional position. Everywhere he turns, he feels himself surrounded, assaulted, besieged by the strident, mocking shock troops of the new order. Especially in Satires 1 and 3 with their crowded, noisy, almost claustrophobic scenes of urban movement, but also in the other 'angry' poems (as at 6.312-13, where he empathizes with the humiliation endured by emasculated husbands of liberated women), the reader is given a strong sense of the speaker's alienation as he takes the role of censorious observer while the new world order unfolds, to his dismay, before his eyes. Given his tangled anxieties, it is no accident that he experiences this broad challenge to his values and sensibilities as a threat of sexual violation, as, in contemporary terminology, a homosexual panic attack: he will not, he insists, meekly become *iniquae / ... patiens urbis* (1.30-1), he will not bend over for the wicked city, he will not allow it to make him its bottom.[13]

Integral to the characterization of the 'angry' speaker is a crude nativist voice that asserts itself most explicitly in the first and the third satires. Repeatedly in Satire 3, Umbricius sets the home-grown and the foreign starkly against one another. He punctuates his lament over the creeping Graecization of Rome, a lament replete with a litany of strange cultural practices now to be endured and exotic foreign terms creeping into the mother tongue (60-8), with appeals to the Roman citizens he imagines to be his audience, in the most old-fashioned nomenclature possible (*Quirites, Quirine*). He indiginantly asks whether a childhood on the Aventine hill, nour-ished by Sabine olives, counts for nothing these days when pitted against the ambition of immigrant hustlers (84-5: *usque adeo nihil est quod nostra infantia caelum / hausit Aventini baca nutrita Sabina?*). Here as in Horace's 'Roman' Odes, as we will see, local names, especially any referring to rural regions, are ideologically loaded. Umbricius' binarism is worked out to the level of food names: locally grown olives are set against the imported figs and damsons that the newcomers bring with them (83). He heatedly asserts that there is no longer any place for a Roman (*non est Romano cuiquam locus hic*) where 'Protogenes and Diphilus and Hermarchus' reign supreme (119-20). But the speaker's nativism, so simplistic on the whole, is in certain ways complex and convoluted: in his mind the issue of national identity and its privileges is fused with his anxieties about emasculation and the corrosion of male prerogatives. This pushes the question of national identity into the vexed field of gender and sexuality, and as a result the speaker's foreigners come to double as symbolic women and male sex deviants, and his women and deviant men are cast as internal foreigners, a conspiratorial state within a state. The restoration of the 'nation' becomes identical with the restoration of male authority.[14] Faced with a ubiquitous and protean foe, the speaker can only define

Romanness in negative terms; as Hobsbawm observes in another context, ' "Germany" was more easily defined by what it was against than in any other way' (1994: 82). Juvenal's speaker offers a niggardly, reductive vision of Romanness, one closing in on itself as the real world was becoming larger and in fact more Roman.

Ideals and anti-types in modern nationalism

The *Satires* of Juvenal would scarcely trip off the tongues of scholars of nationalism if they were to cast about for precursors to modern nationalist rhetoric and ideology (a question which, in reality, they would never entertain, believing as they do that these phenomena are *ipso facto* artefacts of modernity). Nor would I myself argue that there is any debt or influence at work here in a strictly genealogical sense, resulting from conscious or unconscious borrowing from generation to generation. But it is clear that there is a generic structure to what is now taken as nationalist discourse, and that much of the essential outline of this structure asserted itself long before the modern era. If we scrutinize the important European nationalisms of the nineteenth and twentieth centuries, we often find as a basis of national self-definition and as a starting-point for the construction of a national enemy the same potent brew of xenophobia and/or (in modern terms) racism and anxieties about masculinity that determined the shape of Juvenal's anti-types to Romanness. Again, a free-floating misogyny is projected onto those perceived as foreign and/or homosexual (in the period that saw the invention of 'homosexual' as a term and as a category of identity), to generate a set of bogeymen whose shared traits make them interchangeable as targets of indignant native wrath in its search for culprits to blame for the critical condition of the national health.[15] One could, in fact, substitute 'Jew' for *Graeculus* (or one of its symbolic equivalents) at various points in the Juvenalian speaker's rants and have something very like the kind of reactionary nationalist tracts that were being cranked out with some regularity in parts of Europe by the late nineteenth century. As was the case earlier, this kind of discourse has also more recently been driven by an anti-modern impulse and couched in a larger critique of contemporary culture that regards all social change as national decline.

By the fin-de-siècle, these and related ideas were widely accepted in Central Europe in particular, owing to their articulation across a variety of cross-fertilizing registers and their dissemination in several mutually reinforcing spheres: science and 'science' (medicine, psychology, anthropology, criminology, physiognomy, characterology, sexology), politics (from mainstream rhetoric to extremist propaganda), and popular culture (fiction, drama, the popular press). Their progress to this point and beyond was, however, gradual; most efforts to date the genesis of their modern European cycle locate the seeds in eighteenth-century intellectual currents.[16] They gained force during the so-called 'conservative revolution' (1890-1933) in Germany, and the rest, as they say, is history.[17] It is important to remember, though, that the 'social fantasies' (Schulte-Sasse's felicitous term) of National Socialism, far from being *sui generis*, are simply the most grotesque permutation of long established ideas, the logical extension of what had gone before. As Schulte-Sasse puts it, the Nazis' utopian visions were built on a 'fantasy structure that [was] not unique to National Socialism but [took] a particularly pathological form in it'. She continues:

> [F]amiliar elements of this structure include [the] perception of a delimited social body, its juxtaposition of an 'inside' constituting community and an 'outside' marked by Otherness ... , its imaginary mastery of the Other, and its projections of social antagonism or harmony onto certain individuals or groups.
>
> 1996: 232

The relevance of this description of a modern ideological system's generic features to the rhetoric of Juvenal's speaker is obvious.

In fact, one could argue that insofar as both Juvenal's *Satires* and Nazi narratives articulate an extreme version of this rhetoric, thus putting its signature moves in high relief, they are better suited for comparison than might at first appear. It is true that Juvenal the poet assigned his speaker an especially reductive form of an apparently current discourse in order to make it a target of satiric scrutiny, while the Nazis and their predecessors embraced the reductive form in dead earnest (and accordingly, it should be remembered, were often taken as a joke in the early years of their ascendency). Both offer reductions to absurdity, the one by critical design, the others insofar as all extremist discourses are *ipso facto* reductive in spite of themselves. 'The paradox of satire,' observes a recent critic, 'is that, by distorting, it brings into focus; by flattening out, it heightens. By being unfair ... it somehow gets at the truth'.[18] The result here in both instances, though it comes through different processes, is a pellucid distillation, a 'focused, heightened' articulation of the discourse's fundamental characteristic features. Clearly we are dealing with two different worlds here. The ancient and modern incarnations of this discourse rode in on very different cultural and historical tides. The latter emerged as a mutant offspring out of movements so seismic – Romanticism and its vestiges, science (and its bastard children – race science, for example), and the revolutions ushered in by Darwin, Nietzsche, and Freud, to name a few; in a word, modernity – that it seems to be the product of those things alone, with no history prior to their convergence. Yet even under seismic shifts there can be lines of continuity reaching back farther, a persistence in the basic mechanics and central tropes of the rhetoric and an elasticity in the structures of thought behind it that allow for adaptation across very different historical circumstances and ideological systems.[19]

There is almost no limit to the material – primary texts and secondary studies – that could be invoked to demonstrate this continuity; here it is only possible to make a beginning, and to suggest further lines of inquiry. Mosse's (1985) analysis of the gendering of nationalism in nineteenth-century Europe provides a useful base from which to proceed. In his discussion of the emergence of national anti-types in this period (in a chapter called 'Race and Sexuality: The Role of the Outsider'), he stresses the importance of ideas of the normal and the abnormal in early psychology as crucial background.[20] Otto Weininger's *Sex and Character* (*Geschlecht und Charakter*), published in Vienna in 1903, was especially influential in

34

the forging of paradigms of normalcy and deviance; although it was not itself concerned with national identity per se, many of its premises found their way into contemporary nationalist discourses.[21] Like other works of this genre, Weininger's treatise worried about an impending collapse of the duality between male and female and the havoc such a collapse would wreak on the culture. He saw the masculine and the feminine principles as the guiding elements in human life; the first was a positive force, productive, moral, and spiritual, the font of culture, while the second was negative, unproductive, and immoral, confined to the level of physical impulse.[22]

Weininger's pervasive misogyny and his fears about the confusion of sex roles bled into his anti-Semitism (or vice versa) when, in a final chapter, he cast the Jews outside the pale of normative, masculinized humanity along with women, assimilating them with women (or his idea of women) in the process: they were congenitally effeminate, weak in body and character, entirely devoid of virile discipline and self-restraint. (When Weininger said 'Jews', he meant Jewish men, because they needed to be male in order to be pejoratively feminized; one wonders what he – or Juvenal – would have done with female outsiders.) Women and Jews, in his calculus, were functionally identical: slaves of the senses, emotionally and intellectually arrested, strangers to a higher plane of existence. The category of the 'unmanly' was completed by homosexual men, who were further figured as being drawn to life in the 'artificial' world of the city. Since the corrupt modern metropolis was also considered the (un)natural habitat of rootless Jews in reactionary discourses of this period, and since any mention there of the city was a coded reference to criminality (among other things), we can see, *mutatis mutandis*, the same axis of associations (foreigners–sex deviants–the city–criminal activity) that presents itself as a sociological given to Juvenal's speaker (although Weininger himself does not identify Jews with criminality as explicitly as other sources, where the link became a standard part of the stereotype). Moreover, Weininger deploys the theatre as an emblem of Jewish–homosexual–female urban decadence and as a metaphor for the duplicity that is the primary idiom of all three of his out-groups. He believed, according to Mosse, that '[l]ike women and Jews, homosexuals lacked ... appreciation for the genuine in life. They craved "the pose, the audience, the theater" ... while for the true male, "only timeless objects have value." '[23]

Far from being marginal, this kind of thinking was widespread in Central Europe before and after the turn of the century, and the fact that it was routinely dressed up and promulgated in 'respectable' academic tomes lent legitimacy to lower-order articulations of it in nationalist and racialist programmes. These programmes translated 'scientific' notions of sexual health and degeneration for popular consumption and followed the lead of the academics in transposing common stereotypes of sexual deviance onto 'inferior' races. Across registers, diverse groups were blended – again – into a composite outsider, with feminization as the common denominator. Nationalist texts introduced a revolving cast of national anti-types: feminized Jews (or sometimes blacks, or, in the literatures of the pan-German movement before World War I, non-Germanic inhabitants of the multi-ethnic Habsburg empire, or, in German sources after the war, the French, who were of course notoriously effeminate), male homosexuals ('the spawn of dark, dank alleys, estranged from the healing power of nature' [Mosse 1985: 36]), and their supplements the criminal class and the 'insane'. These groups were in turn arrayed against the besieged native male, whose very existence seemed to be threatened by this tide of human detritus. Significantly for its reproduction, the informal organs of education and youth culture in general absorbed this starkly binary world view. Mosse discusses the founding tenets of the German Youth Movement as being entirely consonant with contemporary ideological currents (the movement dates from 1901). Its mission was to seek 'the "genuine" in nature and the nation' and to recover the spirit of the native male, who was set in opposition to the 'ugly human being of modernity, disfigured by disease, debauchery', and the artificiality of city life.[24] By the time of the Weimar Republic, these and related ideas were being channelled into popular fiction in the form of dystopian novels with titles like *Deutschland ohne Deutschen* (*Germany without Germans*, H. Heyck, 1929). This genre was built around horror at the 'jewified and negroidized' commercial culture and the open, emasculating sensuality that had swamped the cities of Germany, flowing in part from the United States, the mongrel nation par excellence, even as the Asiatic garbage in Juvenal's Orontes had flowed from Syria to Rome. As does Juvenal's third satire, these novels often end with 'visions of flight or exile', as the 'last of the true Germans' give up their struggle in the irremediably corrupted cities and set out to establish outposts of authentic Germanness in remote rural hinterlands.[25]

Apart from the general contours of this discourse, which again is not unique to modern Germany but rather just an exceptionally 'loud' version of a generic rhetoric of reactionary nationalism, Mosse emphasizes three particular features of it that especially echo its Roman prototype. The first, already suggested, is the tendency to lump together the nation's perceived enemies by assigning them transferable traits that make disparate groups and individual members of them virtually interchangeable. As Mosse puts it, '[a]ll outsiders were to a large degree rendered homogeneous'.[26] The second is the presence of a distinct iconography of Otherness, which provides a useful guide to what outsiders *look* like physically to supplement the assertions about what they *are* like in terms of character and values. This is a crucial service since, as Mosse says, '[t]he outsider had to be clearly recognizable in order to be punished and excluded from society'; down to the level of physical appearance, he must be 'irrevocably fixed as exemplifying the restlessness, rootlessness, and lack of virility so feared' by respectable members of the national body. Thus, Jews and homosexuals were, like criminals, routinely represented as being ugly or deformed (as measured against the cultural ideal of beauty), and marked by physical signs of dissolute sexuality and a weak nervous constitution (both *ipso facto* 'female'), such as paleness, languor, and shifty eyes. Images of Jews as grotesquely fat capitalists fitted out with all the accoutrements of the nouveau riche were also common.[27] We have seen how the foreigners conjured up by Juvenal's speaker – Crispinus and the unnamed freedman of Satire 1, the oversexed Greekling of 3 – are similarly marked for easy visual identification, by Oriental enervation or nervous energy, by luxurious clothing and ostentatious jewellery. Indeed, the freedman in the dole line seems to understand the indelibility of such signs of difference when he says that the earring-holes in his ears will cry out who he really is, no matter what he himself might claim (1.104-5: *natus ad Euphraten, molles quod in aure fenestrae / arguerint, licet ipse negem*; the adjective *mollis*, as often, oozes effeminacy). His remark points to another contradiction in the discourse in both its ancient and modern forms: the outsider is imagined alternately as clearly recognizable *and* as a master of disguise.

Finally, the Juvenalian speaker betrays the essentially paranoid character of his vision by framing the threat in terms of conspiracy (ubiquitously suggested although never explicitly formulated as such) and contamination (the contagious disease [*morbus, contagio*] of the male 'homosexuals', who stand in for foreigners even as foreigners stand in for them; the insidious spread of Eastern influences through native contact with the city's unavoidable immigrant population). These remain central tropes in modern European articulations of the discourse, including and perhaps especially in the Germanic one that most concerns Mosse. There, embattled natives faced the combined spectres of a conspiracy of homosexuals bent on subverting society's morals and the proverbial world Jewish conspiracy, which not only aimed at overturning accepted sexual morality but also plotted to take over the organs of finance and politics while poisoning the well of culture in all its forms. On a Viennese postcard from 1910, Jewish influence is figured as a secretly injected poison: a caricature Jew applies a needle behind the ear of an unsuspecting, newspaper-reading Gentile, to the caption 'Weg mit der Judenpresse! Sie vergiftet den Geist und tötet deutsches Denken!' ('Away with the Jewish press! It poisons the soul and kills German thought!').[28] This has an analogue in Umbricius' picture of the insinuating Greek dropping poison into the ear of a powerful man whose thoughts and actions he seeks to manipulate: *facilem stillavit in aurem / exiguum de naturae patriaeque veneno* (3.122-3).

To the imagination that could generate such images, there lurked in the nation's heart a cabal of internal enemies who presented a clear and present danger to everything that was healthy, normal, and natural in the eyes of the true native. Furthermore, in modern nationalism homosexuals in particular but also other outsiders, especially Jews, were figured as carriers of disease, which seems to have correlated in some vague way with the sexual promiscuity attributed to both groups (Mosse 1985: 134-8, 143). The nation, in the words of Schulte-Sasse (1996: 232), was in this perspective an 'organic, vulnerable body' open to 'foreign contamination' and corruption by money, among other things; these two threats were interconnected, insofar as 'both involve[d] a circulation permitting penetration of the social body' by a host of colluding enemies with interchangeable traits: Jews, who were internationalists and capitalists; the British, who were capitalists and foreigners, and so on. This critic's description, which reproduces the nationalist equation of foreign cultural and economic incursion with sexual violation, vividly captures the fusion of xenophobia and homosexual panic that have fundamentally shaped old and new editions of this discourse (*quis iniquae / tam patiens urbis ...* ; and see Satire 1.110-14 for 'Juvenal's' most pointed comments on the distorting power of [new] money, which he blames for facilitating his displacement by newcomers).

The German case may furnish the most crystalline example of the *Nachleben* of the rhetoric of Juvenal's indignant speaker and his ilk, but it is scarcely the sole instance in the modern era of racial and ethnic prejudices and anxieties about gender and sexuality combusting to produce a multi-coded imaginary outsider who could play the crucial role of anti-type in the project of national self-definition. As Mosse (1985: 85) points out, the standard cast of villains in British imperial boys' adventure fiction, whose didactic function of instilling Englishness cannot be overestimated, featured German homosexuals, effeminate men from southern Europe, and Jewish thieves (some things never change). In the context of a discussion of the Victorian British classification of Otherness as a background against which the paragon of Englishness, the high bourgeois gentleman, could be brought into focus, McClintock coins the term 'triangulated switchboard analogy' to denote the principle of substitution (race for class for gender and so on) that the process allowed – a term perfectly suited to describing the mechanics of the rhetoric of Juvenal's speaker. She goes on to demonstrate how, according to this principle, the rhetoric of race was used to draw distinctions among genders and classes (women were like the 'lower' races; the poor were like African savages), and the rhetorics of gender and class were used to distinguish races (whites were the male of the species, blacks the female; Zulus were the 'gentlemen' of blacks). McClintock marshals sources that show how black Africans were identified with sexual excess and, in the case of the men, characterized as effeminate, as well as being likened to apes; the Irish were likened to black Africans and apes; working class women to black men and apes; and working class men were figured as female (especially when they were in mobs).[29]

One later parallel is the rhetoric that accompanied the witch hunts for 'perverts' in government positions carried out in the United States during the Cold War. These purges were driven by 'a widespread perception of gay sexuality as an alien infestation, an unnatural because un-American practice, resulting from the entanglement with foreign countries – and foreign nationals – during the war' (Edelman 1992: 269). This incarnation of the discourse resurrects Juvenal in a number of distinct ways: the explicit or implied invocation of a trinity of demons (sexual deviance, the foreign, the female), each of which contains the others within itself; the positioning of this complex as the negation of everything truly American (in the modern case) and as a danger to a vision of national order and cultural integrity that was promulgated as one rooted in tradition, but in fact was in the process of being fabricated even then. As Edelman (269) puts it, the imagined homosexual/communist axis of evil threatened the 'backward-looking nostalgia of domesticity' which was ascendant in the America of the 1950s and 1960s and which was attempting 'to establish ... the fictive cohesiveness of a suburban national cultural identity'.[30] Like all reactionary nationalist programmes including that of the Roman satiric speaker, in other words, this one was grounded in the idea of the recovery and preservation of something that never existed. Additional modern parallels would not be far to seek, as the template, once stamped, has been almost infinitely productive. My own selection of parallels has been guided by their capacity to show that this particular rhetorical system for marking off the native from the not-native, us from them, was current in Roman antiquity and not forged in the crucible of modernity as is often assumed.

Umbricius' pastoral fantasy

The production of nationalist narratives always involves the 'invention of tradition' in some form; a common expression of this is an ideologically loaded opposition between country and city.[31] While not as ubiquitous as it is in Horace, the city/country trope is a key element in the Juvenalian speaker's construction of authentic Romanness and its opposite terms. But whereas Horace lavishes most of his attention on a soft-focus picture of the pastoral past and its exemplary ur-Romans – at least, that is the image we are left with in the 'Roman' Odes – in Juvenal the emphasis shifts almost entirely to the national ruins of the urban present that has swept that world away. In his speaker's selective vision, all the concatenated misfits enumerated above, be they actual foreigners or internal outsiders, have settled and thrive in the big city, to the extent that honest and upright native-born citizens (*ingenui*, repeatedly invoked, as at 3.131) no longer feel at home there. The speaker expresses the point of view of the poor Roman who feels himself disenfranchised, beaten down, and crowded out by swarms of newcomers with their unintelligible languages, loose morals, weird customs, and crass money-making schemes. His innate conservatism is assaulted by the rampant disregard for boundaries of all kinds that he witnesses in the city: female misbehaviour and male sexual deviance go unchecked, and freedmen born as slaves in distant lands shoot ahead of the speaker on the social and economic ladder, as natives once *ipso facto* assured of some status and sustenance are suddenly forced to compete with these enterprising strangers on their terms (an especially vivid dramatization of this competition is the dole scene at 1.95-126). The city that Juvenal's bewildered speaker sees as he converts his anxieties about social change to high moral outrage is a dark and threatening place, full of physical dangers (among them the presence of infectious disease, 3.232-6) and mired in social and moral chaos, market-driven, overcrowded, deeply alienating, and grandly indifferent to his plight. The traditional hierarchies and values that once would have protected him simply by virtue of his being a native male no longer have any meaning here; as Umbricius concludes, there is no place in Rome for real Romans.

Although Satire 1 clearly implicates the city as the spawning ground of all the evils that it catalogues, and the implied urban setting of the transgressions detailed in 2 and 6 suggests an association between the two, it is naturally in the famously urban Satire 3 that the ideological valence of the city as an emblem of the triumph of unhealthy foreign values is worked out most fully. Here, in the opening twenty lines, the first speaker who will serve as Umbricius' interlocutor manages to introduce in a highly concentrated, allusive way a remarkable number of the tropes that structure discourses of reactionary nationalism, ancient and modern, which his friend Umbricius will pick up and develop with a vengeance. The prologue speaker describes how Umbricius has finally decided to leave the cruel city (*saeva urbs*, 8-9) and its daily assaults on his sensibilities and to seek a corrective in the country town of Cumae and the 'pleasant retirement' (*gratum litus amoeni / secessus*, 4-5) that it is imagined to offer. The choice of words recalls the *locus amoenus* of pastoral poetry and so casts a suitably pastoral aura over Umbricius' chosen refuge. This aura descends again toward the close of the poem, when Umbricius himself plunders the literary tradition for a script to accompany his final departure (316, 'the cattle are lowing and the sun is setting: it's time to go', *iumenta vocant et sol inclinat. eundum est*). Thus the poem is framed at beginning and end by fragments of the pastoral fantasy that occupies such a central place in Umbricius' mental map. Back at the beginning, the first speaker accompanies his friend part of the way out of town, through the grove where in the old days, as he notes, King Numa used to meet his favourite nymph and the Muses held court, but which now (*nunc*) has degenerated into the sordid gathering place of mendicant, homeless Jews (13-16). Ferguson identifies the mention of the Jews here as 'the first indication of the nationalism and xenophobia which form a part of Juvenal's satire'.[32]

1. Them and Us

Thus from the outset the fundamental temporal and spatial oppositions – between then and now, there and here – around which this rhetoric is built are put into play, along with an ancillary one, between the natural and authentic (identified with the then and there) and the artificial (with the here and now). The prologue speaker notes with regret the theme-park phoniness of the modern grove's grottoes (*speluncas dissimiles veris*, 17-18) and wishes that green grass and 'native limestone' (*ingenuus tofus*, 20) bordered the fountains instead of imported marble; even stone is enlisted in the struggle between native and foreign. The trope of artifice proceeds to mutate and expand in the course of the poem as Umbricius takes over as the main speaker, moving from manifestations of artifice in the physical world to the realm of human behaviour: no one in the city can be trusted to be what he appears to be, no one's words can be taken as sincere. From the entrepreneurial hustlers to the smooth-talking Greeks and beyond, to the whole population of outsiders (who have now become insiders, to Umbricius' dismay) merging together in his mind and unified by their elastic relationship with the truth, absolute values and fixed correspondences between signifier and signified are nowhere to be found. 'Let us leave our native city,' Umbricius exhorts; 'let those who turn black into white remain' (*cedamus patria ... maneant qui nigrum in candida vertunt*, 29-30). His inchoate anxieties about his own self-definition and his place in this brave new world are stirred up when he observes how the Greek seems positively to embrace instability of identity: 'he has the ability to take his expression from someone else's face,' Umbricius says with a mixture of envy and disgust (*potest aliena sumere vultum / a facie*, 105-6). A congenitally honest man such as himself cannot possibly compete on these terms: 'What can I do in Rome? I don't know how to lie' (*quid Romae faciam? mentiri nescio*, 41), he whines, as usual putting the worst construction on the actions of his rivals in order to turn his inability to adapt into a virtue.

At various intervals in his litany of the horrors of contemporary life in the teeming imperial metropolis, Juvenal's speaker pauses to paint a loving picture of what he imagines to be the alternative, the

43

simple existence of hardy natives in the country towns of Italy still untouched by the alien invasion of his own time, and/or as they existed in the prelapsarian Golden Age of Roman mytho-history; as is generally the case in discourses of this type, when one steps into the country one steps into the past and vice versa. Umbricius dwells longingly on his vision of such a place at 168-79. He signals our entry into the enchanted realm of rustic native virtue with the established cue of the Marsi and the Sabelli, the proverbial salt of the Italian earth (169, 'if you suddenly found yourself among the Marsi or at a Sabine table ...').[33] In these undeveloped and thus untainted rural societies, class distinctions are minimal or at least not marked with ostentatious display, luxury is unknown, and women dutifully nurture infants at their breast as they were meant to do. Even the rustic baby holds a lesson for the city dweller, his wide-eyed credulous fear at the stage monster from whom his mother protects him (*personae pallentis hiatum / in gremio matris formidat rusticus infans*, 175-6) a foil to the calculated dissimulation practised everywhere in Rome. There is, in fact, something rather childlike about the whole population, content to watch the same play (*notum exodium*, 174-5) over and over again: no society of the spectacle this, no need for ever more novel diversions to break through their ennui. The grassy theatre (*herboso ... theatro*, 173) itself is in counterpoint to the artifice of the city, when we remember that the poem's first speaker lamented that marble had crowded out grass in the city's parks.

Pastoral nostalgia interrupts Umbricius' tirade again at 3.223-31, where he imagines the little farmstead that he will be able to buy outright in the country for what he pays to live in a city tenement for a year. The image that he has of his future home is governed by the standard Golden Age motif of a beneficent earth that offers up high yields with minimal effort on the part of her steward: the well in his little garden (*hortulus*, 226) will be so shallow that it will practically water the crops itself (*puteusque brevis nec reste movendus in tenuis plantas facili diffunditur haustu*, 226-7), and soon he will have enough vegetables to throw a party for a hundred vegetarians. Anyone with any real knowledge of farming knows that nothing

44

about it is *facile*. Like the speaker's choice of Cumae, a *Greek* town, as his haven, this passage is one of several where Juvenal hints that the character is to be read as naïve and misinformed if not seriously deluded. But the fact remains that in Umbricius' reality, vestiges of the Golden Age phase of the national narrative are still available in the countryside.

Interjecting a pastoral interlude into his own tirade, the speaker of Satire 6 also articulates a perfect generic version of the fantasy of a national Golden Age that animates nationalist thinking like that of Umbricius, perfect especially in the way it explicitly associates past national health with female chastity and attributes the destruction of that health to decadent foreign influences (6.287-300). Hard work, lack of sleep, and proper martial husbands on constant guard against external enemies gave women no scope for misbehaviour in the days before Rome became an overgrown cosmopolis, he says; but now (*nunc* again, 292) prolonged peace has allowed an invasion of urban(e) luxury (*luxuria*, 293) and foreign customs (*peregrini mores*, 298) from the decadent, effeminate East (*Sybaris, Rhodos, Miletos*, 296). This speaker is so reactionary that he prefers a Golden Age off the historical scale altogether, in the mythic past of the first human beings, as he indicates in his prologue (1-20). Then (*tunc*) when the world was completely pristine (*orbe novo*, 11), families lived in cold caves where the 'mountain wife' (*montana uxor*, 5), 'rougher even than her acorn-belching husband' (*horridior glandem ructante marito*, 10) and entirely unlike the hyper-refined, easy women of the modern city (or Latin love elegy), made beds out of thatch and animal skins and suckled 'robust babies' (*infantes magni*, 9; cf. Horace's 'manly offspring of rustic soldiers', *rusticorum mascula militum proles*, in his pastoral Roman past at *Odes* 3.6.37-8). Now that was truly the high point of Italian pre-urban virtue!

The clearly over-the-top, comic quality of this last vignette smacks of parody, and as Winkler has shown, the Golden Age interludes in Juvenal's *Satires* as a whole are heavily infused with authorial irony – though the speakers are always dead serious. Winkler also reminds us that any talk about Golden Ages, mythic or national/historical, was utterly conventional by the time these texts were produced.[34]

Idealization of the Italian countryside and its identification with a virtuous national past go back through Augustan literature to that of the Republic. Furthermore, the morally freighted comparison of the country with the city had become an established theme in Roman satire, and the *locus communis de saeculo* – the rhetorical common-place about the decline of the age – was a standard item in the exercises of the schools of rhetoric and declamation, and spread from there into literature written by rhetorically trained authors. There is, in fact, very little in the *Satires* that is not in some sense scripted by convention in the form of rhetorical, generic, or more generally literary topoi.[35] But as is the case throughout this book, my interest is not so much in the earlier history of the building blocks at Juvenal's disposal as in the later uses to which they will be put and in the ways in which these texts points to those uses. Whatever their formal antecedents, the Juvenalian speaker's nostalgia for the Golden Age and his horror at city ways, linked as they are with his pervasive concerns about Romanness, anticipate later nationalist uses of city and country as emblems of larger ideological conflicts.

City, country, national identity: later articulations

'From the nineteenth century on,' writes Mosse, 'the guardians of nationalism ... felt menaced by the big city, the apparent center of an artificial and restless age' (1985: 32). He traces the path of a diffuse anti-urbanism that arose early in the century against the backdrop of Romanticism and, later, generalized anxieties about modern life and industrial society. An influential articulation of the latter was Max Nordau's *Degeneration* (*Entartung*) from 1892, which argued that the modern world was witnessing a struggle between the forces of health and decadence, and that urban life was responsible for physical and spiritual sickness and the biological degeneration of the species.[36] Ideas like these were not necessarily tied to nationalist sentiments, but like racism they were easily adaptable to nationalist purposes. Thus by the end of the century, according to Mosse, nativist movements in Central Europe had taken them up and made the city 'a metaphor for everything unnatural' and thus antithetical to authentic native culture (137). In these ideologies the city was associated with the same package of correlated pathologies that Juvenal's speaker lays at its door: artifice in countless forms, restlessness, impermanence, sexual excess, extremes of luxury and poverty, moral and physical degeneration. The city was a breeding ground of vice and conspiracy and, above all for the nativists, the home of outsiders who embodied alien values and practices: Jews, homosexuals, criminals, the 'insane'. The countryside, on the other hand, was figured as the home of the native and acted as the setting for nostalgic fantasies about a healthy national past, when men were men, women were women, values were immutable, and life was settled and 'genuine', ordered according to the stable boundaries and hierarchies that nature ordained (Mosse 1985: 32-3, 137-8). The modern incarnation of this discourse, then, like its Roman predecessor, is built on a rigid set of 'radical antinomies', as Travers puts it; the volkish reactionaries who formed the vanguard of Germanic nationalism 'expounded [an] ontology of nature ... within a highly negative anthropology of the modern world ... that pitted the organic against the artificial, the natural against the mechanistic, the "healthy" against the "sick," the native against the foreign, and morality against license'.[37]

Ideas such as these, given a new lease on life in the atmosphere of national defeat, persisted into the Weimar period and were channelled directly into Nazi ideology and its programme of national regeneration. The demonized city of modernity was a staple in National Socialist media of all kinds. For the sake of illustrating thematic common ground, film is an artefact especially suitable for comparison with Juvenal's texts, whose techniques of representation have been likened to those of cinema, particularly in the sweeping urban panoramas of Satires 1 and 3 (Braund 1996a: 43-4). Schulte-Sasse (1996) discusses several Nazi films in which the city is linked with feminizing foreign contamination and with the concomitant emasculation of the native male. She identifies two common narrative structures in these films; one of them, which involves ' "contained" individuals struggling within a geographic space of contamination', i.e., the city, is also the narrative situation of Juvenal's urban satires with their beleaguered, alienated speakers.[38] The city in these films, variously designated with a nebulously sinister 'Weimar' or more specifically as Berlin with its sexualized, degenerate crowds, stands metonymically for the idea of 'Germany', now an 'infested space needing purgation'. As this critic points out, the Nazi view of the mob as a dangerously feminized, urban phenomenon goes back in the modern era to Le Bon's *Psychologie des foules* of 1895 (255).

Schulte-Sasse examines the film *Hans Westmar* (1933) at some length, and her description of one of its most ideologically dense scenes is worth quoting in full for its resonance with Juvenalian tropes and techniques. Here, the nationalist youth Westmar leads a returning German émigré on a tour of Berlin, which the older man finds 'disfigured beyond recognition' after a period of absence: 'This is Berlin? This is Germany's capital? I don't recognize it,' he exclaims (255). As the two last true Germans make their way indignantly through the city, they are:

... flooded with signifiers of the alien and incomprehensible. Neon signs cut diagonally across the screen from all directions: 'On parle français,' 'English spoken,' names of international restaurants intersect with each other, rendering the otherwise familiar topography of Berlin a disorienting twilight zone. The older man's [favourite tavern] ... now bears the name Chez Ninette, which is emblematic of the encroachment on Berlin of the foreign and feminine ... . Chez Ninette's clientele consists of bald, obese, cigar-smoking, boisterous men, marked throughout Nazi cinema as 'capitalists'. The scene further illustrates the violation of the social body as it foregrounds racial impurity, nakedness, and degradation. In the bar the group is greeted by a black coat boy, and everyone speaks French. To the older man's question, 'Can one speak German here too?' the uncomprehending coat boy answers: 'Naturellement!' and gestures towards the men's toilet, to which the camera pans, showing theater posters advertising 'A Jew Goes through the World' ... . The German language is polluted in this world by excrement.

1996: 255-6

This scene recalls Juvenal not only in its substance – the familiar catalogue of gendered foreign outrages – but also in its technique: both film and literary text align along the same axis the spectator's/reader's view and that of the alienated protagonist, so that the former, sympathetic or not, cannot help but share in the latter's helpless sense of disorientation, assault, and violation. In her discussion of another film, 1940's infamous *Jew Süss*, Schulte-Sasse notes (75) that '[t]he film's two brief mass "Jewish" scenes ... have in common a compositional principle of clutter that lends them a claustrophobic quality' in comparison with the insulated, ordered world of the Gentile court. This is a perfect description of the 'compositional principle' at work and its effect in both of Juvenal's city-based satires (1 and 3), where the accumulation of offending 'clutter' is so relentless that the reader can feel as overwhelmed by the tide as the speaker does.[39]

Juvenal's practice of relieving the urban assault at critical junctures with idyllic pastoral interludes also finds a parallel in the film *Hitler Youth Quex* (1933), which in spite of its entirely urban setting manages to orchestrate its hero Heini Völker's awakening to National Socialism in a forested area on the city's periphery, thus reproducing the ideologically coded opposition between the urban and the rural established in antiquity (Schulte-Sasse 1996: 262-3). The defensive, angry dismay of the eager young patriot Westmar and his companion when confronted by the cosmopolitan dynamism of Berlin clearly echoes the responses of Juvenal's speakers to analogous developments at Rome in spite of the distance between the two worlds that they inhabit. The veterans of World War I who play a prominent thematic role in several of these films represent another parallel with those speakers, in their feeling that they have been betrayed by a society whose rules they had thought they understood, in their resentment at the shifting ground that they are now forced to negotiate, and in the stories that they tell themselves to make sense of the strange new world and their marginal place in it. Thrust from the trenches into the 'feminized world of "Weimar" ' and traumatized to find there that the 'established system of representation' upon which they had depended for their sense of identity has collapsed, they proceed to 'disavow a destabilized male identity' by 'project[ing] it onto external phenomena' – the hybrid, polyglot clutter of the city (Schulte-Sasse 1996: 268-70). Like Juvenal's speakers, especially Umbricius, they turn their inability to adapt to new circumstances into a badge of moral superiority. As Schulte-Sasse (272) puts it, 'male failure and male lack are displaced onto the context of Weimar corruption (the men's "soldierly" integrity dooms them in civilian occupations; they're "too honest" to succeed as auto mechanics, too scrupulous to work in nightclubs, etc.)'. To a critical reader, their excuses are as transparent as those of Umbricius: 'What can I do in Rome? I don't know how to lie.'

The same period that gestated the ideas that in Central Europe reached their ultimate expression in Nazi propaganda saw the beginnings of an English variation on the appeal to pastoral nostalgia in the framing of national identity. In Howkins' account, the process in England emerges as one initiated by elites as a calculated response to a specific economic and social crisis in the later nineteenth century. This process gathered strength and took on a life of its own until rural images came to signify the 'real' England in the collective cultural imagination, while the city represented an unnatural and alienated life cut off from the nation's salutary wellsprings. Rural images were so thoroughly naturalized as signifiers of 'England' that British soldiers went into battle in World War I with their heads full of the peaceful country homesteads that their government-printed inspirational reading had convinced them they were defending even if they themselves came from a smoke-belching industrial city, as in fact most of them did. Howkins' description of the movement to 'revive' purportedly authentic folk music, architecture, and other cultural forms is instructive for its resonance not only with the fanciful, didactic cultural histories promulgated by the volkish nationalists and their heirs in Germany (involving happy, radiant peasants and idealized Teutonic knights as paradigms for emulation by weary moderns), but also with the efforts of Augustus to revive – or invent – traditional values and practices in the interest of national cohesion.[40]

There is, in fact, a vast body of work on the equation of the English countryside with Englishness itself, with many dating the beginnings of this association and its use in constructing a national identity to considerably earlier than Howkins does. Helsinger's is one such study, and in the course of her discussion she makes several lucid comments that are relevant to Juvenal's conventional Golden Age vignettes and to understanding the consequences of nostalgic attachment to a provincial national paradigm – consequences that are especially evident in the attitudes of his speakers. When the rural becomes the premier metaphor for the nation, she writes,

> ... meanings [are] attached to a rural life that is increasingly distant from the everyday experience of British or English subjects. This transfer of meaning often brings with it a certain stylization: images and narratives are simplified and codified as they are staged, performed, and quoted for a national audience.
>
> 1997: 13

Any sense of community that accrues from the strategic deployment of these images and narratives is achieved, as Helsinger points out, 'at a cost'. She explains:

> Tying the heterogeneous nation to an ideal of home or community represented by the tribe or (home)town or village limits the nation's tolerance of social difference ... . The nation as home or nation as community commits itself to excluding what it cannot assimilate.[41]

Helsinger has the English case in mind, but the principles described in these observations appear to have been well established in the discourse of Roman 'nationalists'. When Juvenal's pastoral set-pieces, which commentators often have treated summarily as mechanical reproductions of convention, are situated in this larger context, they acquire a more complex ideological dimension.

On the other side of the equation, the modern industrial metropolis caused as much alarm in certain English circles as it did to Hans Westmar and his ilk (or as the new Rome caused to Juvenal's speakers). As Howkins explains, the growth of the 'new urban world' of London in the nineteenth century and the widespread perception of the city as a place of idleness and corruption provoked expressions of concern and even panic from nervous scions of the ruling bourgeoisie. This discomfort was fed by the widely disseminated knowledge of Gibbon's analysis of Roman imperial decline as a process that began with decay in the metropolitan centre of empire, an idea that gave rise to worry that the British Empire was going the way of its ancient predecessor. Reading Gibbon also encouraged fears about the degeneration of the English 'race' among those who accepted his argument that generations of decadent urban living had turned the Romans into a 'race of pygmies', a 'puny breed' no longer able to resist the tide of virile barbarians from the north. Thus, if the evidence of observation was not enough, the historical example of Rome acted as a warning about the causal connection between city life and racial degeneration. It was the conviction that the nation was in the throes of a racial crisis centred in the cities that provided the impetus for a back-to-the-land movement designed to shore up Englishness in its natural habitat, for, as Howkins puts it, 'the country and country people were seen as the essence of England, uncontaminated by racial degeneration and the false values of cosmopolitan urban life'.[42]

To be sure, there are significant differences between English anti-urban discourse and that articulated by Juvenal's speakers and the pan-German nativists, who again emerge as strangely kindred spirits. In brief, the speaking subject is different here (the propertied middle class invested in preserving the status quo rather than the disaffected reactionary who feels oppressed by it), and so is the focus of fear and loathing: not foreigners so much as the degraded British labourer and the volatile urban proletariat produced by industrialization. In this variation, the natives themselves in a sense become the foreigners; the indigenous working class has been transformed by life at the low end of the modern industrial pyramid from bluff yeoman farmers into semi-bestial urban slum-dwellers, an alien blight on an otherwise healthy national body.[43] Still, in all three versions urban panic is driven by what could be designated as nationalist idées fixes: beliefs that 'true' national character and identity are being destroyed through a process of mongrelization generated by the conditions of urban life; that this development presents serious dangers to the health of the nation as a whole; and that this trend must be reversed by looking to the countryside as a repository of cultural and racial integrity.

But in more general terms what this particular strain of British anti-urbanism lacks to make it a truer parallel with contemporary Germanic discourses (and their Juvenalian predecessor) is the element of anti-modern or anti-liberal revolt. It was not, in other words, a 'war against the West', where the West is identified, as it usually is by 'Occidentalists', with dangerous things like multi-cultural and multi-racial societies, cosmopolitan urban life, materialism and market capitalism, women's liberation, sexual openness, and individual freedom. In their recent history of this 'war', Baruma and Margalit use the term 'Occidentalist' to designate an attitude that has unified a historically sweeping range of revolts against Western post-Enlightenment modernity.[44] Paradoxically enough, as they demonstrate, 'the first Occidentalists were European' (2004: 22); the backlash against the values of Western liberalism began in the West itself, with Germany proving especially fertile soil for reaction. Equally paradoxically, anti-modern tracts generated in the West managed to be simultaneously Occidentalist (in their hatred of the natural consequences of an adherence to Enlightenment values, which in this view led only to the 'decline of the West') and Orientalist (in their systematic disparagement of inferior, 'effeminate' Eastern peoples). Baruma and Margalit trace the systematic dissemination of anti-Western discourses born in the West itself to Asia and the Arab world, where they were central in the formation of the cultural tenets of Islamic fundamentalism.

Most versions of Occidentalist discourse have a nationalist component, and all, according to Baruma and Margalit, are structured by four basic tropes (2002: 4). Foremost among these is the idea of the soul-destroying decadence of urban life:

Anti-liberal revolts almost invariably contain a deep hatred of the City, that is to say, everything represented by urban civi-

lization: commerce, mixed populations, artistic freedom, sexual
license, ... leisure, ... wealth, and its usual concomitant, power.
Mao Zedong, Pol Pot, Hitler, Japanese agrarian fascists, and of
course Islamists all extolled the simple life of the pious peasant,
pure at heart, uncorrupted by city pleasures, used to hard work
and self-denial, tied to the soil, and obedient to authority.

2002: 4

Given the logic of the discourse, two of the other tropes should not
surprise us: the evils of bourgeois capitalism and the immorality of
female emancipation. The fourth, an anti-rationalism that privileges
'soul' and 'instinct', applies less well to Juvenal's reactionary
speakers, and in fact the whole concept of Occidentalism can be properly applied only to modern anti-modern movements, insofar as its
target was not fully formed until after the Enlightenment. Still,
Baruma and Margalit actually invoke Juvenal as a prototype of
Occidentalist anti-urban discourse (2004: 18-19, 28), and indeed
underneath the generic convention, declamatory commonplaces,
parodic exaggerations, and literary play, his speakers have declared
war on a West-in-the-making.

2

Augustan Nation-Building and Horace's 'Roman' Odes (3.2, 3.5, 3.6)

The 'invention of tradition'

The dominant voices coming through in Juvenal's *Satires* and Horace's 'Roman' Odes could not be more different. In the former, especially the earlier satires (Books 1 and 2, containing Satires 1-6), we hear the voice of a disgruntled and powerless 'angry white man' unleashing his fury at the forces he blames for pushing him to the margins of society; in the latter, it is the voice of the Augustan establishment laying out a programme of national renewal after a long period of political and social dislocation. Nevertheless, in their construction of Romanness the *Satires* and the Odes share two basic features which would come to form the backbone of modern nationalist discourses: the idealization of the national past and the implication of issues of gender and sexuality in that process. Chapter 1 examined these features, among others, in the rhetoric of the Juvenalian speaker, constructed as a lonely voice crying in its own reactionary wilderness. In contrast the 'Roman' Odes, like many other Augustan literary texts, seem to articulate an officially sanctioned state programme, albeit one in its infancy at the time when these poems were produced in the 20s BC. Because these two features of national identity construction were central to the Augustan programme as a whole, this is a fitting juncture at which to sketch in more of their theoretical background, developed in connection with modern nationalisms, before taking up its application to the poems of Horace.

Eric Hobsbawm uses the term 'the invention of tradition' to refer to the apparently almost universal tendency of nationalist thought to idealize the collective past, usually through the creation of an ideologically shaped historical romance about the nation. These formulaic narratives are regularly built on notions of cultural authenticity and 'true' national character, which lately have somehow been challenged or allowed to lapse and thus are in need of revitalization through a programme of cultural and moral renewal. Hobsbawm bases his generalizations on a study of the emerging nationalist discourses of Germany and France in the nineteenth century. He argues that the construction of national identity 'rests on exercises in social engineering' that rely on a number of basic strategies to promote a sense of cohesion, common history, and shared destiny, often where little or none had existed before. Chief among these strategies are the institution of public ceremonies and rituals that glorify the people's collective achievements while celebrating supposedly characteristic values, and the mass production of public monuments that use images to establish a new historical narrative, typically with one *pater patriae* figure or a group of them (a cult, as Hobsbawm puts it) cast in central roles. Also important are the inculcation of a belief that the nation's ascendency is historically inevitable, and the identification of a national enemy against whose values the people in question defines its own identity and principles (Hobsbawm 1994: 76-82).

Hobsbawm discusses these strategies as if they were pioneered by the founders of modern nation-states. Yet anyone familiar with Augustan material and literary culture will immediately recognize that each of them has parallels in the Augustan 'nation-building' programme. The idea of a national destiny is the guiding force of the *Aeneid*, and several literary texts helped Augustus to construct Cleopatra and Egypt as the antithesis of Romanness. Furthermore, the role of Augustan monuments in promulgating the new national narrative, and especially in disseminating images of the *princeps* and his family as exemplars of traditional virtue, is well known.[1] Among Hobsbawm's examples of the first strategy is a German youth ceremony practised after the first unification in 1871:

Watched by parents and friends, the boys marched into the school yard singing 'Wacht am Rhein' ... . They formed up facing representatives of each class who held flags decorated with oak leaves ... . The head boy presented these banners to the headmaster ... . The boys then marched under their banners ... before the planting of an 'imperial oak' to the accompaniment of choral singing.

1994: 81-3

This strongly echoes descriptions in Virgil (*Aeneid* 5.545-603) and Suetonius (*Augustus* 43) of the Trojan Games (*lusus Troiae*) for Roman youth instituted by Augustus as a 'theatrical performance of invented community', to use McClintock's words (1996: 274). In the same vein McClintock, under the heading 'Nationalism as Fetish Spectacle', discusses the elaborately staged 1938 centennial re-enactment of the Boer trek from British domination, replete with backward-looking ideas of proper gender roles (1996: 271-7). Clearly this sort of ideologically charged ritual re-enactment of national history and identity is not restricted to any particular period or place.

Hutchinson traces in more detail the recurrence of imperatives of moral regeneration in discourses of national identity. Drawing on a range of modern nationalisms, he identifies several elements in the 'mythic pattern' that informs nationalist historical narratives generically. These narratives typically begin with a migration story, then move from there to a foundation myth, which is in turn followed by an account of a Golden Age of cultural integrity and collective virtue. This perfect past is held up, implicitly or explicitly, as the paradigm against which current inner decay, the last stage in the typical national narrative, is to be measured. This low point does hold out a promise of regeneration, but it can only come through a revival of the pristine and 'authentic' nation that existed before its fragmentation, and through the dutiful shouldering of that nation's proper destiny.[2]

Hutchinson's description of the fourth stage, the obligatory period of social and moral decay, is especially interesting in connection with Augustan ideology. Decay is routinely represented as the result of 'inner degeneration'; external influences help this process along, to be sure, but it is primarily the neglect and 'ossification' of the nation's own traditions that weaken its social and moral fabric and make it vulnerable to the 'materialist corruptions' of 'anomic cosmopolitanism'. We will see how vividly Horace exemplifies this way of constructing the nation's trajectory, and in particular how he develops the notion of inner decay as the most serious obstacle to the realization of the nation's divinely sanctioned destiny. Also noteworthy in connection with Augustan precursors are Hutchinson's comments on the role of the artist in projects of national renewal. Citing cases in point, he shows how artists have often taken up the call to 'create [exemplary texts and images] out of the collective experience of the people, preserved in historical legends, and [to] dramatize their lessons for the present'. A common approach to this task is to 'celebrat[e] heroes who embody the nation's quest for meaning and integration' (1994: 128-9).

The 'invention of tradition' is not exclusively a phenomenon of Western European nationalisms. Boehmer demonstrates that this tendency was, ironically, inherited by the rhetorics of many of the anti-colonial nationalist movements of the twentieth century.[3] These rhetorics showed the same strategic dependence on newly reconstituted foundational narratives and expressed a similar romantic belief in an 'authentic' native cultural integrity that had been eroded, in this case, not so much by inner decay as by the depredations of colonialism. Here the discourse functioned, in other words, as a counter-narrative to the distorting effects of colonialist representations of native peoples. In the process, though, it promulgated another set of distortions based in the generic myth of a cultural wholeness that existed before everything went wrong.

One of the persistent features of idealized pasts in these essentializing post-colonial discourses, as Boehmer notes, is their pastoral ethos: the pre-colonial past is consistently imagined as entirely non-urban. The city is identified with the destructive modernity of the colonizer, while the countryside is made to embody the 'authentic' native cultural traditions and moral values that prevailed before colonization; spatial and temporal dimensions fuse. Miles' succinct formulation of this principle in connection with Augustan literature applies equally well to modern expressions of it: '[I]dealization of the past and the idealization of country life that we find in the literature of Livy's contemporaries are complementary: the one is a temporal, the other a spatial projection of the same ideals and issues' (1997: 175). By positing 'historical beginnings and aetiologies', the writers (Hutchinson's 'artist-creators') who helped shape these anti-colonial nationalist discourses hoped to establish a 'basis for a new selfhood' and a ' "real" or rooted identity' for a people who had assumed a 'false' one – or in these instances had it imposed upon them – as the result of historical circumstances (Boehmer 1995: 115). Smyth (1997: 58-62) concentrates on this syndrome in Irish nationalist discourse, in which the 'equation of the rural with the "real" ' and the 'elevation of the country above the city as a signifier of Irishness' are ubiquitous.

As was the case with the 'invention of tradition' in general, so the ubiquity of a pastoral ethos in the idealized pasts conjured up by post-colonial nationalisms showed them taking a page from their mainstream European predecessors. These too regularly identified 'authentic' national culture with the countryside and with agrarian values, a connection anticipated in the *Satires* of Juvenal and in Latin literature in general, as we saw in Chapter 1. The pastoral strain in nineteenth- and early twentieth-century German and British nationalist rhetoric involved a particularly stark contrast between the country and the city. The former was cast as the home of the robust native, where values were eternal and manliness intact, while the latter came to represent what were regarded as the worst features of modernity: artifice and impermanence, luxury, gender ambiguity, and sexual excess. The city was imagined as the home of suspect foreigners or of an increasingly brutalized native working class; it was a breeding ground for disease, both physical and moral. The country, on the other hand, emerged as a primary symbol of the healthy, ordered world that modernity had allegedly swept away. Reactionary rhetoric of this kind was predictable in societies still grappling with the effects of industrialization and harbouring ambivalent attitudes toward the 'progress' that this and related developments represented. Whole movements grew up out of the perceived need to excavate the 'genuine' – and genuine national consciousness – out of the artifice and bourgeois materialism and/or the unhealthy, sunless existence of degenerate modern urban life. One of the most ominous of these, the German Youth Movement, is a perfect emblem of the links between anti-modern and nationalist discourses in the late nineteenth century, which characterized German nationalism in particular.[4]

The power of the pastoral paradigm in modern nationalist ideology is vividly captured by Howkins (1986), who traces what he calls the 'propaganda process' through which rural England became the 'real' England in that nation's representations of itself in the years leading up to World War I. The process had its roots in the agricultural crisis of the 1870s and the ensuing migration of country people to the cities, developments to which politicians and other public figures responded by encouraging a 'back to the land' movement. This movement in time spawned a full-blown political and cultural discourse in which the land and country life came to represent 'order, stability, and naturalness'; country people were cast as nothing less than 'the essence of England, uncontaminated by racial degeneration and the false values of cosmopolitan, urban life', which were thought to be causally linked (1986: 69). Significantly, the example of Rome was routinely invoked for what it taught about the perils of bread-and-circuses urbanism and the wholesale social and moral decline that followed in its wake.

What is especially striking about the pastoral ethic promulgated in so many texts of the period, as Howkins points out, is that the country, and in particular England's south country, was identified not only with the standard disappearing virtues of 'purity, decency, goodness, [and] honesty', but with 'reality' itself (63). Rural society was constructed as organic and 'real', while the society of the cities was seen as unnatural and somehow 'unreal', a dangerous simulacrum that seduced the genuine nation into becoming a cheap imitation, something other than itself. This fetishization of the 'authentic' is a recurrent feature of nationalist discourses, as we have seen. The irony, of course, is that the work of fixing the land as a centrepiece of nationalist ideology was done for the most part by an urban, elite class, as it had been earlier under Augustus. In the later instance they were so successful that by 1914 when, as Howkins puts it, 'Englishness went into battle', the countryside and the values identified with it were firmly entrenched as the dominant image of what was at stake. Literary anthologies distributed to troops could talk quite seriously about how the average soldier on the front 'in imagination ... [sees] his village home', clearly, as Howkins observes, 'an absurd statement since the majority of soldiers came from the cities' (80). He concludes:

> By 1918 what had begun as a response among a section of the middle class to the problems of 'outcast London' was well on its way to becoming a permanent part of the nationalist ideology ... . So did the ironmaster's grandson, the archetypal product of the industrial revolution, come to associate his country with the countryside.
>
> 1986: 82

The role of gender and sexuality

A related staple of English trench literature and other artefacts of the Great War was the 'consciously stereotyped' image of chaste sweethearts and wives patiently waiting on the homefront for the return of the nation's defenders (Howkins 1986: 80-1). This image brings us to the second of the two basic features of modern nationalist rhetoric that will be especially relevant when we turn to the 'Roman' Odes. McClintock states it unequivocally: 'Nationalism ... is a gendered discourse and cannot be understood without a theory of gender power' (1996: 261). To support this claim she paraphrases the editors of an important anthology on the gendering of nationalist ideology, who offer a succinct formulation of the 'ways in which women have been implicated in nationalism'. Historically, women have functioned uniquely

> as biological reproducers of the members of national collectivities; as reproducers of the boundaries of national groups (through restrictions on sexual or marital relations); as active transmitters and producers of the national culture; as symbolic

61

signifiers of national difference; [and] as active participants in national struggles.[5]

Beyond this generic description, the specific features of the gender and sexual politics associated with particular nationalisms can vary. More often than not, however, nationalist rhetoric, with its stress on tradition and continuity, has incorporated conservative gender ideologies characterized by clear dichotomies and hierarchies. As McClintock puts it, perhaps too absolutely, 'nations have historically amounted to the sanctioned institutionalization of gender difference' (1996: 260).

Nationalism and conservatism in the area of gender and sexuality make natural partners for a number of reasons. Given that nationalist thought is so often structured around tradition and opposition (self/Other, past/present, country/city), it is no surprise that its gender ideologies would conform to that pattern. Especially in manifestly reactionary nationalisms, gender distinctions have played a 'vital role ... in ordering a world that seemed on the brink of chaos', often as a result of rapid social and economic change (Mosse 1985: 102). McClintock offers an explanation for the recurrent articulation of nationalist sentiments, sharp gender distinctions, and efforts to control sexuality. She argues that it is the consequence of the simultaneously forward- and backward-looking character of nationalism generically, which 'presents itself both as a modern project that melts and transforms traditional attachments in favour of new identities and as a reflection of authentic cultural values culled from the depths of a presumed communal past'.[6] The tensions inherent in this dual character are

> resolved by figuring the contradiction in the representation of time as a natural division of gender. Women are represented as the atavistic and authentic body of national tradition ... embodying nationalism's conservative principle of continuity. Men ... represent the progressive agent of national modernity ... embodying nationalism's ... principle of discontinuity. Nationalism's anomalous relation to time is thus managed as a

natural relation to gender ... . Women [are] not seen as inhab-
iting history proper but as existing ... in a permanently anterior
time within the modern nation.

1996: 263-4

Because, furthermore, women 'are subsumed symbolically into the
national body politic as its boundary and metaphoric limit' and as
'the visible markers of national homogeneity', they are subject to
'especially vigilant and violent discipline' when they deviate from
their prescribed roles. Something akin to this last principle has been
applied to the figure of Lucretia in Livy's national narrative of
Rome.[7] Moreover, an interweaving of tradition and change of the sort
that McClintock invokes in connection with modern nationalism is
what gave the Augustan programme its dynamic tension.

An alternative or supplemental explanation would hinge on the
fact that historically nationalism has often arisen in environments
where fears about emasculation are in the cultural air; discourses of
gender and nationalism become intertwined as the reclamation of
masculinity from allegedly feminizing trends becomes part of the
national project. Thus Boehmer, for example, notes the stress in a
variety of anti-colonial nationalist movements (mostly African) on
the resurgent masculinity of native males subordinated under colonialism, along with the corresponding demotion of the female that is
all but inevitable in the logic of this discourse.[8] Derné has studied the
same phenomenon in Indian nationalism, where the subordination of
the female is masked by a compensatory idealization that makes the
domestic sphere 'the realm of authentic Hinduism' (2000: 253).
Discussing Irish nationalist discourse, Smyth observes that this
gendering feature makes the whole enterprise a less than resounding
blow against colonialism, because it merely reproduces on another
level the binary oppositions imposed by the colonial power (gendered
as male) to the disadvantage of the 'feminized colonial Other':

Uncritically adopting the gender division imposed by colonialism, Irish decolonization attempted to deny its
representation as 'an essentially feminine race' by reconfig-

63

uring the national division of the sexes along specific (unequal) lines. Thus, the Irish male was constructed as active, a fighter and earner, occupying the public and political realm outside the home; the Irish woman was passive, a nurturer, mainstay of the family, bastion of the domestic realm of home and hearth. In other words, nationalism imposed *within* Ireland the economy of unequal gender relations that colonialism had constructed *between* Ireland and England.

1997: 55-6

In these instances, colonialism is the emasculating force that precedes a burst of nationalist sentiment, but there have been other culprits, often in some combination: modernism, urbanism, decadent materialism, foreign influences. At this juncture it is worth remembering the frequency with which Roman moralists of the late Republic expressed anxiety about blurred gender boundaries and the emasculation of the Roman citizen male, which they regularly blamed on the invasion of *luxuria* from less virile parts of the empire.[9] This discourse fed directly into the proto-nationalist programme of Augustus.

In nationalist discourses circulating in Germany and England in the nineteenth and early twentieth centuries, the threat to masculinity was modernity itself. Mosse in *Nationalism and Sexuality*, his seminal study of the period, examines how the 'unambiguous gender ideals of nationalism' made it a matter of national importance to define the roles of the sexes and control the behaviour of men and women so that it enacted those roles. Literary, political, and scientific (or pseudo-scientific) texts enshrined clear gender differentiation as a precondition to a flourishing national culture. The resulting focus on family life, together with widespread fears about racial degeneration (the price, allegedly, of urbanization and industrialization) and concerns about declining birthrates among elites made it inevitable that private affairs would become a matter of public interest and regulation. If settled family life was conceived as the bedrock upon which national health rested, then all deviant sex imperilled the nation; there was, as Mosse shows, a widely

64

perceived 'link between sodomy and national catastrophe' that served to justify nationalist attacks on non-procreative sexual activity. In this era of the 'cult of manliness', the nation became a branch of that cult, and the education of its future leaders became a quest by an elite band of males for 'the "genuine" in nature and the nation'. The health of the nation as a whole was thought to depend on men's cultivation of 'manly' virtues such as self-control, sublimation of passion to duty, and devotion to the fatherland, a man's true and proper love. These were set against the dangers of encroaching 'feminine' sensuality and luxury, which were equated with moral decadence and considered to have the potential to lead to national ruin if allowed to go unchecked. Thus for the first time, according to Mosse, 'moral rigor ... became part of the quest for national identity'. In dating this development to the nineteenth century, he betrays the historian of modern Europe's typical blind spot to ancient precedent.[10]

Retreat into a clear gender order was, like nationalism itself, a response to social changes that had followed upon rapid industrialization, turning the old order upside-down since the eighteenth century. By the nineteenth, as Mosse explains, the reaction had given rise in Germany and England to a set of national stereotypes embodying retooled ideas about masculine and feminine virtues and their relationship to a thriving national culture. These stereotypes promoted an idealized masculinity that was equated with national health and became bound up with nationalist ideology as a whole. The ideal male, according to this discourse, was a paragon of self-restraint and freedom from sexual passion, with the physical and moral strength to channel his sexual energy into national leadership and wars of national interest. Anathema to him was any behaviour that was coded as female, in particular any loss of control, with sexual passivity ranking as the most heinous offence. (This was also the era of the apparently contradictory notion of male sexual beastliness, which could also mesh conveniently with nationalist ideas. Ideology does not feel the need to explain its contradictions.)

The understanding of masculine virtue as hinging on control – of self and others – is not unique at all, as Mosse seems to suggest; it is familiar to anyone with a glancing knowledge of the ancient Athenian sex and gender system. Even the modern connection between the practice of this nexus of virtues by male citizens and the maintenance of national health has Greek analogies. In Aeschines' speech *Against Timarchus* (345 BC), for example, the speaker argues that the defendant's 'female' unruliness would make his participation in public life a threat to civic order. Augustan ideology codified these connections by making gender-appropriate comportment an element in the construction of national identity and a cornerstone of national well-being in a programme designed to foster cohesion among disparate citizens of the Roman 'nation'. The culmination of nineteenth-century incarnations of this discourse came, in England at least, with the 'Generation of 1914' and its 'flight from modernity' (in Mosse's words), which was driven in large part by a desire to reclaim an untainted virility from a society that was perceived as 'weak, effeminate, and overrefined'.[11] The tense coexistence within the masculine paradigm of the aggressive masculinity of Nietzschean vitalism alongside the ideal of self-restraint, and the association of resurgent individual masculinity with rejuvenated national strength all converged to help fuel the tragedy of the Great War.

The elaborate discursive system that fixed men in their proper place assigned a complementary role to female citizens of the nation, who were cast as the guardians of traditional order and morality against the threat of foreign vice and the disruptive potential of modernity. Female national symbols came to represent chastity, modesty, and 'eternal' values; they provided a reassuringly static backdrop for male public action and unsettling social change. The ideal woman's expressions of patriotism were confined to those allowed within the practice of traditional female virtues. She could act as a defender and protector of the nation, whose fundamental building blocks were marriage, children, and the well-ordered home, only through her role as wife and mother. The function of female national symbols was, in short, to make 'time stand still in a nervous age', as Mosse puts it. This crucial stabilizing role is the key to understanding why 'new' or 'modern' women were regarded with suspicion and became the target of attempts at social control: they presented a threat to the very order that they were meant to uphold. Accordingly in prescriptive texts these 'unnatural' women were duly punished in the end for their unruliness, and the division between the sexes was thereby restored.

The central position of the cult of domesticity in nationalist ideologies of the modern era is well documented. These ideologies constructed a closed system in which domestic order, national health, and the fulfilment of natural or divine law were imagined to exist in a system of mutual dependence. It was the domestic sphere, however, with woman at its centre that bore an inordinate burden as the foundation upon which the others were thought to rest.[12] Obviously there have been many variations on the general scheme outlined here. McClintock discusses how a feminine ideal was constructed along these lines in Afrikaner nationalism (1996: 275-7). In Germany and Italy these ideological trends culminated in the rigid gender divisions of fascism – an extreme version of nationalism, where the discursive scheme in regard to gender and sexuality is likewise 'merely a particularly feverish example of a more general formation'.[13]

Wanted: manly youths, strict mothers, civic martyrs

An established approach to Augustan texts involves reading against the grain of their apparent 'message' for ironic or even subversive undercurrents.[14] Although the *Odes* are certainly complex poems that admit many levels of reading, here I want to take them at their word, so to speak, on the premise that their overt content articulates emerging aspects of the Augustan programme, which had begun to take a distinctive shape even at this early date, in the years immediately after Actium when *Odes* 1-3 were produced. This approach would make Horace an 'active partner in the creation of ideology' (Santirocco 1995: 232) rather than a mouthpiece of a party line imposed from above, as he has sometimes been imagined as being. All the 'Roman' Odes (3.1-6) show the poet in this nation-building role, but the second, fifth, and sixth are especially striking for the degree to which they prefigure later nationalist discourses. Here the Augustan programme of cultural renewal is a reactionary enterprise directed towards recapturing an authentic, uncontaminated national past while repudiating the corrupted and corrupting aspects of a civilization gone awry. As does later discourse, these poems invent tradition by constructing an idealized vision of that past to serve as the first stage in a national historical narrative and the site of 'true' national values and national identity. This vision is opposed to an implied or explicit narrative of the present as a realm of failure and deficiency, to be measured by the degree to which it has drifted away from the anchoring certainties of the past.

The key elements in Horace's vision of the Roman past anticipate the standard ingredients in modern nostalgia-driven images of national Golden Ages and 'authentic' nations: a pastoral setting where sturdy, uncompromised natives practise the bedrock virtues that distinguish them as a group; the implied interdependence of natural and/or divine order, cultural wholeness, and moral clarity; and the identification of moral clarity with the observance of clearly differentiated gender roles and with corresponding constraints on sexual practices. As we saw in Chapter 1, no Roman writer fabricated this picture of the past out of whole cloth. Nostalgic tendencies and a moralizing streak run through Latin literature and culture, and by the Augustan era the Romans were old hands at inventing tradition. The historian Sallust in particular comes to mind for his paradigmatic Republican formulation of national decline as moral collapse and especially for his stress on invading foreign *luxuria* as the enemy within that robbed the Romans of their toughness and their morality alike (*Catiline* 10-13). This last idea would reappear in the sixth 'Roman' Ode among many other places in Horace, and in fact became a cliché that was ubiquitous in Latin literature.[15] What varied was the purposes that these conventions were made to serve. Part of Augustus' genius lay in the way he recognized the ideological substance of sentimental attachments and rhetorical commonplaces and harnessed them in the service of his own social and political programme by fusing nostalgia with change, the regressive with the progressive in the distinctive manner of modern nationalist ideologies.

The most prominent feature of *Odes* 3.2, 3.5, and 3.6 is their preoccupation with prescriptive and deviant manhood and woman-hood in the context of an overarching call for national renewal. *Virtus* is the explicit theme of 3.2 and 3.5; in the former the concept is foregrounded through the mantralike repetition of the word at the beginnings of stanzas 5 and 6.[16] A literal reading of this word ('manli-ness', or comportment proper to men) is authorized by the comprehensive gender scheme woven into these three poems as well as other 'Augustan' Odes.[17] The robust youth (*robustus puer*) of *Odes* 3.2 is enjoined to cultivate his *virtus* by devoting himself to the hardy military life with its open-air existence and constant dangers (*vitam-que sub divo et trepidis agat / in rebus.* 3.2.5-6). There he will learn the value of the stripped-down life (*pauperies*) and will, it is implied, develop an aversion to its opposite, *luxuria*, the unmanning force that had been identified as the root of social and national catastrophe in Roman moralistic discourse since the late Republic (stanzas 1-2). Any honour worthy of his pursuit lies outside the contaminated world of political compromise ('manliness, a stranger to sordid polit-ical defeat, shines with untainted honour', *virtus repulsae nescia sordidae / intaminatis fulget honoribus*, 3.2.17-18). In battle, facing a clearly doomed tiro (the 'royal bridegroom', *sponsus regius*, with his aura of Eastern despotism), the maturing *puer* ranges '[like] a wild lion, which bloody anger drives through the middle of the slaughter' (*asperum / ... leonem, quem cruenta / per medias rapit ira caedes*, 3.2.10-12). Here the Roman soldier is unambiguously likened to an Iliadic hero; his anger connects him specifically to Achilles and his battle-rage after the death of Patroclus. Archaic warrior values thus appear to be invoked as an appropriate paradigm, at least in some circumstances, for the contemporary young Roman male to embrace.

Porter (1987: 157) argues that 'from line 6 on everything seems calculated to shift the reader's sympathy away from the young Roman ... [including] the extraordinary bloodthirstiness ... in the description' of his battlefield conduct (Porter refers to stanzas 2 and 3, with their image of the mother and the betrothed of the outclassed opponent looking on from the city wall at his doomed stand against the martial fury of the *robustus puer*). This reading is in line with an established critical view of an important contemporary text, which holds that the *Aeneid* ultimately rejects archaic heroic values as ego-driven and socially destructive and offers an alternative in the figure of the restrained and community-minded Aeneas, whose own consumption by *furor* in the second half of the poem marks a tragic disintegration of his personality. Indeed, in the *Iliad* itself, Achilles' rampage is represented as an unsustainable detour outside the boundaries of the social contract, in a world where social obligations form the basis for whatever meaning life has.

Still, there is no reason why Augustan ideology and the texts that articulate it could not admit as models of masculinity both supreme self-restraint and martial rage. We have seen that self-restraint and uninhibited aggression have simultaneously coinhabited modern nationalist paradigms of masculinity as exemplary values. Not all critics agree that Aeneas' *ira* is to be seen as an entirely bad thing, and again, in the *Iliad*, Achilles is at his most torturously heroic when his behaviour reaches its most antisocial extremes.[18] The controlling tone of the first three stanzas of *Odes* 3.2 is unmistakably one of exhortation, with three jussive subjunctives, *condiscat*, *vexet*, and *agat* (3.2.3-5): 'let him learn, let him attack (the Parthians), let him live (an active life)'; this is how the *puer should* behave, this is who he *should* be.[19] Any possible sub-texts should not obscure the positive value of a picture of restored martial virility in a programme concerned to shore up a Roman masculinity reeling from the feminizing depredations of late Republican culture. This picture goes hand in hand with the vaguely *übermenschlich* resonance in the promise of apotheosis apparently extended to the hero in stanza 6 ('manhood, opening up heaven to those who do not deserve to die, tries its journey on a path denied to others, and spurns vulgar gatherings and the wet ground on fleeting wing', *virtus recludens immeritis mori / caelum, negata temptat iter via / coetusque vulgaris et udam / spernit humum fugiente penna*, 3.2.20-4). The presence of these elements makes later militaristic uses to which this poem was put not so wildly at odds with its actual content as some have suggested.[20]

The figure of Regulus in *Odes* 3.5 is a supplement to the *puer*, a different kind of warrior figure who represents the other side of exemplary Roman masculinity. While Regulus indicts his men for losing the capacity for martial aggression that the soldier of *Odes* 3.2 exemplifies, he himself is a paradigm of superhuman self-restraint. Steadfast, impervious to the pleas of loved ones, and immune to appeals to human emotions such as pity which could divert him from his duty (no mercy should be shown to his captive men, he says at 3.5.17-18), he is guided by his devotion to abstract principles, especially honour and the sanctity of oaths, by which he is bound to return to Carthage. To emphasize that these are to be seen as quintessentially masculine virtues, the poet has Regulus make his exit from the senate on his way to the death awaiting him in Carthage with a grand stylized gesture: he sternly casts his 'virile gaze' toward the ground (*fertur ... virilem / torvus humi posuisse vultum*, 3.5.41-4) in a flourish that acknowledges his own sense of shame while producing an unforgettable gendered image of unshakable resolve. This gesture is marked as all the more masculine by the contrasting but complementary presence in the same stanza of his equally exemplary chaste wife (*pudica coniunx*, 3.5.41) in a gender-appropriate position of supplication and powerlessness. The wife embodies the 'female' emotionality that Regulus transcends as he glides purposefully past his grieving family and friends with the kind of impassive detachment from personal relationship that Virgil tried with mixed success to recommend through his man Aeneas. Not only the historical setting but also Regulus' archaic diction (*duello* for *bello*, 3.5.38) situate him squarely in the virtuous national past of invented tradition, as had the anachronistic single combat of the *robustus puer*. [21]

Standing in stark opposition to the virtuous national hero are the Regulus poem's two sets of masculine degenerates, one from the past, that is, from Regulus' time, and one from the Augustan present (although the former group in its degeneracy is to be identified simultaneously with Horace's own day in the economy of this discourse, where time's valence is more metaphorical than chronological and degeneracy by definition belongs to the present). As a foil to Regulus the poem first offers an indignant portrait of the remnants of Crassus' army who have remained in Parthia since his defeat there in 53 BC (stanzas 2 and 3). Once they had been the pris-

71

tine flower of hardy Italic tribal stock, here exemplified by the Marsi and the Apuli, ancient peoples of central and south-eastern Italy respectively. Authentic Romanness is thus identified not with the city itself but with Italian backwaters where old-fashioned virtues were imagined to endure. Thus Horace anticipates later nationalism's identification of country people and their values with the genuine nation and its practice of making them stand metonymically for the nation as a whole (which in this case geographically speaking had included all of Italy south of the Po since the expansion of Roman citizenship after the Social Wars in 91-87 BC). In the task of forging a national identity the poet enlists the sons of rural regions that by his time were becoming, ironically, proverbial for Romanness even as Rome itself was perceived as falling away from it.[22]

From this height the soldiers of Crassus have descended into irredeemable disgrace by allowing themselves to be reduced to their current status as the 'debased husbands of barbarian wives' (*milesne Crassi coniuge barbara / turpis maritus vixit*, 3.5.5-6). This dense phrase succinctly conveys horror at the subordination of Roman citizen males to women and foreigners while linking national disaster to the disruption of a right gender and ethnic order. This is a dangerous reversal of the way things ought to be, an outrage encapsulated in the indignant exclamation 'alas for the Senate and perverted customs!' (*pro curia inversique mores*, 3.5.7). The blurring of boundaries and subsequent loss of identity that the poem condemns are figured in these stanzas in the pointed juxtaposition of ideologically loaded words such as *toga* ('forgetting his name and the citizen's dress', *nominis et togae / oblitus*, 3.5.10-11) and *barbara*; the latter is echoed at the end of the poem in the menacing figure of the barbarian torturer (*barbarus tortor*, 3.5.49-50) who awaits Regulus' return to Carthage. Likewise the close juxtaposition of *Marsus et Apulus* and its archaic Italian ring with the Orientalizing *sub rege Medo* ('under an Eastern king', 3.5.9) creates a concrete image of Roman subjugation.

The fallen men (*deteriores*, 3.5.30) of Regulus' own time are likewise rebuked for allowing their *virtus* to slip; this is represented as a process of degeneration that cannot be turned back and furthermore as a falling away from a 'true' self. This whole complex of ideas is vividly conveyed in the famous comparison of the men's transformation with wool-dying, with its attendant images of true colours and meretricious staining ('wool, once it has been dyed, does not get back its lost colours; nor can true virtue, once it has disappeared, be put back into lesser men', *neque amissos colores / lana refert medicata fuco / nec vera virtus, cum semel excidit / curat reponi deterioribus*, 3.5.27-30). The recurrent image of the captives in humiliating postures of defeat serves to epitomize their failure as Roman citizens and as free men: 'I have seen the arms of free citizens twisted behind their backs', says Regulus (*vidi civium / retorta tergo bracchia libero*, 3.5.21-2), and at 3.5.36-6 he complains that they have 'passively felt the bonds and feared death' (*qui lora restrictis lacertis / sensit iners timuitque mortem*). The operative epithet here is 'passive' (*iners*), which resonates with their shameful relinquishing of agency, the ultimate male taboo. These are not real men but men manqués, who had been prefigured in the fleeing man (*fugax vir*) and the unwarlike youth (*imbellis iuventa*) of *Odes* 3.2.14-15.

Prescriptive images of women are more fleeting in these poems, but when they do occur, they are no less paradigmatic. We have noted the stereotypical chaste wife of Regulus, who takes her proper place in the stylized vignette of family values at 3.5.41-4: stoical *paterfamilias* surrounded by chaste, self-sacrificing wife and obligatory children, whom he loves but cannot put before the greater good. Working silently, so to speak, through complex and powerful ideological associations, this vignette acts as an advertisement for the sanctioned domestic order upon which national health was made to depend in Augustan ideology. The strategic appearance of the stern mother (*severa mater*, 3.6.39-40) toward the end of *Odes* 3.6 likewise provides the focal point in a scene of right domestic and national order. In this last 'Roman' Ode, however, the *mater* is balanced by a negative *exemplum* – the unambiguous counter-type of the bad woman who throws the stability of the domestic unit, and consequently the state, into confusion by her flouting of social rules.

The poem begins as an injunction to the present generation to rebuild the temples and with them a right relationship with the gods.

73

In its initial statement of the problem in the first four stanzas, the poem suggests that Rome's current precarious state is the result of divine disfavour provoked by the neglect of the gods (*di multa neglecti dederunt / Hesperiae mala luctuosae*, 3.6.7-8); when citizens begin to cultivate piety again the empire will be back on track toward its manifest destiny. By stanza 5, however, the logic has shifted and national ruin is attributed directly to the 'decline' of the family in a linear cause-and-effect formulation that could not be clearer: 'Our age, teeming with immorality, has first contaminated marriage, the family and the home; starting from that source, ruin has flowed into the nation and the people as a whole' (*fecunda culpae saecula nuptias / primum inquinavere et genus et domos; / hoc fonte derivata labes / in patriam populumque fluxit*, 3.6.17-20).

The striking image of perverted reproduction – the age is pregnant (*fecunda*) not with children but with immorality – and the preoccupation with contamination are typical of discourses in which ideologies of domesticity and nationalism are fused.[23] Also typical is that the onus of responsibility for the disintegration of the family and consequently for the nation's peril and (implicitly) the alienation of the gods is laid almost entirely on the shoulders of the transgressing *woman*. To the extent that the conniving husband (*conscius maritus*, 3.6.29-30) is to blame, it is through a sin of omission: failing to control his wife, looking the other way while she strays. In a word he is *iners*, like the poor excuses for men in Regulus' army, even if in this instance it is a calculated inertia born of an unsavoury complicity between husband and wife. The details in the enumeration of activities that distract the deviant woman from tending to her domestic duties are significant for their introduction of foreign values and class transgressions into an already lascivious scene. This anticipates the tendency of modern nationalist discourses to blur the categories of gender, race, and class in representations of those who threaten the nation's integrity, a phenomenon examined at length in Chapter 1. Already as a young girl, Horace's demonized female was contemplating forbidden love affairs (*incestos amores*) while eagerly learning lewd Eastern dances (*motus Ionici*) and other inappropriate *artes* (3.6.21-4). Now, hardened in her brazenness and available to

74

any travelling salesman or ship's captain, she lacks the discrimination to choose her adulteries from within her own class, and the sense of shame to pursue them discreetly: 'summoned, she rises to go, openly and with her husband's knowledge, whether it is a salesman who calls, or the captain of a Spanish ship, the lavish purchaser of her disgrace' (... *iussa coram non sine conscio / surgit marito, seu vocat institor / seu navis Hispanae magister, / dedecorum pretiosus emptor*, 3.6.29-32).

The codes upon which this entire scenario is built anticipate to an almost uncanny degree some of the central tropes of modern nationalist rhetoric, not to say propaganda, both verbal and visual. With a few deft strokes Horace conjures up Hutchinson's penultimate stage in the formulaic national narrative, the moral and cultural nadir that gives rise to calls for renewal, the low point when the nation 'falls prey to ... materialist corruptions' and external influences and descends into 'anomic cosmopolitanism' (1994: 129). At the same time the poem implicates Roman women almost exclusively in this disaster by casting a generic bad woman as the primary barometer of social and moral decline and as a symbol of the diseased body politic as a whole.[24]

In close counterpoint to the powerful picture of contemporary urban decadence in this most schematic of poems is the invocation of the Golden Age with which it closes (stanzas 9-12). The ways in which nostalgia works here to produce an image of an uncorrupted pastoral past could match any nationalist mythmaking of the modern era. The military victors of old were not raised in homes such as the one just described, but instead were the 'manly offspring of rustic soldiers' (*rusticorum mascula militum proles*, 3.6.37-8); at a young age they learned discipline through hard work on the family farm wielding 'Sabine hoes' (*Sabellis ligonibus*, 3.6.38), the ideological equivalent of *Marsus et Apulus* in *Odes* 3.5. The omniscient eye of the *severa mater*, a precursor to the ideal woman of later nationalist discourse, watches their every move (3.6.39-41). As is the case with Umbricius' parting words at Juvenal 3.316, the unmistakable echoes of pastoral poetry in stanza 11 plant us firmly in the rural utopia of invented tradition: ' the sun was casting shadows through the mountains and relieving the tired oxen of their yokes, bringing with its departure the time of rest' (*sol ubi montium / mutaret umbras et iuga demeret / bobus fatigatis, amicum / tempus agens abeunte curru*, 3.6.41-4).

Here the past is represented as a place not only of moral and gender clarity but of authenticity itself, and opposed to the false values and materialist illusions of the present age. Its inhabitants are manly youths, not emasculated cowards; rustic natives, not Orientalizing degenerates; bluff soldiers, not lewd salesmen. They devote their lives to hard labour rather than whiling it away with eating, drinking, dancing, and seduction. Overarching these constituent binaries are the larger controlling oppositions between city and country, present and past, and it is in the second dimension, the imaginary time/space of the pre-urban past, where true national identity is firmly located. For this reason going forward with national renewal involves, paradoxically, moving backward toward this lost time.

It is worth comparing this Augustan pastoral fantasy with Eamon De Valera's vision of a regenerated Ireland:

> The Ireland which we have dreamed of would be the home of a people who valued material wealth only as the basis of right living, of a people who were satisfied with frugal comfort and devoted their leisure to things of the spirit; a land whose countryside would be bright with cosy homesteads, whose fields would be joyous with the sound of industry, with the romping of sturdy children, the contests of athletic youths, the laughter of comely maidens; whose firesides would be forums for the wisdom of old age. It would, in a word, be the home of a people living the life that God desires that men should live.[25]

From the reactionary character of the general exhortation down to the details in both texts, perhaps most memorably the sturdy children, the parallels between this passage and the sixth 'Roman' Ode refute any notion that the type of nationalist programme which De Valera's vision represents is unique to modern conditions. Like

Horace's poem, the Irish leader's carefully fashioned reverie perfectly illustrates Hobsbawm's principle that the construction of national identity 'rests on exercises in social engineering' orchestrated by elites (1994: 76). It also supports McClintock's claim that invented national tradition is generated by a 'class of cultural brokers and image makers' who aim to stabilize the social order after a period of trauma, or simply change experienced as trauma by them (1996: 272).

While categorical statements such as these leave aside cases like that of Juvenal's speaker where nationalist sentiment appears to be spontaneously generated, they do apply to the members of the Augustan circle who formulated and articulated his programme. But the dissemination of nationalist values in the modern world has rarely been a simple matter of top-down imposition; instead, the process is complex and dialectical and depends on collective internalization and reproduction of the discourse. This is why many scholars posit the existence of mass media with their capacity for mass mobilization as a *sine qua non* for the existence of nationalism itself. It is difficult to say how far the process of dissemination and reproduction went in the Roman context. The literate audience for poems of this type was quite small, but Augustus did have mass media at his disposal in the form of public monuments and coins on which images suggesting the tenets of his programme could be inscribed, and he used these brilliantly to target segments of the population that poetry would never reach.[26] Still, we can only speculate about how usually urbane Roman elites, not to mention average Romans, responded to injunctions that they rediscover their authentic rural roots and embrace traditional values in the interest of national unity. The processes that enabled such figures to negotiate the gap between ideological fiction and social reality are equally unrecoverable, though it is true that a gentle irony could be the mediating tool of choice for the court poets themselves. Nevertheless, the resistance that met Augustus' efforts to pass specific legislation shoring up marriage and the family probably provides a clue to the tenor of contemporary reception of the programme as a whole.[27]

What is missing from the ancient picture, then, is anything but tenuous evidence about reception. On the production side, however, we are on firmer ground: the ideology promulgated by the Augustan elite, articulated here in three poems of Horace, has a clear proto-nationalist component. The similarities extend beyond the structure of the rhetoric to the impetus behind its formulation and deployment. In each instance there is in the background a trend, event or movement that has dragged the nation down, whose disastrous effects the new programme takes as its mission to set right. The multiple shocks of modernity more often than not have been constructed by modern nationalist movements as the crisis that needs addressing. The Augustan analogy would be the social change and political collapse that occurred together in the course of the first century BC. Roman moralists had been pointing to late Republican social changes in particular – greater fluidity in gender roles and the relative freedom of women, casual attitudes toward divorce and a lower birthrate among elites, indifference toward traditional religion – and casting them in moral terms long before Augustus appropriated this discourse for his own political purposes.[28] Indeed, one of the strongest links between the ancient and modern versions of nationalist discourse and a hallmark of the essential conservatism of both is their habit of reading social change as moral crisis and consequently as a threat to a pure national culture conceived in highly moral terms.

Gaisser has argued that the 'imperial Horace' and the cult of manliness that British readers of the late nineteenth and early twentieth centuries found in their Odes were put there by those very readers, conditioned by the imperialist imperative transmitted in the school curriculum and present in the culture as a whole. She thus implies that finding a concern with empire-building and manliness in the 'Roman' Odes involves anachronistically importing later issues and sensibilities into ancient texts. It is certainly true that much of the Victorian commentary recruiting Horace to the cause of taking up the white man's burden had an over-the-top quality about it, as Gaisser convincingly shows. But to deny any common ground is to deny the evidence of the Latin texts themselves. The same can be said of what looks very much like nationalist rhetoric in the poems.

We can insist that it is not really what it seems because nationalism was not invented until much later, or we can yield to the clear implications of the texts and adjust our understanding of the history and development of nationalist ideology. The latter approach allows us to tap studies of modern nationalism to illuminate its earlier forms, and to situate Augustan proto-nationalist rhetoric at an early point in the development of a discourse with a long and less than illustrious subsequent history.

3

Tacitus and the Rhetoric of Empire

The noble savage and the anxieties of empire

Classicists and others familiar with Greek and Latin texts have long known that their pages are populated with examples of what a later era would call the 'Noble Savage'. In 1935, in their important study *Primitivism and Related Ideas in Antiquity*, Lovejoy and Boas included an entire chapter on 'The Noble Savage in Antiquity', making it clear even then that they were building on earlier work. They trace the long history in Greek and Roman thought of claims for the moral superiority of the culturally primitive state as contrasted with the civilized degeneracy of a given writer's own society. This idea was especially at home in ethnography, but from there it found its way into other genres. From Herodotus (4.59-82) onward the Scythians, a nomadic people living to the north of the Black Sea, had figured prominently in this critical formula. In the Augustan geographer Strabo, for example, they are admired in spite of their savagery as the most straightforward, frugal, and just of all races; exposure to Hellenic civilization, however, with its luxury, greed, and artifice has whittled away at their virtue, he says. Horace contrasts Scythian simplicity and domestic order with contemporary Roman excess and promiscuity, and somewhat later the historian Quintus Curtius puts a critique of Alexander the Great's imperialist overreaching into the mouth of a wise Scythian elder.[1] Before Tacitus the Germans too are idealized into an antitype of metropolitan *luxuria*, notably by Seneca, for whom they exemplify Stoic endurance and life lived in harmony with nature (*De Providentia* 4.14-15). It should be noted, however (and Lovejoy and Boas do), that for Seneca as for other ancient writers the barbarian *exemplum* could cut both

ways. In the *De Ira* (2.15), he faults the same people for the unso-
cialized wildness that makes them especially susceptible to anger,
thus exposing a split in his rhetorical use of the Germans that will be
of more interest as this discussion proceeds.

At several junctures in their survey, Lovejoy and Boas point out
the importance of these and other ancient texts in anticipating later
uses to which the Noble Savage would be put as a vehicle of social
criticism, especially during the Enlightenment. Yet this genealogy
would appear to be lost on the world of post-colonial studies, where
discussions of colonial discourse as it is articulated in early modern
and modern texts regularly imply that it was the Age of Discovery
and the Enlightenment that saw the invention of the Noble Savage
as a rhetorical trope, and Romanticism and the nineteenth-century
heyday of European colonial expansion its maturation. The hand-
book of Ashcroft, Griffiths, and Tiffin reproduces the current
conventional wisdom on this question: 'The concept arises in the
eighteenth century as a [product of] European nostalgia for a simple,
pure, idyllic state of the natural, posed against rising industrialism
and the notion of overcomplications and sophistications of European
urban society' (2000: 210). Even David Spurr, whose insights will
figure prominently in this chapter and the next, falls into line with
this myopic view of the genesis of the noble barbarian when he writes
that 'the tradition of idealizing the savage takes us back to the early
stages of Western European imperial expansion' (1993: 125).

The persistence of these presentist claims suggests that now is a
good time to reaffirm the pre-modern roots of this trope. I propose to
do this by fleshing out earlier readings of Tacitus' treatment of the
native peoples who inhabited the northernmost reaches of the
Roman empire in the first century AD, namely the British and the
Gallo-Germanic tribes living on both sides of the Rhine frontier. My
purpose, however, is not simply to reassert the ancient pedigree of
the noble barbarian per se, which after all is a given among students
of the ancient world even if the nuances of Greek and Roman uses of
the figure have not always been fully explored. More important, I
want to recontextualize the ancient incarnation of the figure, to take
it out of its isolation as a handy tool of moralists or an obligatory

82

feature of ethnography – which indeed is all it sometimes was. Instead, I would like to examine it in contexts where it seems to be emerging as a component in a larger rhetorical system which on the whole prefigures modern colonial discourse or, to borrow Spurr's recent formulation, the Anglo-European 'rhetoric of empire'. It is the continuity of this entire package, so to speak, that is my ultimate concern here. Because Tacitus is being read as a conduit of cultural discourses more than an individual voice, the source study that occupies so much of Tacitus criticism – questions about how far the historian follows or deviates from his sources at particular points – will be of minimal relevance here. Other Roman authors are ripe for similar analysis (Caesar comes to mind), and though in each case there are always special features and angles, the essentials of the imperial rhetoric that they all channel will have been suffused in their cultural air no less than they were in Kipling's.

An assumption that the rhetoric of empire has a transhistorical character is implicit in the work of recent critics who have brought colonial discourse theory to bear on their reading of Greek and Latin 'colonial' texts, including minor works of Tacitus, without engaging in any systematic comparison of ancient and modern articulations of the discourse. O'Gorman and Rutledge, for example, have formulated 'post-colonial' readings of the *Germania* and the *Agricola* respectively. They analyse ways in which 'the text ... acts as an abettor in the colonial process' (Rutledge 2000: 75), but their scope is limited and modern parallels are not developed.[2] This chapter builds on that beginning by reading the *Agricola* and the *Germania* together with the *Histories* and the *Annals* as a sustained narrative of imperial self-assertion across their formal generic differences, and by taking as its central project a synoptic analysis of this expanded narrative's strategies and those of its modern colonialist heirs. When the Tacitean refraction of colonial discourse is viewed from this broader perspective, it becomes clearer that it problematizes as much as abets the colonial process, by combining justifications of Roman hegemony with internal contradictions and complex under-currents.[3] This makes it an especially close precursor of later British and European rhetorics of empire with their built-in ambiguities, tenuous rationalizations, and transparent logical slippages. As we have seen, post-colonial critics have tended to view the Noble Savage as an early modern invention and, with more justification, as a figure of colonial discourse, by which they mean the later European version of it. But in Tacitus too, the Noble Savage is just one term in an interlocking system of sometimes contradictory tropes that are now widely recognized as integral to modern colonial discourse generically.

On this subject a vast amount has been written since Said laid the groundwork for its analysis almost thirty years ago. For my purposes, a useful guide to its basic defining structures is Spurr's 1993 study, *The Rhetoric of Empire: Colonial Discourse in Journalism, Travel Writing, and Imperial Administration*. Spurr isolates eleven rhetorical tropes as the building blocks of modern Western colonial discourse and stresses their durability, that is, their ability to adapt from one colonial situation to another with their essentials left unchanged. Discussing the Noble Savage under the trope of 'idealization', he observes that the figure represents an 'unconscious act of self-reflection', and as such 'is invariably produced by a rhetorical situation in which the writer takes an ethical position in regard to his or her own culture' (125). Moreover, in keeping with the deeply ethnocentric character of colonial discourse, any idealizing gesture, in spite of its apparent expansiveness, is really about 'us', so to speak, involving as it does the colonizer's appropriation of native peoples to mediate his own cultural anxieties. The impulses behind the trope, according to Spurr, are both 'narcissicistic and therapeutic' insofar as 'they betray a desire to recreate, in these unconquered territories or in these unsubdued hearts and minds, one's own image, and to reunite the pieces of a cultural identity divided from itself' (42). Elsewhere he explains that

> ... idealization simply constitutes one more use that can be made of the savage in the realm of Western cultural production .... [I]t takes place *in relation* to Western culture itself: far from being a gesture which turns its back on the West in order to accept some alternative mode of being, it conceives an idea of

the Other that is readily incorporated into the fabric of Western values. [This representation of the savage] stops short of crossing the boundary from one culture to the other; rather, it makes use of the savage in order to expand the territory of the Western imagination, transforming the Other into yet one more term in Western culture's dialogue with itself.[4]

Spurr supports this analysis by looking at idealization in a range of texts from Montaigne, writing at the dawn of European colonial expansion, to neo-colonialist accounts in the contemporary media.[5] Not all, or even most, of these texts are overtly colonial or colonialist in either spirit or chronology in the way that the writings of a Kipling or a Forster are. But Spurr's concern is to trace the evolution and eventual ubiquity of colonial discourse from its beginnings in the initial European encounter with non-Western peoples during the Age of Discovery, along with its protean capacity to inform the thought even of those whose politics, like Melville's, were explicitly anti-colonial.[6] Clearly over the great span of historical moments that these texts represent there will be considerable variation in the specific targets of critique in the 'home' culture, as well as in other particulars in the articulation of the discourse. Rousseau had the social and political institutions of eighteenth-century Europe in his sights, while Melville constructed his picture of Marquesan island life in opposition to Anglo-American sexual puritanism and the 'utilitarian ideology of the industrial middle class' (Spurr 1993: 127); 'nature' meant something different to an Enlightenment thinker than it did to a Romantic novelist (or a Roman historian). Still, working in their own ways toward their own ends, these texts all generate a version of the savage as ethical paradigm, embodying values exactly antithetical to whatever is perceived as wrong with life in the metropolitan centre. As Spurr (127) observes of Melville's islanders, 'the Typee represent ... everything that nineteenth-century America is not', and while his Romantic vision of what constitutes noble savagery is inevitably different in its details from the conception of Tacitus, the crux in both cases is this principle of opposition.

Given the different conditions of production, the core of what has been perceived as wrong in the metropolitan centre has remained remarkably constant in early modern and modern texts, if we can infer this from the recurring catalogue of virtues attributed to idealized savages and their societies. These include, in general terms, a natural sense of justice; a constitutional inability to deceive; exemplary sexual *mores*, that is, practices that mirror inversely any putative excesses of the writer's own culture in this area; and an ethical and psychological integrity untainted by compromise between the inclinations of the 'true' self and the demands of society. The savage is imagined to live in a state of perfect freedom, construed as freedom from any crippling social constraint that would distort his naturally good character. Here, social rules derive from the good instincts of the majority; convention and intuition are in harmony. A basic common denominator unifying disparate Noble Savage narratives is the idea that civilization, by which is meant the writer's civilization, carries within itself the potential to be a debilitating and corrupting force, along with a corresponding elevation of 'nature' and the natural, whatever that might mean. The Noble Savage is an antitype to degenerate civilized man, enervated by metropolitan hyper-refinement and bound up in a straitjacket of stifling social artifice.

Of Spurr's exemplary texts, it is perhaps the accounts of the discovery of a 'lost' Stone Age tribe, the Tasaday, in the popular journalism of the 1970s that best illustrate the durability of the trope of the Noble Savage through time and literary registers (135-40). In keeping with the trope's imperative to invoke an imagined Golden Age in the writer's own cultural tradition, these reports wax positively Edenic in their description of a people who are made to embody an original spiritual and cultural unity that has been, for the rest of us, splintered by the march of civilization in its debilitating aspects. There is no conflict among the Tasaday, the reader is told; no private property, hierarchy, or pretence of any kind, no linear sense of time. Even the idea of good and evil is alien to them, but rather than indicating a dangerous amorality, in this case the gap is construed as evidence of the tribesmen's prelapsarian innocence of cognitive differentiation and of the split consciousness that torments modern man. Noble Savages always exist in both space and time, that is, they live not only at the edges of the earth but also in a metaphorical past whose features correspond to the virtues that flourish in conservative visions of the national past nurtured in advanced metropolitan cultures. In addition to doing this symbolic duty, the Tasaday are imagined as being from the past in a literal sense; they are temporally dislocated throwbacks, pre-historic vestiges who have survived into the modern world.

Also noteworthy is the clarity with which the accounts of the Tasaday exemplify the principle of rhetorical oscillation in the values attached to pre-development societies and peoples, a principle that finds a number of expressions in colonial discourse. In this case, the tribe's defining *lack* – of material possessions, of a sense of history, of psychological complexity – is construed as a positive thing, as a primitive ideal that has somehow survived the corruptions of history. This is an inversion of the standard use of ideas of absence and formlessness in colonial discourse, which more often enlists them as central terms in proving a need for European moral and economic guidance among colonized or to-be-colonized peoples. Absence can be idealized as a lost purity or vilified as a yawning void that needs to be filled with the colonizer's values, depending on whether it is cultural chauvinism or cultural nostalgia, both equally self-absorbed, that is on the leading edge of the speaker's purpose. Finally, this case provides a striking illustration of the spontaneous reproduction of rhetorical figures once they become lodged in the collective consciousness of a cultural tradition. Spurr (136) notes remarkably detailed parallels between contemporary journalism's descriptions of the Tasaday and Melville's of the Typee, yet there is never any question of the reporters' consciously borrowing from Melville. Likewise even by Tacitus' time, the reproduction of these tropes was more a matter of cultural and rhetorical memory than of active literary imitation.

This synthesizing account relegates to the background the large and small distinctions that inevitably exist among Spurr's, and other, modern formulations of the idealized barbarian; likewise, there will be differences between these formulations as a group and those of Tacitus. The important points for my purpose are general ones: first, that for all their differences, the core structure and critical function of Noble Savage narratives are always essentially the same, and second, that later versions of this narrative have played the same role in 'metropolitan self-questioning' (Boehmer 1995: 145) that has long been recognized by students of antiquity as being central to the operation of their classical prototypes. That recognition, however, has not been accompanied by attention to the larger rhetorical environment that these figures often inhabit in ancient texts as well as modern ones, that is, to their status as increasingly central figures in a developing rhetoric of empire.

Tacitus holds up a mirror to imperial society

Like the Noble Savages of later colonial literature, Tacitus' northern barbarians are also regularly constructed in distinct opposition to the moral and political dysfunction that lies, or is thought to lie, at the centre of empire.[7] In episodes guided by this 'therapeutic' purpose, the values of Tacitean barbarians are coloured as virtues and framed in such a way as to imply a point-by-point indictment of contemporary Roman society, whose deficiencies anticipate the deficiencies of the later Anglo-European colonial metropolis in the eyes of its own moral guardians. The Germans, according to Tacitus, are without guile, a 'race without either natural or acquired cunning' (*gens non astuta nec callida)*, in Church and Brodribb's translation.[8] They tend to blurt out their secret thoughts especially at banquets, 'when everyone's heart is exposed and naked' (*detecta et nuda omnium mens*), either untrained or innately unable to calculate or withhold (*G.* 22). This is in stark contrast to Tacitus' picture of banquets at the imperial court. There, fear and suspicion have so distorted the atmosphere that guests maintain a studied artificiality even through the most alarming events – a murder between courses, for example, as at *Ann.* 13.16, where Agrippina and Octavia, long conditioned to hide their true feelings in public, repress any normal response to the poison-induced collapse of Britannicus. The ingenuous openness of the Germans is also illustrated by the lavish and indiscriminate hospitality that they practise toward friend and stranger alike (*G.*

21). Their moral distance from the imperial centre is further marked by the 'fact' that gold, silver, and other precious elements mean nothing to them, and usury has yet to be invented (5, 26, 45).

But it is especially in their domestic arrangements that the Germans prove themselves to be shining antitypes to the degenerate masters of empire. Their society is imagined as being supremely well-ordered in the areas of family life and sexual morality, as it is in its hierarchies of class. Thus, freedmen know their place (25), and wives share in their husbands' labours instead of wasting their time in frivolous pursuits. That marriage is a serious business is signalled by the groom's dowry of practical and martial gifts – livestock and weapons – rather than any luxury items for pampering the bride (*munera non ad delicias muliebres ... nec quibus nova nupta comatur, sed boves et frenatum equum et scutum cum framea gladioque*, 18). A premium is placed on female chastity, which is not exposed to the urban(e) temptations that lurk at the theatres and dinner parties of Rome (*saepta pudicitia agunt, nullis spectaculorum inlecebris, nullis conviviorum inritationibus corruptae*). Flirtation is frowned upon (the idea of a secret correspondence between lovers is alien to men and women alike), and Tacitus writes that 'no one there laughs at vice, or thinks it fashionable to seduce and be seduced' (*nemo enim illic vitia ridet, nec corrumpere et corrumpi saeculum vocatur*, 19). These last details seem calculated to cast the Germans as veritable anti-Ovids. In the same vein, it is considered a crime (*flagitium*) to limit the number of children born into a family (19); there is 'no reward for childlessless' (*nec ulla orbitatis pretia*) in the form of extravagant gifts from legacy-hunters, since any property of the deceased automatically passes to other family members in succession (20). Children are nursed and raised by their own mothers instead of being handed over to wet-nurses and slaves (*sua quemque mater uberibus alit, nec ancillis ac nutricibus delegantur*, 20); this reads like a response to Messalla's complaints about modern Roman child-rearing in Tacitus' roughly contemporary *Dialogue on Orators*.[9] Finally, boy children are not turned into sissies by 'refinements of education' (*educationis deliciae*), and all children are robust, like their robust parents (*robora parentum liberi referunt*, 20). This pervasive concern with cultivating

masculinity is also reflected in the approving mention of the punishment of male sexual deviants (12).

Unlike the imagined communities of many later Noble Savages,
this is hardly a picture of life lived free of social constraint. Tacitus
describes a world where social and sexual rules do exist and are
sometimes transgressed; when that happens, punishment swiftly
follows. He dwells in particular and with apparent approval on the
harsh treatment of unfaithful wives, whose husbands are licensed to
shave their heads, strip them naked, expel them from the house and
flog them through the community (19). Yet the narrative gives the
impression that such incidents are rare exceptions in an overall environment of willing compliance. In fact, Tacitus says explicitly that
the exemplary behaviour of the Germans within their own communities is motivated not so much by the goad of external law as by
their naturally good character, which gives rise to good habits: 'there,
good character has the force that good laws do elsewhere' (19,
plusque ibi boni mores valent quam alibi bonae leges). This rhetorical
commonplace locates Tacitus' account of German society squarely in
the tradition of Golden Age visions of earlier *Roman* society that are
standard in the Republican and early imperial moralists. Sallust, for
example, channelling nostalgia for an imagined past, laments lost
national virtue while idealizing the Romans of an earlier time,
among whom 'what was right and good had force not because of laws
but because of their natural character' (*Catiline* 9: *ius bonumque
apud eos non legibus magis quam natura valebat*).[10]

For Tacitus the moral life equates with a conservative social and
sexual order, which in turn would seem to represent, in some sense,
the 'natural' order as well. Unlike that of the Romans, he implies,
the 'natural' virtue of the Germans has not yet been corrupted by the
depredations of advanced civilization, which for a moralist might
include, among other things, the blurring of gender roles. With its
implied denigration of 'effeminate' metropolitan practices, the
admiring picture of German society in these passages is a heavily
gendered one. Among the Germans, gender roles are clear: women
are supportive, chaste, and devoted to their families, while male
virtue consists largely of martial vigour: cowardice in war is consid-

ered the basest of crimes, and there is an ongoing competition in *virtus* among the men (*G.* 6, 14). This last motif is again lifted from the rhetorical arsenal deployed by Roman moralists in critiques of their own society: Sallust longs for the 'rivalry in glory' (*certamen gloriae*) that supposedly inspired the martial exploits of early Roman youth (*Catiline* 7). It is this martial side of noble barbarism that comes to the fore in the works of Tacitus apart from the *Germania*, which takes an ethnographic interest in social institutions and domestic customs while keeping in the background the traditionally male spheres of action – politics and warfare – that are central to most ancient history and biography.

Male martial vigour is not, to be sure, a consistent feature of later Noble Savage narratives, where savages are often quite peace-loving to counter the militarism that characterizes the 'developed' world. Nevertheless, Tacitus' accounts do follow the general principle that what is considered lost at the centre of empire is what is found on its periphery; in this instance one of those things would be manliness and gender clarity, which are readily demonstrated in war. In the *Annals*, the *Histories*, and the *Agricola*, we meet primarily male barbarians who in their function as Noble Savages are marked by courage in battle, often to the point of recklessness. Thus at *Ann.* 2.17, for example, the German chieftain Arminius swashbuckles his way through an engagement to the apparent admiration of the narrator (there is even here, however, a secondary suggestion that after fighting with abandon Arminius employs *fraus*, or trickery, to escape; this reveals the dormant negative side of even idealized barbarians, which can be moved to the forefront if the rhetorical situation requires it). Pride is another hallmark of manly barbarians, evinced in their refusal to grovel before their Roman conquerors (for example *Ann.* 12.36-7, the British king Caratacus' dignified comportment as a prisoner of war in Rome). Above all, the barbarian warriors of the north are characterized by their love of freedom and hatred of slavery, by which they mean submission to foreign rule. Tacitus has them pledge this at regular intervals, most memorably in the several spirited speeches of resistance to Roman rule that he attributes to prominent barbarian leaders (see below).[11] Not all of

91

these leaders are male, but the manly resolve of the British Queen Boudicca (*Ann.* 14.35) only serves to reinforce the idea of the utter absence of this quality in those whose proper province it ought to be: elite Roman males.

One of the many paradoxes of modern colonial discourse lies in the space that it allows for ambivalence toward the imperial culture that the discourse officially champions, as the anxieties of empire and cultural pessimism on the home front alternate with bracing talk about a civilizing mission. It is this duality that enables the same discourse to generate figures as apparently at odds as the Noble Savage and the debased colonial Other. 'Civilization', whose dissemination is a purported goal of empire, itself becomes a contested term. Likewise in Tacitus, when 'uncivilized' barbarians practise virtues that have disappeared from civilized society, civilization begins to look like a potentially debilitating force. The critiques of Roman rule that appear at regular intervals naturally include the standard complaints about taxes, conscription, graft and corruption, arrogance, lust and rapacity, sometimes put in the mouths of disgruntled provincials but often enough given the ring of legitimacy when they are voiced by the historian himself.[12] But Roman rule and Romanization are also equated repeatedly with slavery, in the obvious political sense but also in the sense of a moral slavery that is thought to result from contact with Rome's seductive culture of pleasure. Tacitus has his star Noble Savages, both German and British, hurl various combinations of these charges in their speeches. Arminius, Caratacus, and Boudicca concentrate on political slavery and Roman oppression (*Ann.* 2.15; 12.34; 14.35), while Calgacus in his famous speech in the *Agricola* adds that it is their voracious appetite for luxury that drives the Romans to ransack the world from east to west for treasures (30; see also 15, where the British commons make the same charge). The same idea is expressed by a group of rebel envoys during the Batavian revolt, who identify *luxuria* as an actual implement of Roman rule when they urge the wavering inhabitants of the Roman colony of Cologne to cast off the pleasures of Roman culture, which keep them subjugated as surely as do arms (*H.* 4.64).

3. Tacitus and the Rhetoric of Empire

One can in fact trace a kind of barbarian hierarchy in the corpus as a whole, in which the hardiest peoples are the most remote, and the most enervated those who have had the most contact with Roman civilization, which in turn represents perfect enervation. Like the figure of the Noble Savage to which it gives rise, the idea that urban civilization is a mixed blessing with the power to make people soft and degenerate was conventional in ancient ethnography.[13] To cite a famous Roman example, Caesar begins the *Gallic War* with the observation that of all the Gauls the Belgae are the most courageous because they are 'farthest from the culture and civilization' (*a cultu atque humanitate*) of the long-Romanized province of Gallia Narbonensis and thus have little exposure to merchants peddling wares that make people effeminate (*ea quae ad effeminandos animos pertinent*) (1.1). Given the contexts, in both cases we can see features of the ethnographic tradition being transformed into tropes of colonial discourse. For Tacitus at least there was a convergence of that tradition and his own intellectual inclinations, both of which dovetail with the rhetorical commonplaces about Roman *luxuria* that also inform these passages. As Rives puts it, 'ethnography had traditionally served as a forum for discussing the sorts of moral and social issues in which Tacitus had ... a keen interest' (1999: 51).

Apart from their conventional aspects, other factors can interfere with taking speeches such as those attributed to Calgacus at face value, most obviously questions about characterization and the reliability of narrators. But the historian himself often appears to endorse the correlation of Roman culture with softness and moral enervation. He does this most notably in the sustained editorial comments inserted into a much studied section of the *Agricola* (21). Here Tacitus appears to impute to Agricola's aggressive programme of Romanization the ulterior motive of habituating the Britons to metropolitan pleasures in order to render them complacent in the face of foreign rule: the colonial governor institutes his measures 'so that they would grow accustomed to peace and leisure because of the pleasures that they offered, whereas before, being uncouth and unsettled, they readily took up arms' (*ut homines dispersi ac rudes eoque in bella faciles quieti et otio per voluptates adsuesceret*). The chapter concludes with Tacitus' famous judgement on his father-in-law's promulgation of the institutions, and diversions, of Roman culture: 'Little by little they [the Britons] were led astray to the things that make vice easy, the outdoor hang-outs, the baths, the elegant banquets. And the naïve called this civilization, when in fact it was a kind of slavery' (*paulatimque discessum ad delenimenta vitiorum, porticus et balineas et conviviorum elegantiam. idque apud imperitos humanitas vocabatur, cum pars servitutis esset*). None of this amounts to a categorical denunciation of civilization or a call back to nature on the scale of, for example, the Romantics. But it does show a belief in, and discomfort with, what is construed as the dark side of advanced, highly complex civilizations, which are seen as bestowing their benefits at the price of the moral and cultural integrity of individuals and societies. In this passage, the historian's essential cultural pessimism momentarily overpowers even the hagiographical imperative of the project at hand.[14]

In sum, several overlapping generic, rhetorical, and ideological factors shaped the idealizing strain in Tacitus' picture of the northern barbarians. First, they have inherited some of the attributes, such as hospitality and sexual continence, already assigned by convention to Noble Savages in the Greek and Roman literary and especially the ethnographic tradition. Further, they are fashioned in such a way as to exemplify values and practices antithetical to those regularly appearing in the catalogues of contemporary vice that form the backbone of the Roman rhetoric of decline. In this scheme, arguably the main structuring mechanism of conservative Roman thought including that of Tacitus, the stock markers of social and moral collapse include misbehaving women, emasculated men, deviant sexuality, frivolous love affairs, and neglect of the family, all set against a backdrop of generalized *luxuria*. Roman society, in this view, has now reached a nadir of hyper-refined effeminacy. Given the ubiquity of this discourse in Latin literature, 'now' could be almost any time, but the call grew shriller with the territorial expansion that transformed Rome into a rich, cosmopolitan imperial capital. It is the Tacitean vision of this imperial capital's court that forms the final term in his contrapuntal fabrication of the barbarians. The formulation of this vision had begun before its full development in the *Annals*, as can be seen from the unflattering glimpses of Domitian and his court in the *Agricola* (39; 42-3). It is informed by conservative indignation at the transgression of established gender and class boundaries: the *Annals* are full of pushy women (notably the younger Agrippina, among many others), pathetic, emasculated men (most of the senate), unconventional pairings, sensationally recounted (Nero's 'marriage' to the eunuch Pythagoras, 15.37), and unsavoury portraits of foreign-born freedmen in government service (the 'effeminate' Polyclitus with his lavish retinue, for example, sent as an envoy to negotiate peace with Boudicca and her manly fighters, with whom he is pointedly juxtaposed, 14.39). To these standard complaints Tacitus adds as evidence of decline his own picture of a culture of artifice in which sycophancy and dissimulation distort all thought and action and the state's chief men are enslaved to the whims of unworthy rulers.[15]

Thus the empire that Tacitus imagines is structured at one level by a systematic antithesis between the defining qualities of degenerate metropolitans at the imperial centre and those of dwellers on the northern frontiers *qua* Noble Savages (duplicity versus honesty; slavishness versus independence; gender transgression versus good gender order, and so on). This system of antitheses is the surest sign, first of all, that we are meant to admire the barbarians, at least sometimes, and second that they are more than anything else rhetorical figures that enable Tacitus to talk about the state of his own culture both in the recent past that his works reconstruct and in his own lifetime, since the depth of the cultural pessimism that animates his accounts of the earlier principate makes it unlikely that it evaporated altogether with the advent of the Antonines, even if there were reasons to be optimistic in the political sphere. As O'Gorman puts it, any Roman literary foray into 'uncivilized' lands is really 'a search for Rome and what are seen as Roman values'.[16] She refers to the *Germania*, but the critical function assigned to the 'unspoiled' cultural and moral foils on the empire's northern edges in the Tacitean corpus as a whole anticipates the essentially 'narcissistic and therapeutic' uses to which later colonial discourse in its more self-critical moments would put its own colonized peoples.

The barbarian as sign of social and moral disorder

The capacity of the discourse to oscillate between self-righteousness and self-doubt, and sometimes to pulsate with both simultaneously, accounts in large part for the fact that what is stressed in Tacitus' depiction of the peoples to the north is far from consistent. His focus can shift with rhetorical expedience or become entangled in the ambivalence that hangs over even 'positive' assessments of subject peoples and those just beyond the reach of empire in the discourse of the colonizer. The same people who in one setting functioned as Noble Savages can later do duty as the 'debased' colonial Other, to use Spurr's term, sometimes even within the same text. Already in antiquity these were the dominant models available to an imperial historian when he came to represent the tribes at and beyond the empire's frontiers. There are certainly passages in Tacitus where the northern barbarians and remote, relatively new provincials are described in neutral terms, or where the picture of their interactions with Rome suggests something of the complexity that could characterize actual relations between provincials and the imperial centre, and native and Roman culture, in the empire within the frontiers.[17] Still, rhetorical pressures keep pulling him back to reliance on 'the prisms of inherited tropes … [of] the Noble Savage or the unregenerate primitive', in the words of a recent critic writing about eighteenth- and nineteenth-century Anglo-European views of Africans (Boehmer 1995: 45). When a bedrock Roman chauvinism supersedes Tacitus' cultural anxieties and moral preoccupations in framing a scene, it is the unregenerate primitive that takes centre stage.

From this angle, high barbarian spirits and devotion to *libertas* become unruliness and lack of self-restraint, displayed in everything from disorder in battle and a tendency to flee when the battle turns against them to utter indolence on the homefront. The picture of German sloth in the face of possible Roman attacks at *Ann.* 1.50 is typical: while the Romans organize their assault, the Germans impose no check on their own habitual revelry. Sentries and other indications of awareness of the impending danger are nowhere to be found; instead, they drink until they pass out at their tables or in bed, creating a scene of carelessness and disorder that from the Roman point of view would be inappropriate even in peacetime. Tacitus at several points remarks that wild barbarian valour is insufficient in itself and needs a generous dose of Roman discipline (*Ann.* 2.45; *G.* 30), and elsewhere deflates their bellicose posturing with accounts of flight from battle even by their leaders (*Ann.* 1.68, Arminius and Inguiomerus). At home, according to Tacitus, the same Germans who with a turn of the rhetorical prism can exemplify good domestic and sexual order spend most of their time in idleness, sleeping, eating, and drinking while the women do all the work; their frequent prolonged drinking bouts often lead to violent quarrels, and in their passion for gambling they throw away their property and even their freedom (*G.* 15; 22-4). To this picture of barbarian squalor could be added bad hygiene: at *Ann.* 13.57 Tacitus notes how effective the clothes of the Ubii were for snuffing out wildfires, owing to the layers of filth left on them by common use. *Libertas*, then, does have its disadvantages; it can be expressed as lack of discipline in all areas of life (*G.* 11, where it is the Germans' failure to be punctual that is offered as proof of this general observation).

When the negative side of barbarian alterity is foregrounded, furthermore, plain-speaking is replaced by perfidy, directed as often at each other as at the Romans (there are many examples, including *Ann.* 2.88 and 12.40, internecine treachery; *H.* 4.37 and 4.57, treachery against Rome). Golden Age virtues are crowded out by superstitious ignorance (for example *Ann.* 13.57, the attempts of the Ubii to use weapons to drive off flames as if they were wild beasts) and gratuitous cruelty. German wartime atrocities come to light early in Tiberius' reign when the Romans stumble upon the site of Varus' defeat in the Teutoburg Forest some six years earlier. There they find skulls nailed to tree-trunks and other evidence of torture and barbarous rites: pillories, ditches, and altars upon which captive Roman soldiers would have been immolated (*Ann.*

1.61). This is the sort of thing that the reader is to imagine Germanicus having in mind in the next book when he attacks the Germans for their flouting of 'divine and human law' (*non divini, non humani iuris memores, Ann.* 2.14), which is presented as universal and as universally known. British rebels are no better: 'In their rage and success they did not omit any type of savagery that comes naturally to barbarians (*Ag.* 16, *nec ullum in barbaris ingeniis saevitiae genus omisit ira et victoria*). Mining another 'debasing' vein in his remarks on the Germans' failure to recognize the value of amber, Tacitus hints at their barbarian obtuseness, though just as often this 'negative' quality contains seeds of virtue – in this case, innocence of *luxuria* (*G.* 45). But the negation of the Britons goes so far as to deny them a history of their own, a defining feature of civilization: 'As usual with barbarians, not much is known about the identity of the island's first inhabitants, whether they were indigenous or came from somewhere else' (*Britanniam qui mortales initio coluerint, indigenae an invecti, ut inter barbaros, parum compertum, Ag.* 11). Here the gesture of erasing the natives' history before the coming of the Romans conveniently clears the way for the narrative of Roman Britain.[18]

When Tacitus arrays barbarians and Roman legions against each other in battle, the whole complex of negative values that the first group is made to bear can be concentrated in especially clear and concise ways. Several such engagements in Britain are cast as classic showdowns between chaos and order and all the attendant values that inhere conventionally in each. At *Ann.* 14.30, when Suetonius Paulinus lands his forces on the island of Mona (Anglesey) where fugitive rebels have found a haven, the Romans are met by a 'motley line' (*diversa acies*) of fighting men, along with frenzied females, inscrutable rituals, and general disorder. Women brandishing torches dash among the ranks like Furies (*in modum Furiarum*) with clothes torn and hair dishevelled; Druid priests raise their hands to heaven and utter 'dire imprecations' (*preces dirae*). Together they create the appearance of a 'fanatic female force' (*muliebre et fanaticum agmen*) whose unnerving novelty momentarily paralyses the Roman soldiers with terror. After defeating the Britons, the Romans find in their sacred groves evidence of the same sort of 'savage superstition' (*saeva superstitio*) – in this case, human sacrifice and divination with human entrails – that the Germans had left behind. When Paulinus prepares to do battle with Boudicca a few chapters later, Tacitus again stresses the contrast between the discipline and good order of the army of Rome and the chaotic rushing about of the barbarians (*Ann.* 14.34).[19]

Whereas the Noble Savage is constructed in direct opposition to Roman vice, this negative of the photograph, so to speak, suggests as its corrective traditional Roman virtues, gathered under the general rubric of good order. Here, as elsewhere, many of the deficiencies attributed to the barbarians in their function as negative *exempla* are the deficiencies assigned to women in Greek and Roman tradition (lack of self-control, emotional excess, duplicity, superstition). In other words, when the northern barbarians are good in Tacitus, they (and their societies) are 'virile', and when they are bad, they are feminized, which is ironic given their superficial virility and their favourable comparison with 'effeminate' Asians by certain characters in the text, albeit predictable ones: at *H.* 4.17 Tacitus has Civilis oppose Oriental slavishness to German love of liberty. In the move from Noble Savage to debased Other there is furthermore a slippage in the valence of 'nature', which is by implication a positive force in the logic of the trope of idealization (interestingly enough, in view of the conventional identification of nature with the female). But in contrast, debased savages are, like women, slaves to a dangerous nature that needs taming by the constraints of civilization, which in turn undergoes its own shift in meaning from 'bad' to 'good'. In these features and others, Tacitus' strategies of othering are consistent with established Greek and Roman ways of constructing alterity.

Indeed it was Greek and Latin texts that established the terms for the othering formulae that have been central to modern colonial discourse. Neither then nor now were these formulae a function of colonial discourse exclusively, but in both cases the twin movements of imperial expansion and colonial settlement provided supremely fertile ground for their cultivation. As Boehmer explains in sketching the background of the 'feminized colonial Other' in modern

99

discourse, the opposite against which elite male agents had long defined themselves 'took the form of woman or slave, servant or beast, and, with the onset of colonization, also became the colonized: a category of representation which subsumed within itself those other [established] significations of difference' (1995: 81; she dates the origins of this system, typically, to the Enlightenment with its exalted conception of rational man). Recognizing that the same principle of appropriation was at work in antiquity, Webster observes that 'late Republican Rome ... took the Greek discourse of the barbarian and turned it into something specifically imperial – a discourse which justified territorial expansion' (1996b: 116). Whether it is colonially situated or otherwise, the basic rhetorical features of alterity construction are by now well understood, as is the operation of the discourse as a 'mechanism of self-legitimation' (Boehmer 1995: 80) that shores up threatened ego and cultural boundaries while fixing the identity of the subject and idealizing the values with which that subject is associated. As Spurr puts it, the debasement of the Other has its genesis in 'anxiety over the preservation of cultural order and in the need to designate the unknown by a set of signs which affirm, by contrast, the value of culturally established norms' (1993: 77).[20]

He goes on to illustrate this process under colonialism with passages from British texts of the high empire in which it is precisely a 'failure to impose a series of distinctions necessary for modern civility' (81) that is projected onto native peoples, and which in turn becomes the source of the deepest consternation in the colonial writer. In Darwin's assessment, for example, offered in both his journal (1839) and *The Descent of Man* (1871), the inferiority of primitive peoples is shown by their habitual confounding of spheres kept assiduously separate by Europeans: work and leisure, public and private, reason and passion. Not surprisingly, any violation of the integrity of the body, the symbolic focus of so many generalized fears about identity and its precariousness, comes in for special reprimand, as Darwin demonstrates when he expresses dismay at a group of Argentine Indians who drink themselves sick and then soil themselves with their own vomit. There is more here to the European response than a simple aversion to dirt, for as Spurr notes, the

'defilement of the self's clean and proper body ... marks the transgression of a crucial boundary between inside and out, between the
self and that which it literally must exclude in order to maintain its
difference from the Other'.[21] The same biases and preoccupations
that shape Darwin's picture are in evidence in the selection of some
aspects of barbarian society over others for foregrounding and
embellishment at strategic junctures in Tacitean texts, in particular
the tendency of the Germans toward drunken disorder and, from the
Roman point of view, their general indolence, exemplified in everything from the idleness in which they spent their days to their failure
to keep themselves clean.

A more overtly colonial text illustrates how the spectacle of
savages trampling on boundaries crucial to European consciousness
– in this case, between the sacred and the profane, human and
animal, life and death – has the power to provoke even more vehe-
ment responses, this time from a young Winston Churchill, covering
a British campaign against hostile tribes on the Indian frontier for
the London *Daily Telegraph* in 1897. Here, the discovery that the
enemy had disinterred and mutilated the bodies of native troops who
had fallen in the service of their imperial masters causes him to
unleash a screed whose ultimate rhetorical effect will be to exclude
the tribes from membership in the human race:

> These tribesmen are among the most miserable and brutal crea-
> tures of the earth. Their intelligence only enables them to be
> more cruel, more dangerous, more destructive than the wild
> beasts. Their religion – fanatic though they are, is only
> respected when it incites to bloodshed and murder. Their habits
> are filthy; their morals cannot be alluded to ...[22]

Churchill's tirade is animated by his sense that a sacred order has
been violated and crucial distinctions have collapsed. By perpetrating
this atrocity, as Spurr observes, the tribesmen are seen to 'violate the
boundaries between life and death, between the body and its
dismemberment or disintegration into the indifferent chaos
surrounding it. In the logic of Churchill's discourse, they have also

violated yet another limit, that between the human and the animal' through their own descent into bestiality (1993: 82). Certainly this is also the spirit behind Tacitus' atmospheric treatment in *Annals* 1 of the Roman discovery of the remains of Varus' army in the Teutoburg Forest, with its pointed mention of the horrific sight of Roman skulls affixed to tree-trunks and 'barbarous altars' where captive soldiers had been immolated, all offered as testimony to the German disregard for human and divine laws which Germanicus lays to their charge explicitly in the next book.

Spurr uses the term 'debasement' to designate rhetorical strategies such as those described above, which attach to the colonized a whole range of values held in contempt in the colonizer's cultural tradition. A related trope is feminization, which he discusses under the rubric of 'eroticization'. The figure of the feminized colonial Other is by now a standard feature in the analysis of colonial discourse, the poster-child, so to speak, of Orientalism. In its purest incarnations it has been at the centre of European moves to dismiss whole cultures, usually Eastern ones, as 'passive, soft, seductive, languid [and] effeminate', in contrast with the 'robustly male personae of the colonizers' whose industrious ways could serve as an example to congenitally enervated native males (Boehmer 1995: 86). What is interesting about this trope is its ability to persist in the absence of any charge of effeminacy in the usual sense, even in contexts where a primary impression conveyed in the representation of uncivilized men is one of a primitive, vitalist virility. Yet lurking behind the beards, bellicosity, and brawling (in the case of the Germans and other Tacitean barbarians) is the malign spectre of the feminine, visible in the identification of this class of savage as well with the 'female' principles of excess and lack of self-restraint.

Spurr cites Kipling's description of the British response to a native revolt in the Sudan in 1897 as an especially telling example of this indirect encoding of the female in modern colonial texts. Kipling recounts with approval the force brought to bear on the rebels:

It was an hysteria of blood and fanaticism; and precisely as an hysterical woman is called to her senses by a dash of cold water,

102

so ... the land was reduced to sanity by applied death on such a scale as the murderer and the torturers at their most unbridled could scarcely have dreamed.[23]

Spurr's analysis of this characterization of the conflict is worth quoting for the clarity with which he articulates a central principle of colonial discourse, ancient as well as modern. What Kipling does in this passage, he writes, is translate 'the difference between colonizer and colonized into a conventional distinction between rational man and irrational woman'. He continues:

> In opposition to images of feminine excess and disorder – hysteria, fanaticism, blood, unbridled nature ... – Kipling erects a male ethic of reason and repressive order: sense, reduction, death 'applied' systematically, precision ... . In this rhetorical strategy, differences in power are reformulated as gender difference, and colonization is naturalized as the relation between the sexes.
>
> 1993: 172

It is difficult to imagine a more incisive formulation of the rhetorical principles underpinning Tacitus' description of the Roman army's encounters with British tribal forces, including those of Boudicca, in *Annals* 14. Those scenes are framed in exactly the terms that Spurr sees operating in Kipling. It is true that in Tacitus the terms are complicated by the queen's function elsewhere, and secondarily even in the battle scenes, as a salutary antitype to metropolitan slavishness and effeminacy. This strain in her characterization does not, however, represent a fundamental subversion or deconstruction of the conventional terms in these episodes (*pace* Roberts) so much as a play on them that leaves the terms themselves, and the relative value that they are assigned, essentially intact: things are so out of joint in the metropolitan centre, this variation goes, that *even* a barbarian woman is more of a man than the Roman emperor. In having it both ways, the Boudicca episodes furnish a sort of telescoped illustration of the 'inconsistencies of a discourse which alternately idealizes and reviles the savage' (Spurr 1993: 159), while betraying the misogyny that inheres in both impulses.[24]

The trope of feminization in modern colonial texts is, of course, only one component in a larger system of binaries in which 'male' culture (and ancillary values) is opposed to and valorized over 'female' nature (and ancillary values). Of the terms that structure this system, 'nature' in particular, always a problematic idea, is rendered especially unstable in colonial contexts, its value oscillating wildly in accordance with the orientation of the speaker toward his own society at the moment of the rhetorical utterance.[25] This is certainly true in modern colonial literature, and the same sort of slippage characterizes the colonial texts of Tacitus, as we have seen. Spurr observes that nature's potential double edge is evident even in Rousseau, whose picture of the savage in his natural state as a stranger to artifice and repository of some original human innocence and freedom would seem to place the French philosopher firmly on the side of the view that posits nature as a positive value. But this Enlightenment formulation of the nature–culture problem still operates within a system that identifies the Other with nature and then defines both in opposition to culture, which by definition carries within itself, alongside the negative qualities foregrounded by Rousseau, notions of 'art, technology, and meaningful social institutions' (Spurr 1993: 158). In other words, as Spurr puts it, '[t]he Rousseauian ideal is easily stood on its head and made into the basis for a natural European superiority' (157).

This is exactly what happens in later colonial discourse, which absorbs both the 'Romantic' and the utilitarian strains of European thinking about nature but leans much more heavily on the latter, keeping any invocation of the idealizing tradition with its noble savages in reserve for special rhetorical situations arising after the subordination of both nature and the savage is assured and a gesture of indulgence can safely be made. Nature's rhetorical elasticity under colonialism is explained by Spurr in the following way:

> The concept of nature, whether implied or explicit ... stands for
> an empty space in the discourse, ready to be charged with any

one of a number of values ... . [It] must be available as a term that shifts in meaning, for example, by idealizing or degrading the savage, according as the need arises at different moments in the colonial situation.

1993: 168

The qualification 'implied or explicit' is relevant here, because attitudes toward nature do not factor into the Tacitean depiction of barbarians in any explicit way. Yet a similarly ambivalent and opportunistic relationship with the idea of nature (as an absence of civilization) stands behind the historian's alternating excoriation and privileging of his own culture, and the corresponding symbiosis of positive and negative paradigms of barbarian representation. And here as later the two paradigms, in spite of appearances, are really just different sides of the same colonialist coin. For as Spurr argues in connection with modern texts, 'malediction and canonization are merely opposing principles of the same rhetorical operation whereby the Other is defined as lying outside the world of the speaking subject'. Invoking Derrida, he notes that idealizing and debasing accounts of other peoples 'are symmetrically opposed, ... have the same dimensions, and arrange themselves around one and the same axis' – the axis of ethnocentrism. The two models supplement rather than contradict one another.[26]

Hybridity and its dangers

Colonial discourse offers a third model of native representation; there is another way of being a 'good' barbarian that further illustrates the zero-sum principles governing this representational system as well as the 'no-win' situation in which the colonized found himself trapped in both ancient and modern versions of the discourse. For if one path to approval in the eyes of the imperial power involved an innocence of civilization's taint, the other required the opposite course: domestication and acceptance of that power's authority and its ways. The figure of the assimilated, 'good' colonial subject who has successfully shaken off his or his people's

105

barbarian past appears frequently in Tacitus. Often this figure is schematically paired with a rebellious, incorrigibly debased 'bad' barbarian (where the lack of civilized constraint is constructed as a liability) so as to allow for no ambiguity about the position each figure is meant to occupy in the moral and cultural calculus.

Such a pair appears in Tacitus' account of the Batavian revolt in AD 69-70, when a loose confederation of subjugated, semi-subjugated, and free Gallic and Germanic tribes exploited the political chaos that followed the death of Nero to launch (according to Tacitus) a rebellion against Roman hegemony in the region. At a point in the narrative when some of the rebels begin to lose resolve, Tacitus stages a council (*H.* 4.68-70) in which the main speakers are Gallic *exempla* of the 'good' and 'bad' subaltern in the senses just described. As their names indicate, the families of both had been Romanized in the long course of the occupation and transformation of Gaul; according to the Roman discourse of assimilation, they were no longer barbarians at all. But Tacitus suggests that in these cases the process has penetrated to different depths. Taking the conciliatory position, Julius Auspex calmly explains the benefits of a peace emanating from Rome and urges an attitude of respect and loyalty (*reverentia* and *fides*) to earlier agreements. The rebel leader Julius Valentinus on the other hand, his debased alterity breaking through, continues to foment rebellion, furiously hurling invective against the Romans and stirring up unruly passions in the others with his 'crazy eloquence' (*vaecors facundia*).

In the account of the earlier German campaigns during the principate of Tiberius in the *Annals*, the role of dangerous counter-type to the cooperative native is taken by Arminius, who also sloughs off his much thinner skin of Romanity without a second thought. A troublemaker (*turbator*) with a naturally violent temper (*insita violentia*), he kicks against the foils of Segestes (1.55-9) and Flavus (2.9-10), in his view acquiescent collaborators who happen to be his father-in-law and brother respectively. Segestes prides himself in the good faith and steadfastness (*fides et constantia*) that he has shown in his relations with the Romans and condemns Arminius as a treaty-breaker; the oppositional relationship of the two types is captured in a concise antithesis at 1.55: 'each of them [was] distinguished, the one for perfidy, the other for loyalty towards us' (*insignem utrumque perfidia in nos aut fide*). Flavus too is *insignis fide*, distinguished for his loyalty to the Romans, a decorated officer in the imperial army who like Segestes attempts to convince his renegade brother of the benefits of submission to Rome, whose treatment of those who cooperate is (he says) characterized by clemency and a sense of fair play.

What is especially interesting in these episodes is how a barely submerged Tacitean ambivalence about empire surfaces unexpectedly, complicating any straightforward reading of the established binary scheme. Although formally Arminius has been cast in the role of the villain here, the qualities that elsewhere make him a Noble Savage manage to assert themselves and threaten to disrupt the train of imperial apologetic that fundamentally structures these episodes. Thus, in a speech urging resistance to Segestes' advice, he offers the usual stark choice between *libertas* and slavery to Roman masters, but also exhorts the Germans to defend a trinity of values that the Romans would recognize as dear to their own hearts: fatherland, ancestors, and ancient ways (*patriam parentes antiqua*, 1.59). And in his argument with Flavus at 2.10, where the positions taken seem to be given equal weight, Arminius insults his brother by calling him a deserter and a traitor (*desertor et proditor*); earlier, he had mocked Flavus' military awards as cheap trinkets with which his servitude has been bought (*inridente Arminio vilia servitii pretia*, 2.9). Given the thematics of slavery and freedom in the *Annals* and the positive values associated with noble barbarians elsewhere in Tacitus, these words cannot be devoid of sympathetic resonances.

One might expect trouble from a tenuously Romanized character like Arminius, but the figure of the reliably 'good', apparently successfully assimilated barbarian who seems to embrace his new identity and harbour no inclination to revert (exemplified above by Julius Auspex) presents its own set of problems. As the treachery of the more thoroughly Romanized Gallic insurgents makes clear, one could never be entirely sure which side such figures were on. Later European colonial literature teems with suspicion, justified or not, of the true motives of cooperative natives, and there a proven devotion to the colonizer's values could generate as much anxiety as their potential faithlessness. This is because such figures, as Spurr explains, came to constitute the site where two basic but conflicting premises of the discourse collide: the pseudo-altruistic claim of a civilizing mission on the one hand, and on the other the need to perpetuate established mechanisms of self-definition by maintaining a distinction between the European colonizer and the peoples he strove, ostensibly, to convert to European customs and values; in other words, the need to keep the Other other in the end, in spite of the promise of acceptance into the fold of civilization and regardless of how whole-heartedly the colonized sought to adopt European ways.

Caught between these two imperatives of the discourse, the colonized was forced into an untenable position, occupying an 'in-between state ... neither one thing nor the other, neither civilized nor savage, but strangely without definition' (Spurr 1993: 84). Worse yet, attempts to mimic Europeans were often met not with approval but instead with a mockery that acted to reassure the colonizer of his own status as the authentic vessel of civilization. The rhetoric about the transformative power of European culture notwithstanding, the colonized could only ever be a pale simulacrum of the 'real' thing. In spite of his famous call for Englishmen of a certain class to 'take up the white man's burden' of imposing English values in the dark corners of the world, Kipling's response to Anglicizing Indians can alternate, as Spurr notes, between condescending amusement (at their scruffy imitations of English Victorian dress) and impatient indignation (at their attempts to participate in the democratic process), depending on the degree of actual danger to British hegemony that the act of appropriation represented. Both responses, however, are shaped by the same paradox, as Spurr explains:

> [The] inner economy of the discourse ... must affirm the potential for civilization in colonized peoples while holding them at arm's length. For Kipling, the domesticated Indian is a kind of child of Frankenstein, both 'Ours' and irremediably Other, a grotesque parody of civilized humanity ... . In such instances

one can see how the logic of colonial discourse careers wildly from one position to its opposite ...[27]

It was the controlling insistence on boundaries – between 'them' and 'us', between barbarian and civilized – as much as any fear of treachery that rendered the figure of the assimilated or assimilating native so problematic in modern articulations of the discourse.[28] He was damned for failing to assimilate, but his efforts to do so were ultimately doomed to failure as well.

In the Roman world the dynamics appear to have been rather different. Romans needed Others too, but the latter were not necessarily consigned to perpetual alterity, and who played that role was constantly shifting with the empire's changing boundaries. The more or less unproblematic acceptance of successive groups of provincials, or at least the political and social elite among them, as Romans in the course of the empire's expansion was after all predicated upon a belief that real assimilation was possible, that civilization – *humanitas* – could be learned. The relative openness of the Romans on this score, and in particular the idea that Romanness was rooted more in culture than in nature, distinguishes them from their Anglo-European heirs in empire (whose pronouncements on this question were riddled with contradictions, as we have seen), as well as from the Greeks, who, as Woolf points out, tended toward an essentialist position that regarded the distinction between barbarian and Hellene as based in race (*ethnos*) and fixed.[29] In contrast, the Roman colonial system had provisions allowing outsiders to become insiders; with the acquisition of Greco-Roman culture and certain legal dispensations from the imperial centre, it was possible for barbarians to be transformed over time into Romans. If the identity of Rome's Others changed in the course of this ongoing process, the definition of who was a Roman changed along with it – of who spoke as a Roman, who articulated dominant discourses. By the early second century the time had long since passed when 'Romans' were produced only by the city of Rome, or even by Italy alone. Tacitus himself, Agricola, and the emperor Trajan were all hybrid figures in the sense that they came from provincial families in Gaul and Spain, but by now their Romanness is a settled matter. This was not always so; for Republican writers the Gauls were as barbaric and menacing as the empire's Germans,[30] though even then this group itself was far from monolithic, as Romanization had begun in the Gallic regions closest to northern Italy as early as 200 BC.

For all the instability of these categories over time, however, in any given period there were Romans, born or made, and there were Others, and there were contact zones where the distinction between them was a matter of urgent negotiation. In the early empire one of these zones was the area of the northern frontiers, including relatively new and sometimes restive provinces like Britain. Here the anxieties about (apparently) assimilating provincials that informed later colonial discourse came into play, including worries that their transformation was tenuous or provisional or, conversely, that they would learn too well, that the process would backfire when the Roman skills that it imparted were turned against the Romans. It is the contact zones of the empire that generate Roman versions of the trope of the assimilated barbarian as dangerous hybrid, akin to Spurr's modern colonial 'child of Frankenstein, both "Ours" and irremediably "Other" ' (1993: 85).

More than any other character Julius Civilis, the mastermind of the Batavian revolt, best exemplifies this figure in Tacitus, especially in the way that any attempt to pin down his identity only opens out onto more ambiguities. Civilis was exactly the sort of scion of the local ruling class upon whose receptivity and cooperation Rome, and the process of top-down Romanization, depended. He was a prince of the Batavi, a Germanic people friendly to Rome who inhabited the militarized imperial province of Germania Inferior on the lower Rhine; he was also a Roman citizen. All of this made his apparent backsliding all the more alarming. According to Tacitus' account in Books 4 (12-37; 54-79) and 5 (14-26) of the *Histories*, Civilis took advantage of the political chaos that set in after the death of Nero to launch a revolt against Roman rule in AD 69-70, enlisting the support first of his own Batavians, then of various 'free' German peoples and eventually of two Gallic tribes, the Treviri and the Lingones under the leadership of another Romanized provincial, Julius Classicus. His goal appears to have been independence and then the establishment of a sort of Gallo-Germanic empire which he himself would rule, although the opacity of his machinations as the narrative represents them leaves room for ambiguity on this question. Tacitus suggests that Civilis initially disguised his rebellious intentions by pretending that his military moves were in support of the claims of Vespasian against Vitellius in the struggle for the principate, but that as the Flavians gained the upper hand his revolt against Rome grew more open (4.13). After various successes, which caused great apprehension in the capital, the Romans regained control of the situation and the momentum behind the insurgent movement weakened. Tacitus' account breaks off as Civilis begins to negotiate the terms of a peace agreement at *H.* 5.26.

In spite of the fact that Tacitus presents this basic outline of the event as fact with a reasonable degree of clarity, it is difficult for a reader to finish the account without a nagging sense of unanswered questions. The narrative leaves just enough room for different and sometimes conflicting readings of Civilis' motives, loyalties, and aims, which have a tendency to shift and splinter just when they seem to have stabilized. Is he driven by private grievances about his treatment by the Romans (suggested at 4.13 and 32), personal political ambition, or genuine nationalist aspirations? If it is a combination of all these things, in what measures? Is he truly making common cause with his German and Gallic allies, or playing them for fools? To what extent is he actually disengaged from the internecine warfare of the Roman factions? Could he really have his sights on being declared *Roman* emperor? Exactly what kind of outcome does he envision? What, in a word, is he really up to?

But perhaps more important, who is he really? Roman or Other? Civilized or barbarian? His identity will not stand still. As Haynes puts it, 'Civilis both is and is not assimilable as one of *us*'; he is 'the space that deconstructs the boundaries that separate 'self' from 'other' ... [thus] undermining Roman identity' (2004: 148-9). On the one hand a sinister undercurrent of reawakened barbarism runs through the account of the revolt, beginning with its leader. Civilis is described as binding the other rebels to himself in a 'barbarian

111

ritual' (*barbaro ritu*) at 4.15, and as making a 'barbarian vow' (*barbaro voto*) to follow the tribal custom of cutting his red-dyed hair only when the Romans have been defeated in battle (4.61). The same chapter includes a report of how he handed over some Roman prisoners to his young son for target practice; this is presented as a jarring deviation from the protocols of war in spite of the fact that the Romans themselves had been known to perpetrate what we would call war crimes. The historian later attributes Civilis' temptation to destroy Cologne, which has baulked at joining the revolt, to his 'natural ferocity' (*saevitia ingenii*), a standard barbarian trait (4.63; in this he is paired with Classicus the Gaul). This strain in the characterization of Civilis is reinforced by the representation of his forces in stereotypically barbarian terms, from their noisy wildness in battle (4.18, 22-3, 28-9) to their motley, heterogeneous appearance: at 4.37 they are a 'mongrel army' (*mixtus ... exercitus*).

This picture of Civilis as *barbarus redux* is open to interpretation. One possibility is that it reflects the author's real, and typical, anxieties about the potential of less established provincials to revert to their barbarian roots, whether this one really did or not; in the latter case, that is, if it was in fact all a ruse (see below), it was precisely these anxieties that caused Tacitus to take the bait and give credence to the performance. Or does he? Another reading says that Civilis is to be understood as 'more Roman than Roman' (Haynes 2004: 157), especially in his astute grasp of the workings of power. In this view his barbarism, including all his boilerplate talk about freedom and slavery (4.14, 17, 32), is an act calculated to win over the truly barbarous Germans to advancing his cause, which is in reality little more than his own political aggrandizement (so Haynes 2004: 148, 'Civilis appears to play rather than be a barbarian'; also Keitel 1993: 47-51, 57). The historian, according to this reading, recognizes all the posturing of Civilis for what it was and presents it as such.[31]

The lack of consensus among modern scholars reflects the text's openness on the question of how the renegade's psychological relationship to his words and actions is to be understood. Tacitus never offers any clarifying editorial pronouncements that would authorize the reader to settle this question definitively one way or the other. Instead he seems to allow his own uncertainty about how to read some aspects of these events and especially the mind of Civilis to creep into his narrative, where he plants a range of possibilities without finally endorsing any of them. Certainly Civilis, in his Tacitean incarnation, has a demonstrated capacity for duplicity. The narrative makes repeated reference to his inclination to proceed by guile, and in the initial sketch of his character at 4.13 notes that he was craftier than the average barbarian (*ultra quam barbaris solitum ingenio sollers*). Just as he originally masked his disloyalty to Rome by posing as a Flavian partisan, so he later hid his vision of German ascendency from his useful Gallic allies (4.61). But the cunning itself is hard to read given that in the rhetoric of empire, artifice can be both an identifying trait of debased savages on the periphery and a property of the decadent denizens of the imperial centre. Is duplicity in Civilis' primitive blood, or did he learn it from the Romans? Did they create this monster, or is his deeper nature simply reasserting itself?

While the question of whether peoples acquired through expansion are insiders or outsiders always hangs in any imperial air, these events unfolded at a moment of particularly high anxiety for Roman national identity, when the civil war of AD 68-70 threatened to erase the distinction between Roman and foreigner. Instead of showing a clear-cut Roman front against an external enemy, the conflict swept up Romans battling one another with interference from outsiders and outsiders caught up in the internal politics of the Roman state. As Brunt puts it, 'in 70 Rome had to fight at once against revolted provincials, citizens (the Vitellian legions) and foreigners from outside the empire' (1960: 507). Tacitus recognizes that this was a hybrid war, both foreign and civil (2.69; 3.46; 4.12 and 22), and in fact part of his design in the *Histories* seems to be to use his reconstruction of the crisis to explore what it means to be a Roman.

Apart from the basic, boundary-confounding facts of the situation, the picture he gives us is further clouded when Romans and foreigners trade identities, each taking on signature traits of the other. In succession the Roman forces of Otho, Vitellius, and Vespasian plunder and pillage their way through Italy like foreign conquerors (2.12, 87, 89; 3.15, 49); Roman military discipline gives way to disorder, cowardice, and mutiny (4.20, 33, 36-7). At the same time the Batavian rebels exhibit 'Roman' behaviour mixed in with their barbarian tendencies, noted above: Civilis keeps order in his ranks while discipline collapses on the Roman side (4.24-5; 34-5), and he and other rebel leaders resort to the language of Roman imperialism to describe the independent state they claim as their goal (4.59, 63, 69), in passages that surely suggest nefarious payback for the Roman investment in provincial acculturation. Efforts are made to reassert boundaries. The strategy of Vocula, a Gallic commander loyal to Rome, is to 'emphasize the difference between "us" and "them" and encourage his men to identify with the right group' (4.58; see Haynes 2004: 159-60). The Roman general who eventually crushes the rebellion, Petellius Cerialis, gives a speech in which he appeals to the errant Gauls on the basis of their past closeness to Rome and sets them against the clearly foreign Germans (4.73-4). By this point the war has begun to be comfortably characterized as foreign (4.72), and the rebels as more unambiguously barbaric, especially in their preoccupation with booty (4.78, 5.15, 17). Order is restored, but it has been a close call. The entire episode has been fashioned in such a way as to flag the special capacity of figures of colonial fusion like Civilis to complicate Roman notions of self and Other.

Justifying empire

In Tacitus we see the deployment of all of these paradigms of barbarian representation in the context of a larger, and very unsettled, dialectic on the imperial project. While the Noble Savage trope implies a critique of the colonizer's own culture and of its dissemination through conquest, the trope of debasement correlates with an affirmation of the rightness of empire, implying as it does one set of justifications for intervention by outside powers in the badly-managed affairs of native peoples. Spurr analyses at length the elaborate rhetorical systems constructed around the rationalization of empire by the modern Western powers.[32] Although this system showed, and shows, national variations, in its essential outline it relies on, as he demonstrates, 'the rhetorical strategies of repetition and self-idealization' (1993: 110) to create a 'closed world of imperial belief' (Boehmer 1995: 43) whose claims acquire the status of truth through constant reiteration. The performative element is crucial: through sheer repetition over time in oral and written declarations supported by images, spectacles, rituals and other non-verbal discourses, the political and moral order constructed by the rhetoric insinuates itself as a natural fact into the collective consciousness of both colonizer and colonized. Rhetoric and reality become one.

The declarations that sustain imperial reality regularly make reference to the superiority of the moral system and cultural traditions of the colonizer as a self-evident justification for his position as the arbiter of the systems and traditions of others. Further appeal is made to a divine order into which this earthly hierarchy conveniently fits. Assertions of altruism also figure prominently in imperial self-fashioning. Territorial expansion, economic exploitation, and the imposition of cultural hegemony are glossed as the benevolent dissemination of the colonizer's exemplary institutions and values, which are unproblematically equated with universal human ideals. The colonial power is constructed as the selfless agent of an enlightened moral purpose, committed to transforming the petty tribal interests that have kept the natives in their debased and benighted condition; its actions are principled efforts to counter the savage instincts and chronically self-destructive behaviours of the colonized. It is represented, in short, as the salutary instrument of civilization, doing its part to tame the chaotic forces of barbarism at loose in the world.[33]

One of the texts invoked by Spurr to illustrate this nexus of rhetorical moves is Kipling's poem 'The White Man's Burden', published in 1899. If this is a predictable choice in this context, there are compelling reasons for it: the poem deploys in a concentrated form virtually all of the characteristic strategies of imperial rationalization enumerated above, including the sort of self-actualizing repetition that inadvertently calls attention to the status of the text's assertions as 'mere' rhetorical constructs. It thus exemplifies the tendency of colonial discourse as a whole to deconstruct itself, in spite of itself, along a number of different fault lines. As Spurr points out, the famous imperative 'Take up the white man's burden' opens each of the poem's seven stanzas. This, along with its pervasive argument from assertion rather than proof, is behind Spurr's observation that:

> ... the veiled burden or meaning of Kipling's poem is that the White Man's authority over and responsibility for the 'silent, sullen peoples' must constantly be reiterated in order to survive: 'By open speech and simple, / An hundred times made plain.' While appearing merely to celebrate the selfless humanity of the civilizing mission, Kipling in fact points to its deeply rhetorical nature, implying that in the face of the silent, sullen races, the white man's power resides in his own language.
>
> 1993: 113

We also see here a hint of another principle that Spurr identifies as intrinsic to the trope of colonial affirmation: the inverse relationship between the rootedness – the reality, one might say – of colonial power and the insistence with which that reality is asserted; in other words, the tendency of the rhetoric to intensify under stress. It is precisely at those moments when the colonizer's control begins to unravel that the 'self-evident' premises upon which colonial power rests are reiterated with the most fervour, as if the words will have a stabilizing effect on a newly uncooperative reality. As Boehmer puts it in discussing shifts in British discourse at the twilight of the empire, '[t]he threat of imperial reversal brought dogged reassertions of colonial values' (1995: 157). Under siege, a rhetoric that is already dualistic grows starker in its division of the world into a collective subject unified by its devotion to order and reason on the one hand, and, on the other, the forces of chaos and disintegration (see Spurr 1993: 121-4). Kipling's poem was not in fact produced in an environment of threat to the colonial values that it extols; its purpose seems to have been to support the fledgling American imperial project in the Philippines. Still, the unusual transparency of its rhetoric makes it a perfect illustration of that rhetoric's potential to retreat entirely into itself as a way of diverting attention from its lack of correspondence with reality.

Finally, Spurr notes the extent to which the rhetoric of imperial self-justification relies on the tactic of appropriating the point of view of the native and even his voice as it presumes to speak for him in the ongoing negotiation of relations between the two sides. Here colonial activity is imagined as a response to an appeal from the colonized themselves for outside intervention in the face of their own incapacity to lift themselves out of their state of arrested development. They need help; how can the colonizer, in good conscience, not heed the call? Appropriation is at work as well when native acquiescence is read as approval of colonial values, and collaboration as moral identification with them; other explanations are not entertained in a situation that imposes the necessity of devising complex strategies of accommodation and allows for only muted gestures of resistance. Not surprisingly, the idealized image of himself that the colonizer has constructed is reflected back to him in the thoughts and words of the natives who populate his imaginary and appear in his texts. In those rarified spaces, the unifying power of his culture's institutions momentarily erases elsewhere intractable differences, gathering the colonized into the fold of civilization – for which they are undyingly grateful.[34]

With the march of expansion abroad during the middle and later Republic, Roman writers had begun to formulate justifications for empire including the claim that benefits accrue to both sides when barbarians are tamed by a superior civilization.[35] We can look to Tacitus for an idea of the extent to which the Roman discourse in its prime was structured by the same rhetorical strategies of imperial self-justification that permeated later colonial discourse. At apparent variance with the sympathetic glimpses of barbarian freedom-fighters and the suggestions about the dangers of Romanization that appear at other points in these texts, there is no shortage of passages that advance claims of Roman moral and cultural superiority to justify Roman hegemony. These claims often rely on pronouncements of divine favour that conflate the political and the cosmic order, suffusing that hegemony with an air of rightness and inevitability.

In his exhortation to his men before the decisive battle in the *Agricola*, for example, the hero attributes previous Roman successes in Britain to their role in the fulfilment of 'imperial Rome's divinely guided greatness' (*virtute et auspiciis imperii Romani*), in Mattingly's translation (*Ag.* 33).[36] At *Germania* 33, the historian himself submits the favour of the gods towards the Roman imperial project (*favore quodam erga nos deorum*) as a possible cause of German inter-tribal warfare, and expresses the hope that the Germans will continue thus inadvertently to aid and abet the inexorable movement of Rome toward her imperial destiny.[37] And at *Ann.* 13.56, he has the general Avitus respond to an incident of unsanctioned German land-grabbing with a lecture about the necessity for subjects to submit to the rule of their betters, into whose power the gods have entrusted all decisions about territorial boundaries and allotment of resources (*patienda meliorum imperia; id dis ... placitum, ut arbitrium penes Romanos maneret, quid darent quid adimerent ...*). At least that is the official line reproduced by Avitus for public consumption; behind the scenes, according to Tacitus, he attempts to strike a private deal with the offending chieftain. In its layering, then, this passage, like others, both articulates the rhetoric of imperial self-justification and distances itself from it, in this case by implying a gap between the rhetoric's inflated claims and the facts on the ground.

But again, at other points the historian himself appears to buy wholeheartedly into those claims. For each passage where the text deviates from the dominant key of the colonialist script by giving us freedom fighters and suggestions of sympathy with the grievances of the colonized, there are more that fall back on the less complicated default settings of colonial discourse. Descriptions of Roman activity on the frontiers often speak of the need to habituate the natives to the rule of law and to treat them, when vanquished, with magnanimity – both quintessentially colonialist rhetorical gestures (*Ann.* 12.32, the presence of a colony at Camulodunum in Britain is meant to remind native allies of their legal obligations to Rome; 15.31, the

Parthian prince Tiridates need not fear being treated with arrogance [*superbia*], the attribute of lesser empires). Moreover, the occasional Calgacus notwithstanding, the standard Tacitean treatment of rebellions and their quotidian perpetrators is consistently 'party line'. In these cases resistance to Roman rule or attempts to throw it off are represented as irrational acts of destruction perpetrated against the world's sole guarantor of reason and harmony. Rebels, regardless of their particular background and motivation, are routinely dismissed simply as traitors, hotheads, criminals, and ingrates.[38]

The rightness of Roman rule is so self-evident that British insurgents are conscious of their guilt even as they engage the legions in battle (*Ann.* 12.31). In contrast to such troublemakers there are the 'good' natives, who are characterized with 'appropriating' strokes that impute to them an eager embrace of Roman values, or at least an agreeable acquiescence to them, all with the effect of corroborating the colonizer's idealized image of himself. Thus, for example, the faithful subalterns Segestes, Flavus, and Auspex, all discussed above, take great pride in their identification with Rome, and in their speeches urge the benefits of submission on their restive compatriots (see especially *Ann.* 1.58; 2.9-10; *H.* 4.69). Reverence for Rome and the desire of the right-thinking to join their destiny with hers are imagined on a grand scale at *G.* 29 in the description of Roman relations with the Mattiaci, a Germanic people living on the eastern bank of the Rhine: 'The greatness of the Roman people has introduced such reverence of her rule beyond the Rhine and the old boundaries that, although they have their home on their own side of the river, they nevertheless are one with us in spirit and intent.'[39]

The most concentrated articulation of the rhetoric of imperial self-justification in Tacitus comes in a speech given at *H.* 4.73-4 by the Roman general Cerialis to the Treviri and the Lingones, Gallic peoples who had joined in Civilis' revolt. This speech exemplifies virtually every rhetorical principle extracted by Spurr from much later colonial texts, beginning with the strategy of performative iteration to reassert a 'right' world view that has been destabilized by actual events. Appeal is made to the antiquity of Roman authority and to the unifying political and cultural system emanating from

Rome, the sole principle of order in an unruly world. The gods themselves ought to baulk at a Roman withdrawal, Cerialis warns, for such an action would only leave a void into which warfare and chaos would once again rush.[40] He insists that Rome, far from being motivated by greed or a desire for dominion, is a selfless, benevolent force sacrificing her own blood and treasure to bring peace and justice to the troubled regions of the world, and even then acting only at the behest of the inhabitants: 'The Romans have entered your land not driven by their greed but invited by your elders' (*terram vestram ... ingressi sunt ... Romani nulla cupidine, sed maioribus vestris invocantibus*, 73). We are only here, he says, to protect you from your own self-destructive impulses and from the threat of the Germans across the Rhine, yet your disloyalty is the thanks that we get for our efforts.

Systematically marshalling his topoi, Cerialis further brings in the idea of the unifying power of the colonizer's institutions to gather colonizer and colonized alike into the fold of civilization. Our interests are common, he tells the Gauls, if you would only devote yourselves to the Roman peace and the capital city that we all, victors and vanquished alike, possess under the same right (74). Cerialis deflects a charge of language manipulation that could be levelled against the Romans themselves when he insists that it is the Germans who are the true imperialists, using the watchword of *libertas* to screen their *libido* and greed (*avaritia*). Ostensibly referring to them, he adds that no one has ever sought the submission of others and domination for himself without thus twisting these very words (*nec quisquam alienum servitium et dominationem sibi concupivit ut non eadem ista vocabula usurparet*, 73).

This last cryptic touch in particular seems to raise the question of whether the beliefs articulated here by Cerialis are to be taken seriously, so to speak, or whether they are being called into question or even satirized by authorial irony. We have seen that what distinguishes the histories of Tacitus is their persistent, and very modern(ist), undercurrent of imperial doubt. This undercurrent runs through the critique of the empire's home culture embodied in the trope of the Noble Savage; it runs through the characterizations of Roman rule as slavery and of assimilation as a process of moral corruption. When the indictment of Rome is delivered by a figure of resistance such as Calgacus, it raises the question of how that indictment is to be read: is it being endorsed or rather held up, along with its speaker, for critical scrutiny? The same sort of ambiguity can be introduced when a figure of Roman authority, in this case Cerialis, is made to articulate the dominant ideology that Calgacus resists: is the speaker a vehicle of imperial affirmation or a sower of imperial doubt? What kind of dialectic does the speech represent?

Reading against the conventional wisdom which holds that in his apology for empire Cerialis speaks for Tacitus himself, a recent critic has detected an ironic exposé of imperial modes of rationalization in a system of cross-references that have the effect of 'turn[ing] upside down everything that Cerialis says'.[41] But one could argue in support of the imperial Tacitus that the historian never, in his own voice, explicitly questions the Roman right to rule others or the necessity of putting down provincial revolts, and that in the balance he seems to accept the idea of a *pax Romana* under *good* administration as a self-evident good, as indeed most Romans would. The fact is that a range of apparently conflicting positions on empire surfaces in these texts, and that attempts to reconcile them, and especially any attempt to tease out some monolithic view held by the historian himself, will always be inconclusive. This is first of all because such attempts fail to recognize that shifts in attitude toward the imperial project and the export of imperial culture are to be expected in a corpus that was produced over several decades and represents the less than linear process of the historian working out his own views. Furthermore, Tacitus stands at the beginning of the development of a distinct rhetorical formation – colonial discourse or the rhetoric of empire – which is now widely seen as inherently self-deconstructing. Our difficulty in understanding the relationship between Tacitus' articulation of imperialist sentiments and his misgivings about this very enterprise, especially as it involved the dissemination of a Roman culture about which he was deeply ambivalent, is mitigated when we consider that jingoism in foreign affairs and anxieties about social and moral decline at home have gone hand-in-hand in more than one modern instance.

Imperial doubt and the displaced aristocrat

The intrinsic self-contradiction of colonial discourse can be illustrated by one final recurring trope identified by Spurr as typical of modern colonial texts but which also has a precursor in Tacitus. This trope belongs to the larger system of rhetorical strategies for 'affirming' the imperial project, in that it involves the idealization of the aristocratic colonizer and his cultural tradition. Here, the colonizer is constructed as a natural ruler 'whose noble blood and gentlemanly character entitle [him] to sovereignty' over the less advanced peoples whom he encounters in the parts of the world that he appropriates for himself (Spurr 1993: 114-15). This knightly figure is a product of an upper-class nostalgia that casts him as the last hope for a 'twilight revival of aristocratic values that otherwise exist only in a racial memory', now that 'capitalist forces ... have destroyed the traditional order'. If England itself is now in the hands of the philistines, then the frontiers of her empire offer the only field for the enactment of traditional aristocratic virtues: 'England's spirit of nobility is now to be found only in her colonies' (116). Spurr draws on texts of Karen Blixen and Evelyn Waugh to illustrate the 'chivalric ethos' common at least in British colonial discourse, even if it is reproduced in the first case by the Danish Blixen. In *Out of Africa* (1937) she represents her friends, the Englishmen Denys Finch-Hatton and Berkeley Cole, as (in Spurr's words) 'belonging to another century': 'theirs was an earlier England,' Blixen writes, 'a world which no longer existed'. Likewise Waugh, in *Remote People* (1931), describes British settlers in East Africa in the 1920s and 1930s as 'respectable Englishmen, out of sympathy with their own age ... [who] wish to transplant and perpetuate a habit of life traditional to them, which England has ceased to accommodate'.[42]

Clearly the discourse takes a deeply reactionary stance here, staking out colonized lands as a space where aristocrats can continue to live as though modernity, with its levelling tendencies and vulgar sensibilities, had never happened. In particular these lands become a place where a strain of aristocratic masculinity, endangered by social changes at home, can be practised and preserved. As Spurr notes, in the universe that Blixen builds around Finch-Hatton and Cole, 'Africa itself [offers] a field on which the ancient symbols of European honour and courage are emblazoned. Men born too late to walk with Drake and Sidney can still recover that lost spirit of nobility amidst the atavism of a landscape yet to be subdued' (116). In addition to honour and courage, there is here a notion of a certain aristocratic magnanimity that inspires kindness, albeit paternalistic, toward the natives, not only because it is the gentlemanly thing to do, but also out of a perception that the natives, innocent of civilization as they are, are also innocent of the perversions that come with its advanced forms, and thus share more with the old-fashioned, principled English nobleman than do the utilitarian riff-raff back at home. For these reasons Blixen is convinced that 'white men of the past' (among whom she includes the living men Finch-Hatton and Cole) 'would have been in better sympathy with the Africans than those of the present industrial age' (Spurr 1993: 115, paraphrasing Blixen). It is easy to see why the 'chivalric ethos' of colonial discourse often dovetails with the trope of the Noble Savage.

Indeed, a recent book has argued that British empire-building was motivated not so much by racial chauvinism or greed for raw resources as it was by aristocratic cultural nostalgia: the desire to recreate and preserve in the colonies the disappearing values and highly stratified social structure of an obsolete class, along with the countless rituals, ceremonies, costumes, and other artefacts that signified them (Cannadine 2001). As is often the case, close consideration reveals an absence of internal consistency both within the trope of the courtly colonizer itself and in its relation with other premises of the discourse as a whole. At one level, the trope is unapologetically imperialistic, accepting as a given this figure's right to subjugate other peoples; he is a natural aristocrat assuming his proper place in the natural order. In addition it implies another justification for empire in its suggestion that colonization offers a crucial means of preserving what is 'best' in the cultural tradition of the colonizer, even if this conservative rationale is at odds with the ideas of modern progress that are used to prop up the rhetoric of empire at other points. Thus the trope acts as a tool of affirmation, in Spurr's terms, but this function comes close to being cancelled out by the thread of alienation from the colonizer's society that runs through it at another level. This is a pessimistic vision of imperial culture, a back-handed affirmation that loops back to the critical disposition behind the trope of the Noble Savage and its implied critique of empire. Like that figure, this one also illustrates with particular clarity the 'narcissistic and therapeutic' bent of much of colonial discourse, which foregrounds the colonizer himself and his cultural conflicts so consistently as to suggest that other peoples and lands exist solely to aid him in their resolution.

One can discern in Tacitus' imperial narrative the outlines of the later colonial trope of the displaced aristocrat who escapes intolerable social and political changes on the home front and uses the 'empty' space of the frontier to re-enact the traditional values of his class. Agricola and, in the later books of the *Annals*, Corbulo are not colonizers or settlers in the sense of Waugh's expatriates, but rather generals engaged in securing the frontiers with the expectation of returning to Rome when the task is completed. Still, they are imagined as lonely, anachronistic figures, out of step with their contemporaries and out of place in the imperial centre with its pernicious 'modern' trends.[43] On the edges of the empire – in Britain or, in Corbulo's case, Parthia – they both find a field where they can practise the Republican virtues that have long since fallen out of fashion in the capital without fear of being interfered with by a depraved and inscrutable *princeps*, his corrupt court, and the ascendent mob. The virtuous hero's anachronism is one of the most important leitmotifs running through the *Agricola*, though his pragmatism and diplomatic skills do allow him to find a way to bridge the gap between himself and his anti-types and to succeed in their world. The impression of anachronism is just as strong, although not always as explicitly pointed, in the picture of Corbulo.

Military prowess naturally heads the list of lost archaic virtues that are brought to life again in the persons of Agricola and Corbulo. Agricola is relentlessly energetic in this arena, setting an example by marching in the first ranks, collecting his forces for another campaign when everyone else is ready for a winter break, and showing intelligence and perseverence (*ratio et constantia*) in finding a way to cross the army to the island of Anglesey. All this impresses everyone, including the natives, who begin to respect him in Great White Father fashion (*clarus ac magnus haberi*, 'he was considered a great and special man') (*Ag.* 18, 20). In the climactic battle of his career, he is the model of calm comportment under duress, anticipating every move of the enemy with his seasoned combination of intelligence and experience (36-7). Corbulo is the same type, whipping his army into shape by sharing in the troops' labours and discomforts while making it clear that slackers will be disciplined; he is humane but demanding, a prudent, patient, and fearless leader (for example at *Ann.* 13.35, 14.24, 15.12). In the early part of his stay in Britain when others would have devoted their energies to 'empty display and official obligations' (*quod tempus alii per ostentationem et officiorum ambitum transigunt, Ag.* 18), Agricola works to clean up the corruption and abuse that had set in during previous provincial administrations. He puts an end to nepotism, lightens the tax burden, and in general governs with fairness and restraint, making an effort to be 'attentive to the feelings of the province' (*animorum provinciae prudens, Ag.* 19).

Indeed, like their descendants in later colonial discourse, both these figures are represented as being more in sympathy in important ways with their barbarian subjects than with their fellow Romans. Tacitus has Agricola declare, in a pre-battle exhortation to his troops, that 'an honourable death is better than a base life' (*honesta mors turpi vita potior, Ag.* 33). This is of course a hackneyed sentiment going back to the *Iliad*, but the archaic echo may be part of the point, and the identification of Agricola with this ethic, cliché though it may be, aligns him with epic heroes – and with noble barbarian warriors. Of all the Romans sent their way Corbulo alone is trusted by the Parthians, who regard him with nothing of the hatred they usually reserve for their enemies. His diplomatic tête-à-tête with Tiridates as orchestrated by Tacitus (*Ann.* 15.28, 30) carries strong suggestions of an essential affinity over cultural differences and of a mutual respect grounded in their sharing of a set of values – honour, courage, loyalty, generosity to guests – that marks Corbulo as an anachronism in the capital. As if to drive the point home, this moment of dignity and magnanimity is immediately followed by a sensational account of untoward goings-on back in Rome, including Nero's theatrical pursuits and his 'marriage' to a eunuch during a nocturnal seaside orgy (15.32-7). Like Finch-Hatton and the African chieftains, Corbulo and Tiridates understand each other.

Each figure has a foil in the form of a 'bad' emperor – Domitian for Agricola, Nero for Corbulo – who is a kind of distillation of 'modern' metropolitan vices. What is of interest here is not primarily that these Tacitean heroes are represented as almost superhumanly virtuous. That is to be expected especially in the case of Agricola, given the eulogistic character of much of Greco-Roman biography as well as the author's family connection to the subject and his desire to dispel any aura of complicity in Domitian's misrule that may have hung over his father-in-law. What is of greater interest is the way in which their virtue is framed. An almost melancholy sense of displacement from their own societies, of homelessness, so to speak, runs through a larger scheme that enlists Agricola and Corbulo as symbols of a virtuous Old Rome which has been exiled to the fringes of the empire, crowded out by the crass, decadent New Rome ascendant in the imperial centre. It is this particular convergence of features in their characterization that makes them seem to anticipate the Finch-Hattons of later colonial literature. Correspondingly modern is the ambiguous 'message' about the imperial project as a whole that these Roman figures convey as they conform to the image of the idealized benevolent conqueror on one level while labouring on another against a background of cultural pessimism that undercuts any belief in their civilizing work. This is the same split impulse that allows Noble Savages and ferocious barbarian hordes to coexist under the same colonialist umbrella, be it ancient or modern.

4

'Crazy Egypt' and Colonial Discourse in Juvenal's Fifteenth Satire

An incident in Egypt

It was not only those living in the northernmost provinces and hinterlands of the empire who tried the patience of the imperial centre, in Tacitus' telling. At *Histories* 1.11, in the context of laying out the disposition of the empire at the time of Nero's death, he notes that Egypt had remained an imperial province since the Augustan settlement because it was 'difficult to reach, rich in grain, fractious and unstable on account of superstition and licentiousness, and ignorant of the rule of law and of civil government' (*provinciam aditu difficilem, annonae fecundam, superstitione ac lascivia discordem et mobilem, insciam legum, ignaram magistratuum*). What is perhaps most striking to us about this statement is its sweeping generalization. Does Tacitus mean that all who called the ethnic pastiche of Greco-Roman Egypt home were equally responsible for its unruliness? Excluding, presumably, the segment of the population who were Roman citizens, is he condemning everyone else alike, from the hyper-refined urban Greeks (and Jews) of the large semi-autonomous cities like Alexandria, to the Hellenizing elite of the district capitals, to the largely indigenous inhabitants of the rural towns and villages? Who exactly constituted the trouble-making *provincia* of which Tacitus speaks?

The historian does not say who he has in mind, but instead, by characterizing the province in such general terms, seems to tar all its main component groups, as well as everyone in between on the social and ethnic continuum, with the same debasing brush.[1] The eliding tendency extends to his list of defining provincial vices, with *super-*

stitio smacking more of the primitive end of barbarism and the notion of civilization's absence (according to Tacitus, the Britons were superstitious), while *lascivia* resonates with the 'decadent' East and with an excess rather than a deficit of culture. In later European colonial stereotyping, as Hulme (1986: 2) notes, there existed 'a discursive divide between those native peoples perceived as being in some sense "civilized" and those not'. As a rule this model also applies reasonably well to Roman (and Greek) constructions of cultural Others, colonial or otherwise. Here, however, Tacitus suggests that the inhabitants of Egypt, whoever they are, occupy a special (and especially unsettling) category of barbarism, partaking of both the primitive and the decadent simultaneously.[2]

Though Egypt-bashing was common in Latin literature, as we will see, the sentiment in Tacitus' note is especially well developed in his contemporary Juvenal's fifteenth satire. Like Tacitus, the satiric speaker erases the complexity of the society of Greco-Roman Egypt, this time by targeting a particular sub-group – the Egyptians of the country towns – and then making them and their alleged bad behaviour stand for 'crazy Egypt' (*demens Aegyptos*) as an apparently monolithic whole. Juvenal's Egyptians are also simultaneously decadent and primitive in equal parts. On the one hand they incline toward *luxuria* and effeminacy, coded here in more conventional terms than those used in the feminization of northern barbarians; on the other they are capable of ripping apart and devouring raw human flesh without a second thought. In the end, however, the primitive qualities of these Egyptians overwhelm any impression of degeneracy or civilization gone awry, in large part because the poem's speaker robs them of any claim to a civilization from or within which they could degenerate. Pharaonic civilization in all its antiquity, which made the Greeks and certainly the Romans look like parvenus, is wiped out with the stroke of a pen. Like the New World natives of later colonial discourse, the Egyptians are imagined, in their imputed ignorance of Greco-Roman civilization, as having no authentic civilization at all.

We met the Juvenalian speaker in Chapter 1 in his guise as a spokesman of reactionary 'nationalism'. It should be clear by now that there are many points of contact between the discourses of nationalism and colonialism in both their ancient and their modern articulations, most obviously in their construction of cultural difference. In this respect the discourses might differ only in the physical location of the Other being demonized. In Juvenal, the speaker's scorn for Egyptians is colonialist when they are still restricted to the safely distant space of the subdued province, but they become a challenge to national identity when they begin to infiltrate the metropolitan centre of empire. We might compare the shifting position, physically and symbolically, of Algerians still in North Africa under French colonial rule as opposed to crowded into the suburbs of Paris raising unwelcome questions about the nature of Frenchness. In the latter case the discourse takes a defensive stance, striving to exclude those newly arrived on the capital's doorstep who threaten the integrity of the nation; in the former it goes on the offensive, marshalling ideas of civilizing mission and related rhetorical ploys to support the subjugation of foreigners in their own lands. Juvenal's poems have long been studied as prime illustrations of the highly rhetorical character of early imperial literature, which was shot through with the devices purveyed in the schools of declamation.[3] This chapter will examine how Satire 15 is structured by rhetoric of a different kind. Drawing on disparate conventional elements in the Greek and Roman cultural and literary tradition, the poem reassembles them to form a prototype of the rhetoric of empire in Spurr's sense, especially in the way it frames the Egyptians as abject colonial subjects of a sort that would have been at home in the imperialist literature of Victorian England.

Satire 15 offers a dramatic account of an event that the speaker claims has recently occurred in the countryside of Egypt, the heart of the Orient in Roman cultural geography. It tells the story of a sudden rupture in whatever thin veneer of civilization the Egyptians had managed to acquire, and the resulting descent of two townfuls of them into a spontaneous orgy of cannibalism. The speaker is very specific as to the date of the affair: he states that it happened 'recently, in the consulship of Juncus' (*nuper consule Iunco*, 27) – that is, in AD 127, but there is no indication of sources, nor does the poet allow his speaker to provide any other details that could shed light on whether the narrative has any relation to historical reality. The thinking on this question has varied wildly. Some critics and commentators have taken the report of cannibalism at face value and searched for documented parallels, while others have explained it as a misreading (or a misreading imputed to the speaker) of Egyptian cultic practice, specifically ritual re-enactments of the mythic conflict between the gods Seth and Osiris/Horus. Still others observe that cannibalism seems to have been a topos in declamation and in satire.[4] The tendency to put the worst construction on native religious rites has been a regular feature of later colonial encounters; moreover the fact that the charge of cannibalism had a history as a 'mere' literary convention did not preclude its being turned to other, more clearly ideological purposes. The charge, after all, was also conventional in another sense: already in antiquity it was a standard tool in political and cultural programmes invested in the radical othering of outsiders (see n. 14 below). Juvenal's speaker is clearly engaged in exactly that, in an attack that acquires a colonialist cast by being directed at Roman provincials. When we also consider that according to *persona* theory everything the speaker says is explicitly marked off as a particular type of discourse, the question of the event's historicity seems less and less pressing in the interpretation of this poem.

The narrative begins with a burst of Juvenalian *indignatio* in the form of a rhetorical question: 'Who is there who doesn't know what monstrosities (*portenta*) those crazy Egyptians worship?' (1-2, *quis nescit ... qualia demens / Aegyptos portenta colat?*).[5] With this opening salvo the speaker from the outset aligns the Egyptians with the superstition, irrationality, and outright madness long identified with the female principle in Greek and Roman thought. After this initial loaded question, the bizarre and barbaric strangeness of Egyptian religion is further suggested in the catalogue of animals named as objects of veneration, some of them designated by exotic foreign words that would add to their aura of outlandishness as religious figures from a Roman point of view: 'Some of them worship the crocodile, others quake in awe at a bird with snakes stuffed in its mouth, and they have gilded statues of sacred long-tailed apes ... ;

there, whole towns venerate cats, fish, and dogs, but no one Diana' (2-8, *crocodilon adorat / pars haec, illa pavet saturam serpentibus ibin. / effigies sacri nitet aurea cercopitheci / ... illic aeluros, hic piscem fluminis, illic / oppida tota canem venerantur, nemo Dianam*). With this solemn line-end the speaker sets up the unified standard against which the chaotic mish-mash of Egyptian religion and culture is to be measured. 'Over there,' he continues, 'it is a religious crime to eat leeks, onions, or mutton, or to sacrifice a kid' (all, of course, common practices in Roman culinary and religious culture), 'but it is considered acceptable to feed on human flesh' (9-13, *porrum et caepe nefas violare et frangere morsu / ... lanatis animalibus abstinet omnis / mensa, nefas illic fetum iugulare capellae: / carnibus humanis vesci licet*). With these confident pronouncements, the speaker displays his tendency to deal with unfamiliar cultural prac- tices by reducing them to absurdity; in this case, he trivializes the Egyptian penchant for zoömorphic divinities while garbling some of his facts.[6] 'A blessed race it is, whose gods are born in the garden!' he smirks at 10-11 (*o sanctas gentes, quibus haec nascuntur in hortis / numina!*). Certainly the overall effect of the speaker's introductory remarks is to establish that in their central cultural practices the Egyptians invert and make a mockery of all normal human values.

At this point in the proem, the epic figure of Odysseus is intro- duced as a device for conveying just how incredible, how remote from accepted norms Egyptian behaviour can be. When the wandering hero landed on the island of Alcinoös and told of his encounters with man-eating monsters (in the episodes of the Cyclops at *Odyssey* 9.287-566 and of the Laestrygonians at 10.80- 132), surely this report was greeted with the most skepticism and derision, as if he were a 'lying teller of wonder-tales' (*mendax areta- logus*, 16), says the speaker. This choice of words catapults both the epic and the 'historical' incidents of cannibalism out of 'our' world altogether and into the realm of paradoxography (Odysseus is called a creator of fictions, *fingens*, at 18). Yet, Juvenal's speaker goes on to say, unbelievable as it is, this very thing happened *in our own day*: 'I am about to relate something incredible that occurred recently beyond the walls of seething Coptus, I am about to relate the crime of a mob and deeds more tragic than all the tragedies; for in tragedy no entire people ever commits a crime. Hear what precedent dreadful savagery has produced in our lifetime' (27-32, *nos miranda ... / gesta super calidae referemus moenia Copti, / nos volgi scelus et cunctis graviora coturnis; / nam scelus ... / nullus apud tragicos populus facit. accipe nostro / dira quod exemplum feritas produxerit aevo*). The dramatic culmination of the proem employs several tropes that will become standard in later colonial discourse: the assimilation of 'strange' doings to familiar artistic forms as a strategy of alterity management;[7] the idea of the degenerative effects of a hot climate;[8] the reduction of the native population to a faceless, volatile mob (*volgus*; elsewhere in the poem, a *turba*); and, finally, the attribution to these people of *feritas*, wildness, as a defining trait. Etymologically this is an animal word, and it subtly raises the possibility that the Egyptians are less than full members of the human race – a proposition that will be developed more fully toward the end of the poem.

Now that he has his audience correctly positioned, the speaker proceeds to the narrative proper. It all began with an 'ancient and inveterate rivalry, an undying hatred' (33-4, *vetus atque antiqua simultas, inmortale odium*) between the towns of Ombi and Tentyra over the issue of who had more legitimate divinities. Apparently forgetting that he had launched his own account with a burst of religious intolerance, here the speaker modulates his position into one of reasonable open-mindedness as he expresses impatience with Egyptian intolerance and suggests the absurdity of their disagreement as a *casus belli* – a war over gods 'born in gardens', no less. The antagonism between the two towns is called a 'hungry hatred' (*ieiunum odium*, 51), and is also characterized as ancient beyond memory (33, *vetus atque antiqua simultas*), a 'wound that cannot be healed' (34 *numquam sanabile vulnus*), and a *furor* (36) that continues to burn (35, *ardet*; 52, *animis ardentibus*) from generation to generation. Such descriptions of the rivalry support the overall representation of the Egyptians as irrational and atavistic. Along with the imputation of superstition, these terms again identify them with the female principle and in particular with primitive forms of justice such as vendetta, as opposed to the rational deliberation of civilized men.

This ancient hatred breaks out into open violence while the Ombites are celebrating a festival, which the Tentyrites see as a good opportunity for attacking. The description of this celebration is packed with highly charged images and code-words that reinforce the ideological framework of the account as a whole. The comportment of the participants is marked by 'Oriental' decadence, an unexpected attribute of rustics which the speaker explains with the knowing observation, 'Egypt is an uncivilized place, of course, but when it comes to self-indulgence, the uncouth country mob has no trouble keeping up with the urban sophisticates of Canopus' (44-6, *horrida sane / Aegyptos, sed luxuria ... / barbara famoso non cedit turba Canopo*). This in itself is a telling characterization of Egypt, inasmuch as it allows the speaker to brand the province (and by implication his chosen targets) simultaneously with both the signs of barbarism standard in Roman discourse, though they operate more often in separate spheres: uncultured roughness, usually identified with non-urbanized natives, and the hyper-refined decadence of the more stereotypical Orient, which in many Roman moralists encompassed things Greek as well (Canopus was in fact highly Hellenized).[9] The speaker goes on to flesh out the scene with a deftly painted picture of the activities at the Ombite festival, which presented an irresistible opening to the rival town: 'There was an easy victory to be had in view of the drunken reeling about and the slurring of speech. On top of that, men were dancing about to the tune of a black flute-player, drenched with perfume and wearing flower garlands in their hair' (47-50, *facilis victoria de madidis et / blaesis atque mero titubantibus. inde virorum / saltatus nigro tibicine ... / unguenta et flores multaeque in fronte coronae*). The outrage of the speaker is palpable: the drunken revelry, the effeminate luxury, the race mixing, the spectacle of men dancing (note the suspenseful juxtaposition of *virorum / saltatus*, 48-9) are all too much for him. Along with the suggestion of cowardice on the side of the aggressors, the undisciplined and transgressive behaviour attributed to the party-goers here strengthens the classification of the Egyptians as essentially feminine.

135

The speaker frames his report of the ensuing battle in mock-epic and mock-military language, with all its trivializing implications.[10] The row begins with a heated exchange of insults, but quickly breaks out into a bare-fisted brawl (54, *saevit nuda manus*). The details in the description of the injuries sustained at this point in the conflict are of great interest in view of the Juvenalian speaker's preoccupation with defending the physical and symbolic integrity of the Roman male person from foreign intrusions of every sort. 'Scarcely anybody had a whole nose (*nasus integer*) anymore,' he says; 'you could see half faces, features other than what they had been and bones gaping through broken cheeks, fists full of blood from eyes' (55-8, *voltus / dimidios, alias facies et hiantia ruptis / ossa genis, plenos oculorum sanguine pugnos*). These jarring images are a translation of the speaker's anxieties about fluidity of any kind and boundary violation in all its forms, from ruptures in bodily integrity to contaminating cultural contact, reduced to their most literal level. They represent a nightmare version of the threats posed in Satires 1 and 3 by the transplanted metropolitan Others discussed in Chapter 1, Egyptian immigrants prominent among them, who symbolically violate, engulf, and cannibalize the beleaguered native male every day in the city of his birth.

The rest of the poem's narrative section describes the acceleration of the conflict as it spins completely out of control. The combatants move from fist-fights to rock-throwing, and then, quite suddenly, to a spontaneous act of cannibalism as the Ombites pounce on a faltering foe. In the narrative, there is no preparation for this development; the first bite is completely unexpected: 'Here someone slipped out of fear as he hurried along, and was captured; the victorious mob hacked him into many small pieces so that one dead man would suffice for a crowd, and gobbled every bit down to the bones' (77-81: *labitur hic quidam nimia formidine cursum / praecipitans capiturque. ast illum in plurima sectum / frusta et particulas, ut multis mortuus unus / sufficeret, totum corrosis ossibus edit / victrix turba*). The speaker lingers on the depravity in the details: how the offenders do not even bother to cook their prey, but devour him raw (they are 'happy with an uncooked corpse', *contenta cadavere crudo,*

83); how they relish their forbidden meal so much (it gives them *voluptas*, pleasure) that they scrape the dust with their fingernails for a taste of blood when the rest has disappeared (90-2). What is most striking about this account is how easily the animal instinct surfaces in the Egyptians; whatever civilization they pretend to crumbles at the slightest provocation. As represented here, they are developmentally arrested primitives stuck in evolutionary time, still slaves to the bestial impulses that humane culture has tamed in other peoples.

The speaker tries a humanitarian approach

The second half of the poem consists of a commentary on the events just narrated, as if the manner of narrating did not in itself constitute a commentary. The speaker acknowledges that history has preserved other allegations of cannibalism, but he asserts that in those cases 'things were different' (*res diversa*, 94). Then, he argues, events were driven by extenuating circumstances – specifically, the hunger of cities besieged in war – that excused the desperate measures taken as a last resort to ensure survival. It is worth noting that the two instances of forgivable cannibalism cited by the speaker (at 93-106 and 113-15) are attributed to Spaniards, pressed by starvation during sieges conducted by the Romans in 72 BC and by Hannibal in 218 BC. What the speaker essentially does in this section is begin to construct a hierarchy of alterity that mitigates any barbarism of western or northern Others while relegating the Oriental Egyptians to the lowest position on the scale. But it is not only desperation that excuses these earlier descents into cannibalism. This happened before the offenders were exposed to the civilizing benefits of Greco-Roman culture, specifically philosophy; how, asks the speaker, can they be blamed for not knowing any better? 'But now,' he explains with glib self-satisfaction, 'the whole world enjoys Greek and Roman education; the Gauls have learned rhetoric and now they're training the Britons to be lawyers; there's even talk of hiring professors in the North Pole' (110-12, *nunc totus Graias nostrasque habet orbis*

137

Athenas, / Gallia causidicos docuit facunda Britannos, / de conducendo loquitur iam rhetore Thyle). With the general dissemination of Greco-Roman culture, he suggests, we can be sure that atrocities such as this will never again be committed in these now civilized regions.

The reverent praise of Greek culture and its fusion with Roman culture into a universal beacon of enlightenment for all nations may come as a surprise to readers familiar with the xenophobic speaker of Juvenal's earlier satires. That speaker directed his wrath at Greeks and Egyptians indiscriminately, and saw Rome not as the capital of high culture suggested here but as the central sewer of the empire into which all its sludge flowed. This one presents himself as a proud cosmopolitan; we seem to have come a long way from Satire 3. Of course the poet is under no obligation to be consistent in the characterization of his speakers, and in any case this one is guilty of his fair share of inconsistencies and rhetorical sleights of hand all on his own. His position on the Greeks is fluid; here he praises Greek culture, whereas earlier he had implicitly incriminated it in the 'softness' of urban Egypt. Still, if we take him at his word here that Hellenization is good, then Egypt should have pride of place; the process of 'civilizing' Egypt began almost three centuries before Caesar's conquest of Gaul. To be sure it would barely have touched large segments of the indigenous population, especially in the country towns and rural districts that provide the setting for this satire, but Greek learning did manage to filter down even to those levels.[11] In general, some four centuries of intermingling between Greeks and natives had created more grey areas than official social distinctions admitted. Even leaving aside these possibilities, the summary erasure of any Greek presence from Egypt as a whole in the speaker's critique can only be read as a blatant act of historical revisionism on his part. In the end, however, all this talk about culture recedes into irrelevance anyway, as his cosmopolitan mask slips and he begins to look more familiar. Whereas in this section of the poem he presents it as an article of faith that the acquisition of culture – or the right culture – can civilize anyone, twenty lines later he will shift to the premise that from the beginning *nature* has separated civilized

4. 'Crazy Egypt' and Colonial Discourse in Juvenal's Fifteenth Satire

people from barbarians, with the implication that these categories are fixed.

After a brief nod to another savage custom found in remote lands, against which Egyptian savagery is to be measured and found infinitely worse – the practice of human sacrifice among the Taurians of the Crimea, who at least (says the speaker) do not eat their victims (115-19) – the poem returns to the Egyptians. In their case, there were no mitigating circumstances; they have no excuse. They have committed the most heinous of crimes, the most monstrous violation (*detestabile monstrum*, 121) of the social contract out of sheer, apparently innate blood-lust. The gendering tendency in the speaker's choice of *comparanda* for the indictment's final flourishes is unmistakable: 'A madness that has never seized the ferocious Germans or the Britons or the bellicose Slavic tribes or the hulking Rumanians rages in that unwarlike and useless rabble who unfurl the pint-sized sails of their clay-pot rafts and lean on the short little oars of their brightly painted pieces of tile' (124-8, *qua nec terribiles Cimbri nec Brittones umquam | Sauromataeque truces aut inmanes Agathyrsi | hac saevit rabie inbelle et inutile volgus | parvula fictilibus solitum dare vela phaselis | et brevibus pictae remis incumbere testae*). In this hostile description of something as apparently ideologically neutral as the common people's customary means of navigating the Nile, we can already discern a fully-formed version of the 'feminized colonial Other' so central in later colonialist and Orientalist discourses. The emasculated and entirely contemptible Egyptians are opposed to the manly barbarians to the north and west; feminizing adjectives (*inbelle*, 'unwarlike', an apparent contradiction of the charge that they are *too* bellicose) and vicious diminutives with undertones of sexual impotence contrast sharply with the virile attributes assigned to the uncivilized tribes cast as foils here.

Alterity in all its forms traumatizes the Juvenalian speaker, but the clear suggestion here is that if one has to be a barbarian, it is infinitely better to be a manly one. This alone has the power to redeem the subaltern and to transform him into the idealized, hypermasculine figure of the Noble Savage, that inverted doppelgänger of the feminized Other who conventionally serves as one of the last repositories of manly virtue in a world perceived as increasingly degenerate. Most often that world is the colonizer's home culture, as in Tacitus or, in Juvenal, at the end of Satire 2 (163-70), where rough barbarians are made effeminate through contact with their conqueror's 'homosexual subculture', in Richlin's terms (1993). In Satire 15, more unusually, the Noble Savage is deployed as a counter-type against another set of savages, but radically debased ones. The first section of commentary concludes with the assertion that there can never be a punishment equal to the crime of the Egyptians, who failed to distinguish hunger from irrational rage (129-30, *in quorum mente pares sunt / et similes ira atque fames*). These Egyptians suffer from hopeless moral confusion; they are incapable of drawing even the most rudimentary ethical distinctions.

In his final comments, the speaker waxes philosophical. Abruptly shifting the terms of the argument, he abandons his encomium on the power of culture and introduces nature as the crucial element in the forging of humane values and practices. 'By giving us the ability to cry, nature shows that she has put sympathetic hearts in the human race. This is our finest sense ... . It is at nature's behest that we feel compassion,' he begins expansively (131-8, *mollissima corda / humano generi dare se natura fatetur / quae lacrimas dedit. haec nostri pars optima sensus ... / naturae imperio gemimus ...*). What needs special tracking in the peroration is the insidious deployment of 'we', 'our' (*nos, noster*), and the first person plural verbs. In modern colonial discourse the colonizer routinely presents himself as embodying and promoting universal human values as a screen for cloaking the narrow self-interest behind his actions. Similarly in Satire 15, 'we' and 'our' are universalized to stand for the whole human race when in fact what they really mean in the speaker's code is 'people like us'. Now, if nature gave compassion to 'us' humans, and Egyptians lack compassion, where does that leave them? On the margins of the human race if not outside it altogether, incorrigible deviants from whom nature herself has withheld her favours, not like 'us' at all. Braund (1997) has argued that the identification of 'humanity' (*humanitas*) with Romanness was ubiquitous and unabashed in Roman texts. Rather than signifying the abstract universalism associated with the English word 'humanity', *humanitas* was more often a term of exclusion, a 'highly specific cultural construct ... a way of distinguishing the in-crowd from the rest' (25). This is reflected in the common translation of *humanitas* as 'civilization'. While Juvenal's speaker does not use this term explicitly, what he seems to be doing here is masking his restricting use of the *idea* with an overlay of its inclusive use, which also existed (see Braund 1997: 18-20).

As was noted above, the invocation of nature here would appear to contradict the speaker's earlier identification of culture as the agent that separates civilized men from savages. Thus the rhetoric becomes entangled in the conflicting claims of nature and culture upon which modern colonial discourse ultimately founders (see Chapter 3, pp. 104-5). The speaker's confusion on this point only becomes more pronounced as the poem moves toward its finale. The most salient feature of this section, however, is its humanitarian posturing (which past commentators have actually taken as an expression of Juvenal's finest impulses), and the way this posturing acts as a cover for a subtle rhetorical strategy of exclusion and dehumanization. The Egyptians, because they are not like 'us', have lost any claim to membership in the human race as a whole. Schulte-Sasse (1996: 80, paraphrasing Link 1990) encapsulates the process this way:

> The enemy lacking subject status is symbolically coded as 'chaos'; he is located outside the boundaries of a system centered on reason. These enemies ... cannot be conceived as partners or even really as opponents. Their lack of subject status disqualifies them as rationally thinking beings 'like us' ...

Juvenal's speaker continues to mine this vein at some length, drawing on hackneyed rhetorical and philosophical commonplaces. Compassion and empathy, he says, are what separate 'us' from the mute beasts and make 'us' akin to the gods, unlike the animals, which travel 'prone and with their eyes on the ground' (142-6, *separat hoc nos / a grege mutorum ... divinorumque capaces / ... sensum a caelesti ... traximus arce, / cuius egent prona et terram spec-*

141

tantia). Because it has already been established that the Egyptians lack the characteristic capacity of the *genus humanum*, namely compassion, it is clear that they are being classified here with the mute beasts, the *grex mutorum*; the use of *grex*, which properly refers to animals (like the English 'herd'), reinforces the classification, which reiterates the earlier characterization of the Egyptians as feral.[12] Muteness is a traditional literary attribute of beasts, but in this context it is also worth noting that muteness and linguistic incoherence came to be common metaphors for the overall inscrutability of the Other in later colonial discourse (see Spurr 1993: 102-8).

At this point the terms of the argument shift from compassion to reason, which of course the Egyptians also lack. The common creator (replacing nature now as the cosmic demiurge) has endowed the beasts with the breath of life alone, but on 'us' human beings he has bestowed in addition a rational intellect, the speaker asserts (148-9, *indulsit communis conditor illis | tantum animas, nobis animum quoque*). It is this faculty that first set 'us' on the road to social and technological advancement. There follows a stereotypical narrative of progress with a standard catalogue of advancements: seeking and accepting aid, collecting scattered people together into cohesive groups, leaving behind the ancestors' woods and groves, building houses and living with neighbours in a state of collective security (149-58).[13] One detail in the catalogue of behavioural improvements that signal the march of progress is especially pointed: men learn 'to protect with arms the citizen who has slipped or is weakened by a grave wound in battle' (155-6, *protegere armis | lapsum aut ingenti nutantem volnere civem*). This is, of course, exactly what the Egyptians do not do; instead, they fail to intervene as their fallen comrade is eaten alive.

Once again, the reader accustomed to the pessimistic speaker of the other satires will be thrown off balance by this one's faith in progress and rational coexistence. But this is a different speaker – or is it? For here his rhetoric, never a seamless affair, begins to unravel wildly as he slips back toward the myth of decline with which he is much more comfortable; it is as if he were constitutionally incapable of sustaining a narrative of progress. Just when he has brought us to the pinnacle of human achievement, he delivers himself of this epigram: 'But now there is greater harmony among snakes than human beings' (159, *sed iam serpentum maior concordia*). This unexpected shift in the argument's direction forces a re-evaluation of the paean to civilization that immediately preceded: is it to be read as the end point in a narrative of progress, as we had thought, or as a Golden Age starting point in a narrative of degeneration? It begins to look more like the latter as the speaker suddenly pivots to a narrative of social decline (159-68), moving from the peaceable kingdom of the animal world to the abuse of technology for the forging of weapons in more recent human society – an application that never would have occurred to earlier blacksmiths, accustomed to fashioning only agricultural implements. Especially striking in view of positions taken by the speaker earlier in the poem are the abrupt recasting of the mute beasts as positive *exempla* of prelapsarian innocence (they never attack members of their own species: 159-60, *parcit / cognatis maculis similis fera*), and the transformation of technology from mark and tool of progress into means of wrongdoing.

The Egyptians are now reintroduced and made to represent the nadir in this process of decline: for them it is not enough to satisfy their wrath simply by killing people; they have to consider the body parts of their victims a type of food as well (169-71, *aspicimus populos quorum non sufficit irae / occidisse aliquem, sed pectora, bracchia, voltum / crediderint genus esse cibi*). Are they, then, incorrigibly deviant renegades, anachronistic blots on a generally unblemished record of human progress, or simply the worst of a by now apparently universally bad human lot? Wavering between the conventional narratives of decline and progress as the most effective rhetorical framework for debasing the Egyptians, the speaker's account conflates the two. The internal incoherence of the result cannot escape careful readers. Here Juvenal echoes Tacitus' proto-colonialist vacillation between the narratives of decline and progress, manifested primarily in the historian's alternation between Noble Savage (nature good, culture bad) and debased barbarian (nature bad, culture good).

Still, if the logic is not scrutinized too closely, this final section

143

leaves an unambiguous general impression. On the one hand, there are 'we', interchangeable with the human race as a whole, who have advanced from the roughest beginnings to high civilization; on the other, there are the Egyptians, sub-human creatures who have been left behind in a time and space outside the history of progress. Whether it was nature or culture that gave 'us' the capacity for improvement, the Egyptians do not appear to figure in the equation. Even in the grim picture of decline toward the end of the poem that seems to shift the speaker's premises by denying any capacity for sustained human improvement, the scene of apparently universal degeneration recedes from view as the Egyptians are made its sole emblem.

The slippage in Juvenal's speaker's account of the nature/culture question prefigures a defining paradox in modern colonial discourse, which also fractures along the faultline where the colonizer's claim of his own natural superiority, and thus of his right to a position of authority, meets the contradictory principle that with the proper mentoring advancement is open to all. This notion of improvement through culture – the colonizer's culture – is central to the moral pretensions of the colonial enterprise. Thus the colonized is 'naturally' inferior, yet at the same time the possibility of catching up is extended to him, at least in theory. Under Roman imperialism, as we saw in Chapter 3, the possibility of assimilation was on the whole more than theoretical, and notions of superiority were grounded more often in culture than in nature. But if Romans were made and not born, and if civilization was considered an acquired property rather than an innate quality, then the Egyptians of this poem represent a significant exception to those rules. They are more akin to Kipling's Indians, seen as so different in essence that they are permanently excluded from membership in authentically civilized society (read: the human race), no matter how mightily they might strive to bridge the gap (see Chapter 3, pp. 108-9).

When it came to demonizing the Egyptians, the discourse of the speaker in Satire 15 was no creation *ex nihilo*; it drew on established strategies of enemy construction and on established views of this particular 'enemy'. As Courtney (1980: 607) points out, disparaging remarks about Egyptians can be found in Greek authors as diverse as Theocritus, Polybius, Strabo, Philo, and Dio Chrysostom. Sometimes such attacks even included charges of cannibalism, which is not surprising given its status as a sign of radical alterity in the ancient and modern worlds alike.[14] In Latin literature prejudices against Egyptians came into focus most sharply in the flurry of poetry produced in the years immediately after 31 BC to commemorate the victory of Augustus over the forces of Antony and Cleopatra. In their depictions of the conflict, Horace, Virgil, and Propertius famously homogenize the queen and the diverse Greeks, Egyptians, and Greco-Egyptians who served her into an indiscriminate mass of malignant Oriental fury aiming straight for the Capitoline hill. Like Juvenal's speaker, the Augustan poets construct an image of the Egyptians (or in this case, 'Egyptians', including their queen, who was in reality the farthest from being a 'real' Egyptian of them all) that is a fusion of 'primitive' and 'degenerate', i.e., Eastern features: raging fury, lack of self-restraint, and superstition on the one hand; gender ambiguity, sexual licentiousness, hedonism, cowardice, treachery, and (female) despotism on the other. As in Satire 15, any Greco-Egyptian cultural mixing is entirely erased to expose an imagined unalloyed barbarism – an especially brazen trick in view of the thoroughly Greek and eminently civilized historical figure of the monarch herself – and the whole package is opposed to a rational Roman male subject whose tribal interests conveniently align with the divine and natural order.

This hostile and distorted vision of Egyptian culture, driven in this case by the need for a scapegoat to disguise the actual, civil nature of the conflict, was reproduced in subsequent texts that followed the Augustan tradition in their treatment of the Antony and Cleopatra episode.[15] In the process of attacking the Macedonian court, these texts exploit an apparently established view of Egyptians that would immediately resonate with Roman readers. At the same time Augustus could count on an awareness of the Greekness of Egypt, conspicuous in the Augustan poets by its absence, to be another factor in rendering the country pernicious in the eyes of those Romans who regarded Greek culture as no less Oriental than

Egyptian culture was thought to be. This 'stealth' element is lurking in the background of Satire 15 as well (witness the otherwise gratuitous mention of Canopus), in spite of the speaker's opportunistic praise of Greek culture and his explicit targeting of non-Greek country folk.

It is important to remember that this hostile tradition developed alongside a more positive assessment of Egyptian culture and a general acknowledgement of Egyptian contributions to Greek and Roman medicine, philosophy, religion, and architecture. This counter-tradition included an Egyptomania that waxed and waned in the course of Roman cultural history, in fact waxing among elites under Hadrian when this poem was written. One way of understanding this tension is by reading it as a variation on the Noble Savage/debased Other dichotomy, where even the embrace of things Egyptian could have a colonialist edge. One might consider the latent ethnocentrism in Victorian Egyptomania, Gaugin on Tahiti, or any number of comparable modern love affairs with the colonial exotic. A similar faux multi-culturalism marks Plutarch's *On Isis and Osiris*, where his ability to take Egyptian religion seriously hinges to a great extent on his understanding of it in Greek, that is 'universal' terms – primarily as Platonic allegory. When he grapples with real people and popular religion, as he does in a brief description of an inter-city rivalry similar to the one in Juvenal but without the elaboration or the cannibalism (380b-c), his tone can be as impatient as the satiric speaker's.[16]

Subsequent history: 'more cruel, more dangerous, more destructive than the wild beasts'

Many of the representations of Egypt in Greek and Latin literature before and after Juvenal, and especially the overtly negative ones, could be considered proto-colonialist in a general sense. In Satire 15 the parallel with modern colonial discourse is sharpened because the text is an artefact of Rome's explicitly colonial relationship with Egypt in this period, a relationship which is reflected in the unequal dynamic between the Roman speaker and the objectified provincials whose representation he entirely controls. Moreover, the poem has an unusually concentrated yet comprehensive quality that makes it an especially lucid preview of later colonial discourse. Many of the key rhetorical strategies that defined this discourse in the nineteenth century seem to come naturally to the lips of Juvenal's cultural imperialist.

We saw in Chapter 3 that one of the most basic of these strategies has been the 'rhetorical debasement of the cultural Other', to turn again to the central tropes of the rhetoric of empire as identified by Spurr. He locates the origins of the impulse to debase in the need of the subject to shore up his own ego and cultural boundaries by fixing them in opposition to 'subterranean or reverse selves [and] dark mirror-images' (Boehmer 1995: 81) of the values with which he identifies; conveniently, the colonizer finds such images in abundance in parts of the world where there is economic benefit to be reaped. Thus in colonial contexts perhaps more than others, debasement is motivated by a nexus of utilitarian and psychological factors. Spurr sees evidence of the latter especially where there is an insistent reiteration of the publicly stated values of the colonizer, which are presented as universal values to which all people aspire. This rhetorical sleight of hand removes from the human pool those who apparently do not aspire to them while inadvertently raising the question of why values that are universal need constantly to be reasserted. 'The insistence on European standards of civility becomes an act of self-preservation,' Spurr argues, which exposes 'the precarious state of the European subject who is constantly menaced by the [threat of] collapse into a chaos of indifferentiation' (1993: 80; see Chapter 3, pp. 100-2 above).

The fear of indifferentiation that the colonial Other can inspire is expressed in starkly concrete terms by Juvenal's speaker, in whose imagination the 'failure to impose a series of distinctions necessary for modern civility' (Spurr 1993: 81) culminates in wanton disregard for the bodily integrity of individuals and in the physical fusion of self and other, inside and outside that is represented in the taboo act of cannibalism. The speaker's response to the Egyptians is akin to Darwin's disgust at the South American Indians who throw up on themselves and each other in the midst of their revels. The offences, real or imputed, would seem to be of different orders of magnitude, but the horror of the reporter in each case is driven by an inchoate sense that a crucial boundary has been transgressed, and that this transgression exposes 'the frailty of a symbolic order based on difference' (Spurr 1993: 81).

A hallmark of the discourse, then, is colonial alarm (in various disguises) at the assaults of the colonized on the limits, boundaries, and differences that structure the world of the colonizer and give it meaning, along with a tendency to elevate this cultural conflict to a grand struggle between civilization and barbarism. To illustrate this Spurr cites Churchill's reaction to the failure of rebellious Indian tribesmen to observe European protocols for the treatment of enemy dead (see Chapter 3, pp. 101-2 above). Churchill's references to the 'fanatic religion' of the natives and his insinuation that it is a travesty of true religion which only gives rise to bloodshed and murder are almost identical in shape and content to the Juvenalian 'colonizer's' indictment of Egyptian religion as a perverse and dangerous mockery of any proper sacred order. The pronouncements of the future Prime Minister also betray anxiety about bodily integrity (in his mind a great part of the crime of the Mohmands, as Spurr [1993: 82] sees, was to violate the boundary 'between the body and its dismemberment or disintegration into the indifferent chaos surrounding it'), as well as unease at the breakdown of any clear distinction between the human and the animal: the tribesmen are 'more cruel, more dangerous, more destructive than the wild beasts,' rails Churchill (quoted in Spurr 1993: 82).

Concerns such as this also inform Satire 15's strategies for constructing cultural difference, especially its representation of the Egyptians as a feral sub-branch of humanity, if they are human at all. What is omitted from the discussion of this passage in Chapter 3 is the end-point of Churchill's thought process, which causes him to write:

With every feeling of respect for that wide sentiment of human sympathy which characterises a Christian civilisation, I find it impossible to come to any other conclusion than that, in propor-

148

tion as these valleys are purged from the pernicious vermin that infest them, so will the happiness of humanity be increased, and the progress of mankind accelerated.[17]

Like Juvenal's speaker, Churchill uses rhetorical sleight of hand to equate those who subscribe to his own cultural practices with the human race as a whole, and to consign those who do not to a non-human status that could license the use of extreme measures against them. The aim in both cases is to reconstitute man and beast as distinct categories and at the same time to execute a 'rhetorical act of exclusion', as Spurr writes in connection with the later text: '[H]aving descended to the bestial, the Mohmands must be excluded from humanity ... in order that the idea of humanity may retain its proper value.' He continues by observing that '[t]his act of exclusion, multiplied and elaborated in all its variants, establishes the foundation of a colonizing system' (82, 84).

The tendency of the colonizer to project his own insecurities about boundaries onto his representation of colonial Others also accounts for the stock depiction of these groups as teeming, indiscriminate masses, lacking individuality and merging into the fluid, sinister landscapes that surround them. The trope of the menacing crowd was a staple in colonial writing under the modern imperial powers, and it has adapted itself to the visual media of contemporary Western journalism in its encounters with what used to be called the Third World; one only need consider the extent to which images of angry and unruly mobs have come to represent the Arab world as a whole on American television news. Even before this high-tech incarnation, the reduction of native peoples to irrational, uncontrollable masses of surging humanity had become such a cliché in colonialist representation that Frantz Fanon could turn it ironically against the colonizer when he spoke of 'those hordes ... those hysterical masses, those faces bereft of all humanity ... that mob without beginning or end' in *The Wretched of the Earth*.[18] Spurr cites a passage from Etienne Dennery's *La Foule d'Asie* (translated into English as *Asia's Teeming Millions*) that especially resonates with Juvenal's Oriental mob both in its tone and in some of its details: 'Crowds in the great Chinese cities, half sunk in dirt and mud, swarming like ants in the dark, narrow, winding alleys ... . Crowds that leave the solid ground of the town to huddle upon the canals, rivers, even the sea, in their little junks with their crooked sails ... .'[19] Apart from the general impression of (as Spurr puts it) 'malignant fusion', we can see the pairing of the mob's abject qualities with a certain absurdity, embodied here in their rickety little boats, a striking echo of the ridiculous miniature boats of the otherwise ravenous Egyptians in Satire 15.

As Spurr (165) points out, the practice of depersonalizing the natives by merging them into amorphous, sinister mobs is related to the larger trope of 'naturalization', which assimilates the colonized to nature in its dangerous and destructive aspects. This encourages the view that 'chaos and disorder are somehow a natural condition' of non-Western peoples, and that their primitive passions are always on the verge of boiling to the surface in the absence of the law and reason that constrain behaviour in more advanced civilizations. Boehmer locates the genesis of the crowd motif in the colonizer's discomfort with the recalcitrance of the Other to yield familiar meanings, an unease that is projected onto representation. Europeans translated their own anxieties onto an idea of native peoples as 'unruly, inscrutable, or malign'. 'Crowd imagery,' she continues, 'came in handy to suggest a lack of character and individual will' (1995: 95). The crazed Egyptian mob of Satire 15 stands at the head of this tradition of colonialist representation. Indeed, the remarks of Spurr and Boehmer are typical of contemporary analysis of this trope in the ways they could have been written with the Juvenalian *barbara turba* in mind.

So could any number of descriptive analyses of the 'feminized colonial Other' in European colonial texts, for which a better classical parallel could not be found than the girly Egyptians in the vision of Juvenal's speaker, swishing around the Nile on their toy boats or saturated with perfume at the dance party. And like later versions of this figure, this one harbours a murderous streak alongside the softer, more predictable signs of effeminacy. There is an apparent contradiction in the pairing of charges of an unmanly deficiency in bellicosity and a capacity to be stirred, in Kipling's words, to a 'hysteria of blood and fanaticism', but this latter capacity shares with the less aggressive symptoms of emasculation the common denominator of the 'female' tendency to excess and lack of discipline. On the whole, in fact, the way in which the difference between the speaker and his objects is constructed in Satire 15 is a perfect illustration of the principle that the difference between colonizer and colonized is regularly cast in terms of 'a conventional distinction between rational man and irrational woman' (Spurr 1993: 172). Furthermore, all the speaker's talk about the superiority of his own culture – the suggestion that it is synonymous with culture itself and the sole vehicle of enlightened progress in the world – along with his self-presentation as the voice of reason remind us that the opposition between 'male' and 'female' values is a just one ingredient in larger Orientalizing rhetorical systems that divide the world between the male, culture, reason, the West, and the 'modern' on the one side and the female, nature, passion, the East, and the primitive on the other.

There was a strong association in later colonial discourse between fears of the female, specifically of engulfment by the female, and cannibal fantasies. The gender anxieties threaded through the fifteenth satire suggest ancient precedents for this association and especially for its appearance in colonial contexts. Modern anthropology has long understood the cross-cultural function of cannibalism as a 'marker of the inhuman, the hostile "Other" ' (Alston 1996: 101); this signification has a long history reaching back into Greco-Roman culture, as we have seen. Once established as an all-purpose othering strategy, the charge that one's enemies were eaters of human flesh was easily taken up by colonial discourses as they forged their ethnic hierarchies. For European colonialism this process began very early on, in the earliest years of the Age of Discovery. McClintock (1995: 25-7) discusses a Dutch print from 1575 which represents the discovery of America, and the first European contact with indigenous Americans, as an encounter between a man, the explorer Vespucci, accessorized as the bearer of culture and technology, and a suppliant female figure symbolizing the wild, uncultivated and compliant New World. Here the male colonizer is clearly in control, but in the background the viewer can glimpse 'riotous scenes of cannibalism' in which the diners appear to be female.

McClintock describes the contrast thus:

> In the foreground, the explorer is ... fully armored, erect and magisterial, the incarnation of male imperial power. Caught in his gaze, the woman is naked, subservient and vulnerable to his advance. In the background, however, the male body is quite literally in pieces, while the women are actively and powerfully engaged. The dismembered leg roasting on the spit evokes a disordering of the body so catastrophic as to be fatal.
>
> 1995: 26

What is most interesting about this image is the way in which supreme imperial self-confidence and deep imperial anxieties are encoded side by side, in a juxtaposition that recalls a similar strain of tension in Satire 15. In McClintock's formulation, the drawing clearly shows 'dread of catastrophic boundary loss ... associated with fears of impotence', but this is 'attended by an excess of boundary order and fantasies of unlimited power' (26). The cannibal trope became a standard means of expressing and managing the worries in the first half of this equation as they arose with the multiplication of colonial encounters. In this context even the cartographic practice of designating areas of the unknown on maps with the single word 'cannibals' could be viewed as apotropaic – as a feeble gesture of control and containment. Once again the colonized, in representation, becomes a reflection of the colonizer's fears. The victim, so to speak, is made the perpetrator.[20]

Another later colonialist trope prefigured in Juvenal 15 is 'negation', which Spurr defines as a 'rhetorical strategy by which Western writing conceives of the Other as absence, emptiness, [and] nothingness'. Negation 'acts as a kind of providential erasure, clearing a space for the expansion of the colonial imagination' (1993: 92-3). It can be deployed in relation to, among other things, the history and space of the colonized, rhetorically nullifying them so that they can be reinscribed by the colonizer in his own terms and to his own advantage. If the native landscape is a vast and empty void and if native history was non-existent before the advent of the intruder-saviours, then nothing stands in the way of the colonizer's appropriation of them as props in his own master narrative; in fact, given the obvious need and his own culture's self-evident goodness, filling in the void becomes a moral obligation.

What is relevant to Satire 15 in Spurr's discussion of 'negative space' (93-7) is his observation that the process can be shifted to the inhabitants of that space so that 'colonized peoples are [also] systematically represented in terms of negation and absence – absence of order, of limits, of light, of spirit' (96).[21] His comments about 'negative history', made in the context of discussing European rationalizations of the 'scramble for Africa', are also germane:

> The discourse of negation denies history ... constituting the past as absence ... . The savage, in this view, lives in a continual state of self-presence, unable to leave that trace on the world which serves as the beginning of difference ... and hence progress ... . This way of defining the African, as without history and without progress, makes way for the moral necessity of cultural transformation.
>
> 1993: 98-9

The outlines of this principle are visible behind the satiric speaker's picture of the Egyptians as a pre- or extra-historical people, existing outside the narrative of progress, badly in need of Greco-Roman intervention to set them on a proper, linear historical and cultural path (but at the same time denied the capacity for improvement). Any pre-Roman history, whether Pharaonic or Ptolemaic, has been wiped out, replaced by the animal urges of a 'continual state of self-presence'.

In all texts, ancient or modern, devoted to building and perpetuating a 'closed world of imperial belief' (Boehmer 1995: 43), all these ways of consigning the colonized to the realm of absence and deficiency are closely bound up with the discourse of a civilizing mission in which any less than altruistic motives for conquest and control are wrapped. As we saw in Chapter 3, the self-presentation of the colonizer relies on performative reiterations of the claim that his own cultural tradition and moral system are superior and that this system represents the proper aspirations of all humankind. Once these premises are accepted, it is only a small step to the idea that the aggressive dissemination of those institutions and morals is a benevolent act that simply corrects for any factors (petty tribalism, for example) that have obstructed the march of universal values. Spurr captures the self-serving loftiness of modern colonial discourse when he notes that it posits the colonizer as 'a figure of ennobled subjectivity defined by enlightened human ideals rather than by the narrow interests of a tribe' (1993: 111).

These ideas are evident in the identification of Greco-Roman values with human values in Satire 15, and in the glowing picture of the salutary effect of a Roman presence in the provinces; it is as if authentic culture appeared there only with the advent of the Romans, and as if the Romans went there only to bestow this gift. The clear dualism in the speaker's construction of the relationship between Egyptian and Greco-Roman culture also prefigures the structure of the universe in later colonial discourse, where the forces of reason, unity, and order are regularly set against savage impulses and moral and cultural entropy. Moreover, the appropriation of the native point of view and in particular the reading into it of enthusiasm for the colonial enterprise that are such staples in later colonial texts are anticipated in Satire 15 in the speaker's depiction of Gaul and Britain as more Roman than Rome in their hearty and apparently unanimous embrace of Greco-Roman *paideia*. Spurr charts this phenomenon in its later appearances, but *mutatis mutandis* his words apply no less to earlier ones: 'To see non-Western peoples as having themselves become the standard-bearers of Western culture is in some ways a more profound form of colonization than that which treats them merely as sources of labour or religious conversion.'[22]

Finally, there is the tension between the promise that the unifying power of the colonizer's institutions can gather the colonized into the fold of civilization, and the need to maintain a distinction between native and colonizer that is based in natural difference. In later colonial texts this tension is ubiquitous, and can be expressed in the figure of the imperfectly assimilated barbarian who strives to embody the values of his colonial masters, but always inevitably falls short in great or small ways. In a tradition in which Romanness was widely regarded as genuinely acquirable, the discourse of Juvenal's speaker is unusual for the very nineteenth-century message of immutable cultural exclusiveness that it ultimately sends.[23] This message fatally undermines the speaker's faux-magnanimous professions of liberalism on this score. The tension manifests itself in the conflict between his elevated talk about Greco-Roman culture as a great leveller in some parts of the poem, and his assertion in the peroration that it is nature that determines our place in the human hierarchy. His failure in the end to come down on the side of either progress or decline also reflects the bifurcation of his discourse in this area. To do the former implies a faith in culture, particularly technology, and an assumption that nature needs taming, while the latter course locates the impetus for decline in culture, particularly technology (remember the ploughshares being fashioned into swords), and finds positive *exempla* in the natural world (unlike human beings, animals do not attack members of their own species). Juvenal's speaker, like later colonialists, wants to have it both ways.

Epilogue

To dispel any illusions that colonial discourse vanished with the end of the British Empire, we might consider a text that recently appeared under the title 'From Tyranny to Freedom' in an American journal of political commentary. In it, the neoconservative pundit Michael Ledeen reacts to the killing and mutilation of four American contractors working for the occupation authority in Iraq in April 2004:

Recent acts of barbarism against coalition forces in Iraq have revived an old ... debate: Are these terrorists the products of fanatic tyrannies, or are the tyrannies the logical expression of the true nature of the peoples of the region? ... [I]f fanaticism

155

and barbarism are intrinsically part and parcel of the region's culture, mere regime change cannot possibly eliminate this sort of terrorism. Some way would have to be found to change the culture … . The barbarians in Fallujah are part of a culture that is both bloody and peaceful, just like the Western culture that produced fascism and communism. The central issue … is which elements in that culture will prevail.[24]

One can only wonder at the extent to which the rhetoric's basic tropes have remained intact over time. Like his predecessors, including the Juvenalian speaker, Ledeen wavers between attributing the behaviour of the Iraqis to an irredeemably degenerate culture or to their 'true nature', although certainly it is the latter that insinuates itself into the mind of the reader and colours his or her assessment of whether any attempt to 'change the culture' could meet with success. Does the 'true nature' of the Iraqis doom them to exist forever on a lower plane than civilized people, or can they harness the good aspects of their culture – the ones that look like ours – to lift themselves out of their squalor? In spite of his controlling air of certainty, there is equivocation in Ledeen's rhetorical interstices.

Noteworthy also is how automatically he reaches for the formula 'fanaticism and barbarism' to explain the violence, with no consideration of any provocation on the part of the occupying army to which the contractors were attached. These acts of brutality are thus robbed of any context and presented as completely gratuitous, as an expression of pure pathology. On another level, there is the quintessentially colonialist sense of surprise that the natives, having been engaged, are not playing by 'our' rules. Finally, the acknowledgement that 'Western culture' too has had its low moments rings hollow as a gesture of even-handedness because of the way the writer distances himself from those events: they were in our past, like the incidents of human flesh-eating at the sieges in pre-Roman Spain, and 'we' have since moved beyond any possibility of recurrence. 'We' arrived at our advanced state long ago; the Iraqis just need to catch up to our level – but do they have the right stuff for doing so? Like Juvenal's speaker, Ledeen seems to forget that the civilization that he infantilizes here is infinitely older than the one he holds up as a paradigm.

This seems a very serious juncture at which to remind the reader that in Juvenal there is a current of authorial irony exposing the creaky rhetorical underpinnings of views such as this to critical scrutiny.[25] By weaving in the critical subtext, the poet would appear in this case to be poking fun not at extremist views but at mainstream ones, if we can judge by the presence of at least a kernel of them in sources no less sober than Tacitus and Plutarch, and in spite of the insinuation of the Egyptian into multiple facets of Roman life. Rather than laughing with his audience at someone else's benighted views, in Satire 15 Juvenal wittily challenges his peers, or some of them, to examine their own. In this he anticipates the spirit of Swift, who turned the colonialist trope of the Irish cannibal against the English, or the late colonial critical distance of a Conrad or a Waugh, expressed in satiric swipes at the tired tropes of imperial self-satisfaction and evident in the ironic title of the former's story, 'An Outpost of Progress'. Casting around for reading material in the remote Congo river station of this tale, the two doomed 'pioneers of trade and progress' who man the post find an old pamphlet that 'discussed what it was pleased to call "Our Colonial Expansion" in high-flown language. It spoke much of the rights and duties of civilization, of the sacredness of the civilizing work, and extolled the merits of those who went about bringing light and faith and commerce to the dark places of the earth.'

Send-ups such as these, however, are embedded in material whose tone suggests an internalization by the author of other colonialist premises: the air is heavy with a fear of contamination by the primitive; the natives are inscrutable and malign; the wilderness is 'strange and incomprehensible', outside historical time.[26] It is not so easy for one steeped in the enabling fictions of an ideological system to divest himself of them, or fundamentally to unsettle the system's categories. As Boehmer observes about this class of modern writers, '[e]ven as they interrogated, mocked, and despaired, ... dark parodic

157

effects formed part of the self-constituting project of imperialism'.[27] In this respect there may have been less distance between poet and *persona* than recent critics – and possibly Juvenal himself – have imagined.

Notes

Introduction

1. Bernstein et al. (1992: 179, quoted in Webster 1996a: 2) offer useful general definitions of imperialism and colonialism in relation to one another: 'Whereas colonialism means direct rule of a people by a foreign state, imperialism refers to a general system of domination by a state (or states) of other states, regions or the whole world. Thus political domination through colonialism is only one form this domination might take: imperialism also encompasses different kinds of indirect control.' Colonialism, then, is a subformation, both a consequence and an implement of imperialism, and though the apparatus of Roman colonial control could involve arrangements more complex than 'direct rule', this relationship still obtained. Both terms can be applied to Roman interactions with the rest of the world, and I will use both, alternating as the context seems to require. On ancient versus modern incarnations of these -isms, see below.

2. De Ste Croix (1981) is unique in applying Marxist historiography, especially notions of class struggle, to the study of the ancient (Greek) world.

3. On British imperialism's use and abuse of the classics see most recently Goff (2005), where this perspective is balanced by discussions of the reworking of classical motifs in anti-imperial and post-colonial literature.

4. Harris 1979: 4. He also likes the definition of Zevin (*Journal of Economic History* 32 [1972] 319): 'Activity on the part of any state which establishes or subsequently exercises and maintains qualified or unqualified rights of sovereignty beyond the previous boundaries within which such rights were exercised', but for 'sovereignty' he would substitute 'power' (4 n. 1).

5. Webster continues: '[W]hen Philip de Souza [in Webster and Cooper 1996: 125-33] compares nineteenth-century French writing on the Barbary Corsairs with Classical accounts of Rome's pirate wars, he is not drawing a direct analogy between French imperialism and Roman imperialism: he is comparing the discursive strategies which made territorial expansion possible in either case ...' (1996a: 9).

6. See, for example, the essays in the section 'Writing the "Other": Colonial Representations', in Webster and Cooper 1996: 99-144; Habinek 1998: 151-69 (ch. 8, '*Pannonia Domanda Est*: The Construction of the Imperial Subject through Ovid's Poetry from Exile'); and Rutledge's (2000) reading of Tacitus' *Agricola*.

159

7. See Loomba 1998: 49-57 for a short history of critiques of Said and *Orientalism*.

8. On 'imperial themes' (Brunt's term) in Caesar and Cicero, see Brunt 1978; in Cicero alone e.g. Steel 2001; Habinek 1995; in Virgil e.g. Hardie 1986; Rudd 1986. On national identity in the *Aeneid*, in addition to Toll 1991 and 1997, see e.g. Syed 2004.

9. On this question I follow what has become the critical consensus, which insists that a clear distinction must be made between the poet and the dramatic characters that he creates to speak in his poems. In the satires discussed here the main speaker is a 'narrow-minded and cynical bigot who blindly condemns what he does not like' (Winkler 1983: 218). His credibility as a moral authority is called into question as he repeatedly exposes himself as irrational, dogmatic, hypocritical, and profoundly lacking in self-knowledge. The target of the satire, then, is this speaker's reactionary discourse and its moral blind spots as much as the behaviours and trends that he catalogues for derision. See Anderson 1964, 1970; Winkler 1983; and Braund 1996a.

1. Them and Us

1. On Athenian binarism, see conveniently Just 1989: 153-93 (ch. 8, 'The Attributes of Gender'). Major studies of ancient alterity construction include, on the Greek side, Cartledge 1993, Hartog 1998, and Hall 1989; for the Romans, Dauge 1981 and Wyke 1992.

2. See e.g. the comments of Sedgwick 1992: 239: '... the trope of the Other [in] current understandings of nationalism ... must almost *a priori* fail to do justice to the complex activity, creativity, and engagement of those whom it figures simply as relegated objects ... .'

3. Winkler 1983: 223 applies the term 'redneck' to Umbricius, the speaker of the third satire.

4. It is now widely accepted that 'homosexual' as a term and as an identity category is a modern invention, and that in Greek and Roman antiquity the designation of a man as a sexual deviant had more to do with his generally 'effeminate' comportment than with the biological sex of his erotic objects, though the two could converge. For a good overview of this complex subject, see C. Williams 1999, esp. 3-14 and 125-59. See Richlin 1993 for a dissenting view; she argues that Rome had a 'homosexual subculture' that corresponded to the modern idea of this group.

5. All citations are from Clausen's Oxford text (rev. 1992). In this and subsequent chapters, translations are my own unless otherwise indicated.

6. The locus classicus in Latin literature for the theatre as a transgressive space and in particular as a place of seduction and female moral backsliding is Ovid, *Ars Amatoria* 1.89-100, but there the attitude of the speaker as 'professor of love' is, of course, very different.

7. 'Out-group' is a term adopted by Richlin (at e.g. 1984: 67) to designate powerless, marginalized social groups whose difference makes them easy targets for stereotyping and abuse by Roman satirists. What especially provokes Juvenal's speaker is his perception that the out-groups are becoming in-groups and that he and his kind are on their way out.

8. See below and e.g. Mosse 1985: 144; Gilman 1985 passim. On the figure of the effeminate womanizer in Roman culture see e.g. Edwards 1993: 63-97. Juvenal 6.O1-34 is the famous Oxford or Winstedt fragment, which Clausen takes to be authentic.

9. Aristotle, *On the Generation of Animals* 727b18, 765b8, 783b26.

10. For a fully developed *mulier audax* as sower of social and political discord and conventional sign that things in general are out of joint, see the wicked Tullia in Livy 1.46-8.

11. Both Konstan (1993) and Nappa (1998) understand that the speaker of Satire 2 is provoked by the whole package of social inversions that the deviants in the poem represent and not just by their 'homosexuality' per se; Nappa further connects the speaker's fears to a belief in the capacity of these inversions to weaken the Roman state, constructed as masculine.

12. As Richlin 1993: 549 has pointed out, the conception here of 'homosexuality' in biological terms would appear to problematize the now established idea that the Greeks and Romans were not essentialist in their thinking about sexual preferences.

13. Richlin 1992: 197 was the first to observe the sexual overtones of the language here: the speaker 'is not *patiens urbis*, that is, he will not submit to the city passively ... [he] will not be a pathic for the city's vices ...'. See also her comments on the speaker's strategies for creating a sense of solidarity between himself and any other losers under the new regime who might be listening to him – a sort of brotherhood of the downtrodden (200, 207).

14. Schulte-Sasse makes the same connection in her discussion of National Socialist ideology. Describing a scene in a Nazi film in which a henpecked husband's metamorphosis into masterful patriarch corresponds with his awakening to the Nazi version of nationalism, she calls the transformation 'the ultimate paradigm for ... the restoration of male cultural authority necessary for reinstating Germany as *Heimat*' (1996: 272-3). This is not as far from Juvenal as it might seem, as we will see.

15. The projection of misogyny onto male Others allowed (native) women themselves (exorcised of their threatening qualities) to remain inside the nation, where they were needed, while satisfying the need to cast out their Otherness at least on a metaphorical level. This move points to the perennial dual status of women and to their liminal position as both inside and outside, same and other. In nationalist discourses the female is often split; the 'bad' woman is cast out in the person of feminized male Others, while the 'good' woman is retained in the form of the chaste, conventionally virtuous, happily subordinate female ideal of nationalist fantasies. Juvenal's speaker has no use for even 'good' women, but a similar split is clearly articulated by Horace in *Odes* 3.6, as we will see in Chapter 2.

16. See e.g. Hermann, Blitz, and Mossman 1996, whose title (*Nationalismus, Männlichkeit, und Fremdenhass im Vaterlandsdiskurs deutscher Schriftsteller des 18. Jahrhunderts*) has a strikingly Juvenalian ring, at least in the first half.

17. Travers 2001 calls this 'revolution' a 'vague and amorphous movement of intellectual and cultural protest' (2). He identifies as one of its central myths 'the notion of an embattled community' (11), a notion that would certainly resonate with Juvenal's speaker. See also e.g. Ketelson 1976, who covers the same territory in German.

18. Stephen Metcalf in *The New York Times Book Review* (10 October 2004) 21.

19. This is not to minimize what really was new in the formulations of the modern-day Umbricii. Germanic volkish racism in particular seems to come close to being in a class by itself, and the conceptualization of race in biological terms is generally viewed as uniquely modern. As Travers 2001: 126 observes, in late nineteenth-century racialist tracts, 'Jews are represented not simply as evil, but as irremediably evil, their negative characteristics: avarice, materialism, sexual licentiousness, faults not of character ... but of biological identity ... . The work of these racist theorists ... are [*sic*] imbued with an organicist/eugenicist discourse that construes the hostile "otherness" of Jewishness in terms of a "disease" or an "infection" ...'. And yet in Juvenal there are intimations even of this in the speaker's talk about effeminacy as a disease and Greek vice as something innate to Greeks as a *gens*. See the recent important work of Isaac (2004) who argues, against the conventional wisdom, that race and racism in their modern senses originated in antiquity.

20. Interestingly enough, Richlin 1992 discusses the dualistic world of Juvenal's speaker as breaking down along lines of normal and abnormal, as when she notes the 'claustrophobic positioning of the [normal] poet amongst the abnormal', where he is 'jostled, contaminated, injured by [their] touch ...' (200).

21. For accessible background on Weininger, see e.g. Harrowitz and Hyams 1995; Sengoopta 2000, especially ch. 2, 'Weiningers's Worlds: Identity, Politics, and Philosophy in Central Europe'. As Harrowitz and Hyams (16) point out, Weininger's work was 'a continuation of intellectual trends already present in *fin-de-siècle* Vienna', but at the same time 'the first text to introduce the notion of scientific racism to a popular Viennese readership'.

22. The time-honoured identification of the male with reason and self-control, which Weininger follows, fractured in later nationalist discourses that drew on his ideas but were fed by other influences (e.g. Nietzschean vitalism) as well. Thus, the ideal male might practise reasoned self-restraint, or he might be the agent of a rampaging violence not subject to conventional moral codes, as the rhetorical situation required (his cathartic loss of control was always in connection with killing, not sex); female weakness becomes male strength. There is no such oscillation in the value of loss of self-control in Juvenal, where it is exclusively female; but the characteristic virtue of the male national ideal does seem to range between martial rage and Stoic self-restraint in the 'Roman' Odes (3.2 versus 3.5); see Chapter 2, pp. 69-71.

23. This paraphrase of Weininger follows Mosse 1985: 17, 24, 145-7 and notes (the quotation is from 146). Hoberman's summary (1995: 142) of Weininger on Jews and women (with homosexuals the invisible third member of the trinity) calls up an even more Juvenalian picture: 'Jews and women lack "personality", they "stick together", they are drawn to art galleries and the theater ... , they possess a chameleonlike quality ... and ... are unable to grasp Kantian reason.'

24. Mosse 1985: 45-6; see also 24-5.

25. Hermand 1992: 102-4, and in toto on the volkish utopian tradition and National Socialism.

26. Mosse 1985: 151; see also e.g. Schulte-Sasse 1996: 232-3: 'All of these narrative configurations [i.e., the Nazi conflation of Jews, foreigners/inter-nationalists, capitalists, and so on] aim at constructing a unified subject position that is based on an artificial linkage of contingent elements. There is ... no essential connection between Jews and money or "foreigners" and capitalism, but Nazism naturalizes contingent elements into a relatively cohesive *Weltanschauung* ... . This process is the same one that condenses contradictory negative features of Nazism's "Jew" (wealth and filth, commu-nism and capitalism, impotence and licentiousness, etc.).'

27. Mosse 1985: 134-6, 142-4; the quotations are from 135 and 143. See also Gilman 1985 and 1991; and Schulte-Sasse 1996: 67-91 on 'The Project of 'Jewish' Otherness'. As she notes (67), 'myths linking Jews with money, abstractness, a distorting rationality, rootlessness, deception, and sexual degeneracy can all be connected to social, economic, and psychological fears of modernity'. This diagnosis could easily apply to Juvenal's speaker if we substitute 'Greeks' for 'Jews' and excise 'abstractness' and 'rationality', although the cunning of the Greek could be seen as a form of amoral utili-tarian reason.

28. From the catalogue to the exhibit 'Prelude to a Nightmare: Art, Politics, and Hitler's Early Years in Vienna, 1906-1913' at the Williams College Museum of Art, Williamstown, MA, 13 July – 27 October, 2002.

29. McClintock 1995: 41-4, 52-6, 104-14, 119, 403 n. 92. While both were fundamentally concerned with fixing national self-definition by means of the 'development of a conventional vocabulary and set of signs through which the alien is represented' (Boehmer 1995: 79), it should be said that the British and the German translations of this discourse of alterity were signif-icantly different in the interests that they served. In England, to generalize, it served the status quo, while in Germany it challenged it. In the first instance, it was a tool of bourgeois captains of industry and empire who believed in progress, capitalism, and modernity; these very things were the targets of its wrath in Germany, where it was at least initially a fringe discourse that arose among those who felt themselves disenfranchised by the ascendency of these new values. In this respect the rhetoric of Juvenal's speaker is closer in spirit to that of reactionary German nationalists. It is the 'triangulated switchboard analogy' and its framing of a national 'identity ... based on a distinction of the self from what is believed to be not-self' (Boehmer 1995: 79) that binds all three together.

30. Edelman's piece is a brilliant analysis of a particular episode of Cold War gay-baiting. As background he identifies earlier English connections between homosexuality and foreign entanglements, and notes a 'structural analogy between homosexuality and communism' in American fiction of the 1950s and 1960s, among other media (n. 22).

31. For fuller discussion of the 'invention of tradition' (Hobsbawm's term) as a nationalist strategy, see Chapter 2, pp. 55-6.

32. Ferguson 1979: 137. He fails, however, to follow this theme in any systematic way in the remainder of his commentary on the poem. Other commentators and critics have anticipated some of my observations about the binary character of Umbricius' reactionary world view without connecting this to later ideological currents, specifically modern nationalism. See, for example, Braund's commentary on the poem and especially her concluding essay (1996b: 173-236).

33. For the ideological resonance of the names of certain Italian tribes (the Marsi, Apuli, Sabelli), see Chapter 2, pp. 71-2.

34. Winkler 1983: 23-58 (ch. 2, 'The Good Old Days in Juvenal's *Satires*') and references; see too Bellandi 1991 and Singleton 1972, who also stress the irony and ambiguity in Juvenalian redactions of the Golden Age, especially in Satire 6.

35. See Leach 1974: 25-69 on the idealization of the countryside in Latin literature, and Lovejoy and Boas 1935: 23-102 for a more general survey of ideas of a Golden Age in Greek and Roman culture. On 'City and Country in Roman Satire', see Braund 1989 and Bond 2001 (Braund points out that the city is a stock setting for much of later satire as well, while Bond suggests parallels between Juvenal and twentieth-century urban critics such as Spengler). On rhetoric in Juvenal, see De Decker 1913 (22-38 on the satirist's use of the *locus de saeculo*), Anderson 1961, Kenney 1963, and Braund 1996a: 1-9, 44-7. On the conventions of invective against women in Roman satire, see Richlin 1984. In connection with generic composition I am reminded of Johnson's observation that 'to mark [a] statement as a topos ... as a convention ... answers nothing. Only less than mediocre writers grab their topoi willy-nilly. To select a cliché carefully, for a given context and purpose, is usually to transform it ...' (1987: 11 n. 13).

36. For an overview of the nineteenth-century obsession with the threat of biological and cultural degeneration, including Nordau's work, see Herman 1997: 109-44 (ch. 4, 'Degeneration: Liberalism's Doom').

37. Travers 2001: 116-17. He continues, 'völkisch writers such as ... Hans Grimm ... sought to substantiate their anti-urbanism by juxtaposing the health and vitality of their rural heroes to the decadent or atrophied inhabitants of the city ...'. For these writers, 'the landscape and *mores* of rural Germany, with their eternal rhythms of organic growth and seasonal change, offered a point of stasis in an increasingly unstable world' (161). See also e.g. Hermand 1992.

38. Schulte-Sasse 1996: 254. The second narrative type shows the 'contamination of an individual body within an otherwise healthy organism'. She gives as an example of this type 'the feminized musician Klaus' (simultaneously an emblem of internationalism) in *Kolberg* (1945), who dies in a flood trying to save his violin, 'the metaphoric representation for corrupt, soft "civilization".'

39. For another perspective (urban clutter as convention in Roman satire), see Braund 1989: 23-5; she draws on Kernan (1959: 7-8) and Hodgart (1969: 129, 135-7), who characterizes satire generically as 'an urban art'.

40. See Howkins 1986 and Chapter 2, pp. 60-1 below.

41. Helsinger 1997: 16-17. For other studies of pastoral nostalgia and English national identity, see the references in notes 8, 9, 36, and 53 of her Introduction.

42. Howkins 1986: 65-9; quotation from 69. Gibbon's famous description of the Romans as pygmies appears early in the history, toward the end of ch. 2 in the context of his ruminations on the seeds of decline germinating even in the Antonine Age.

43. See Stedman Jones 1971 for a full study of the idea of urban crisis in nineteenth-century England.

44. 2002; expanded in 2004.

2. Augustan Nation-Building and Horace's 'Roman' Odes

1. See Chapter 4, p. 145 on Cleopatra in Augustan poetry; Zanker 1988 on the propaganda value of Augustan monuments.

2. Hutchinson 1994: 123-4. On the idea of 'The "Golden Age" and National Renewal' in modern nationalist discourse, see also Smith 1997.

3. Boehmer 1995: 98-137 (ch. 3, 'The Stirrings of New Nationalism'), with extensive illustration.

4. See Mosse 1985: 32-47 for a discussion of the anti-urban and anti-modern bias of German and English nationalist discourses, especially as it related to fears of racial degeneration.

5. McClintock 1996: 261, citing Yuval-Davis and Anthias 1989: 7. In recent years there has been a proliferation of studies of the role played by gender ideologies in the formation of national identity. To name a few: Mosse

1985; Parker, Russo, Sommer, and Yaeger 1992; Pickering and Kehde 1997; Yuval-Davis 1997; Mayer 2000; the more specialized studies of Innes 1993 and Moghadam 1994; and special issues of *Journal of Gender Studies* and *Feminist Review* (1992, 1993).

6. McClintock 1996: 263, quoting Kandiyoti 1991: 431.

7. McClintock 1996: 261, 268. On Lucretia, see Joplin 1990; Joshel 1992.

8. Boehmer 1995: 117, 122, 148, and ch. 3 in toto.

9. See conveniently Edwards 1993: 63-97 (ch. 2, *'Mollitia*: Reading the Body') for a sampling of such texts from the Republic, as well as later.

10. Mosse 1985, esp. 16-17, 24, 34-6, 43-5, 72, 78-80, 88-9, 93, 103, 111, with extensive documentation.

11. Mosse 1985: 13, 17-18, 78-9, 103, 116-17, and ch. 6 ('War, Youth, and Beauty'). On the 'cult of manliness' in England see e.g. Vance 1985.

12. Mosse 1985: 90-102 and ch. 5 ('What Kind of Woman?'), with documentation.

13. Spackman in Pickering-Iazzi 1995: 100. See also Mosse 1985: ch. 8 ('Fascism and Sexuality'); DeGrazia 1992; Koonz 1987.

14. For this approach to the 'Roman' Odes, see e.g. Jameson 1984 (on 3.2); Lohmann 1991 (on 3.2); Maleuvre 1995 (on the cycle as a whole). On the other side, taking Horace's 'Augustanism' straight, see e.g. Kraggerud 1995 (on 3.6) and Welwei and Meier 1997 (on 3.2).

15. On literary idealizations of the countryside in this period, see again Leach 1974: 25-69; see also Miles 1997: 168-71 and 175-8 on the tension between Roman nostalgia and not only competing ideals (*urbanitas*) but social reality. In keeping with his general argument that Latin literature served elite interests, Habinek sees invocations of the *mos maiorum* as an almost certain sign of self-interested elite innovation, even as far back as Cato the Elder, who in the *De agricultura* '[sought] to naturalize the radical innovations in Roman agriculture by associating them with tradition' (1998: 56).

16. All citations are from Shackleton Bailey's 1985 Teubner text.

17. See Seager 1993: 26-8 for a survey of the Odes that deal with Augustan themes, including 'the revival of old time morality and old time religion, the sanctity of marriage and family life, the link between the simple rustic virtues and Italian agriculture, the restoration of dignity to the established orders of Roman society' (23).

18. See Galinsky 1988 on the anger of Aeneas.

19. But see Lohmann 1991, who reads the subjunctives as elements in a priamel that rejects martial values. Taken at their word, the injunctions to the *puer* eerily prefigure an exhortation to youth in Kurt Gerlach's 1923 racialist utopian novel *Fernstenliebe*: '[L]et us make our spoiled and effete boys both manly and valiant, let us push them to posts on the Rhine and build camps for them, let us issue passwords and kindle signal fires' (quoted in Hermand 1992: 114).

20. Gaisser, for example, on whose reading see below. On the apparently anticlimactic final two stanzas of the poem see Davis, who includes a survey of their critical history (1983: 10-13).

21. For another reading of this poem see e.g. Arieti 1990, who sees in Regulus a more ambiguous figure.

22. For similar invocations of natives of the Italian countryside as embodiments of old-fashioned 'Roman' virtues see e.g. *Odes* 1.2.39; Virgil, *Georg.* 2.167-9: Italy is the mother of a 'hardy race of men, the Marsi and the Sabellan youth … ' (*haec genus acre virum, Marsos pubemque Sabellam … extulit*). The Sabelli (in practice used interchangeably with *Sabini*) figure in the 'Roman' Odes too (see below). See Habinek 1998: 88-93 on Horace's career-long working out of the relationship between Rome and Italy.

23. Wallace-Hadrill 1982 notes the connection commonly made in Roman texts between increased sexual freedom (especially for women) and political calamity, but seems to accept the Roman equation of social change with moral decline more or less at face value. See Edwards 1993: 35-6 with n. 4 for other scholars who have made the same mistake.

24. Among other parallels, Sallust's loose 'modern' woman Sempronia has a similar function at *Cat.* 25.

25. Quoted in Trevor 1995: 26-7.

26. See again Zanker 1988.

27. On this resistance see e.g. Suetonius, *Aug.* 34.1; Tacitus, *Ann.* 3.25; Dio Cassius 56.1.2. Gordon Williams (1969: 65) argues that the pessimistic ending of *Odes* 3.6 is to be connected with the failure of Augustus' earliest efforts (in 28 BC) to pass 'moral' legislation.

28. See Edwards 1993: 34-62 (ch. 1, 'A Moral Revolution? The Law Against Adultery') for an analysis of how the moralists scapegoated 'women's liberation' to explain all the ills that befell Rome in the late Republic.

3. Tacitus and the Rhetoric of Empire

1. Strabo, *Geog.* 7.3.7-9; Hor. *Odes* 3.24.9-24; Q. Curtius, *Hist. of Alexander* 7.8.12-30. On the Scythians, especially as treated in Herodotus, see most recently Hartog 1988: 3-206. For a survey of the figure of the Noble Savage, including the Scythians, in Greek and Latin texts, see Lovejoy and Boas 1935: 287-367. See also (e.g.) Blundell 1986: 203-24 (ch. 8, 'Hard Primitivism and the Noble Savage').

2. Rutledge and I appear to have recognized independently of one another how well Spurr's study of colonial discourse applies to some Latin texts. For his analytical frame he also draws on some of Spurr's basic tropes, emphasizing those with special relevance to the *Agricola* which I will largely omit – especially 'negation' (the construction of lands marked for conquest as empty voids awaiting colonial moulding) and 'surveillance' (the correlation between naming/mapping and physical appropriation). These are also important terms in O'Gorman's (1993) reading of the *Germania*, although her debt to contemporary theory is less explicit. See Dupont 1995 for a related approach to the *Germania*.

3. See Benario 1991 for a survey of previous efforts to tease out Tacitus' position on Roman imperialism and colonial expansion, which come to a wide range of conclusions.

4. Spurr 1993: 128. Boehmer 1995 discerns the same principle at work in European modernism's love affair with the 'primitive': far from bringing 'Western ideological categories ... into question', modernist reference to non-Western cultures in the end functioned as a 'corroboration of European points of view ... [and] an expression of Europe's concern with itself ... . [M]etropolitan modernism [was] a latter-day colonialist discourse even in its apparently revivifying recognition of 'exotic' arts' (145).

5. Spurr's sources include Montaigne, *On Cannibals* (1580); Rousseau, *Discourse on Inequality* (1754); Melville, *Typee* (1846); and reports in *Time* (18 October 1971), *National Geographic* (August 1972), and *The New York Times Magazine* (8 October 1972) about the Tasaday, a supposedly Stone Age tribe 'discovered' on an island in the Philippines, later revealed as a hoax perpetrated by the Marcos government.

6. 'Melville's ideal of the savage, notwithstanding his attacks on colonialism in the Pacific, is fundamentally more conservative than Rousseau's ... . Melville's savages are the product of a Romantic nostalgia that in the end lies comfortably within the *ethos* of industrial capitalism' (Spurr 1993: 128); or as Sanborn (2004: 3) puts it, 'In the post-colonial era, it has become extremely difficult to champion writers who equate nonwhites with nature and who presume that a sojourn among them will heal the wounds of modernity.'

7. This general principle has long been recognized, especially in connection with the *Germania*, without being identified as a component in a larger Tacitean rhetoric of empire which in turn is seen as a prototype of later colonial discourse. See O'Gorman 1993: 135 n. 2 for earlier statements of the principle, and most recently Rives 1999 (16, 51, 61-2, 202-7), who stresses the ethnographic roots of the device. Tacitus was scarcely the only Roman writer to use the Germans for ideological purposes. See Rives 1999: 24-7 on Caesar's construction of the Germans (*Gallic War* 6.11-28); his purpose was less moral than political. On Roman images of the Germans in general, see Lund 1990; Trzaska-Richter 1991.

8. A.J. Church and W.J. Brodribb, *The Complete Works of Tacitus*, New York: 1942. For the *Germania* and *Agricola* I use the text of Koestermann 1970; *Histories*, Wellesley 1989; *Annals*, Borzsák 1992 and Wellesley 1986.

9. *Dialogue on Orators* 28-9: In the good old days, 'each man's son was brought up not in the room of a hired wet-nurse but in the lap and bosom of the chaste mother who bore him, whose special glory it was to watch over the home and be devoted to her children', whereas now, 'the baby, as soon as it is born, is handed over to some little Greek slave, along with one or two other especially worthless slaves who are not suited to any serious employment'.

10. See Rives 1999: 206 for further examples of the commonplace; and O'Gorman's comments on Tacitus' Germans as primitive Romans (1993: 146-9).

11. There has been much discussion of the meaning of *libertas* in Tacitus. Clearly it is not an absolute good; its value depends on the context or, in my terms here, whether barbarians are being idealized or debased. See Rives 1999: 62-3 on the undisciplined freedom of the Germans. Rutledge (2000: 86-90) argues that Calgacus' devotion to *libertas* marks him as an extremist, unwilling to bend to political realities. But the apologetic requirements of the *Agricola* make its author an advocate of *realpolitik* there, and in spite of that Calgacus' nobility shines through. It is difficult not to read any freedom-loving barbarians in the *Annals* as foils to the shameful servitude of the senate which is a pervasive theme, even if at another level they are a threat to the empire's *pax* (so Straub 1977). For full discussion see Jens 1956; Morford 1991; Shotter 1978.

12. As they are at e.g. *Ann.* 4.72 (revolt of the Frisii) and 14.31-2 (background to Boudicca's revolt); *H.* 4.14 (background to the Batavian revolt).

13. Lovejoy and Boas (1935) call this idea 'hard primitivism' and trace it in the philosophical schools, especially the Cynics (117-52) and the Stoics (260-86). For the barbarian hierarchy in Tacitus, see e.g. *Ag.* 11, *G.* 28, *Ann.* 3.46 (the Gauls made soft by civilization, as opposed to the still hardy Britons or Germans); *Ann.* 3.40, *H.* 4.17 (the Gauls themselves and the Batavian rebel Civilis on the enervated Italians as opposed to the vigorous peoples of the north).

14. Many efforts have been made to reconcile the abruptly critical tone of this passage with the eulogistic orientation of the work as a whole; none of them consider the contradictions inherent in colonial discourse generically. See e.g. Woolf 1998: 69-70; Rutledge 2000: 85-6; Baldwin 1990.

15. These last themes are too pervasive for citation of specific episodes, especially in the *Annals*; see Shumate 1997.

16. 1993: 148. She develops this idea at some length, noting that when the barbarians are cast as symbolic pristine Romans, the identity/difference dichotomy upon which ethnographic – and colonial – discourse turns is fundamentally destabilized.

17. There is a vast bibliography on the dynamics of cultural exchange in the contact zones of the empire. Studies range from the local (Woolf 1998 on Romanization in Gaul) to the synoptic (MacMullen 2000, which looks at the Eastern Mediterranean, Africa, Spain, and Gaul). The latter's forty-page bibliography could serve as a guide to further reading. Because such studies tend to stress syncretism and provincial receptivity, it is worth remembering that there was resistance: see MacMullen himself (1966); Dyson 1971; Bowersock 1986.

18. Rutledge 2000 is very good on Tacitus' invocation of the 'negative history' and 'negative space' of Britain in the *Agricola*. In this quintessential move of colonial discourse, any pre-conquest history is rhetorically erased, and the landscape itself is constructed as a formless void awaiting the shaping hand of the colonizer, before whose advent the land in effect did not exist. O'Gorman's reading of the *Germania* (1993) runs along similar lines.

19. Cf. Roberts, who argues that the conventional oppositions structuring these episodes do create the impression that 'Roman victory is presented as a triumph for civilization over the dark forces of unreason and superstition, of ethnic and religious fanaticism' (1988: 122), but that the clarity of this opposition is clouded by a subtext about the 'effeminacy' of Nero and the obsequiousness of his court.

20. Cf. Boehmer's succinct account of the role of othering in European self-definition: 'The feminized colonial Other allowed the European the more intensively to realize himself ... . Images of the native, alien, or Other, reflected *by contrast* Western conceptions of selfhood – of mastery and control, of rationality and cultural superiority, of energy, thrift, technological skilfulness. Europe ceaselessly reconfirmed its own identity and individuality by finding for itself around the globe subterranean or reverse selves, dark mirror-images: the Oriental, the Thug, the African, the New World Indian, the Quashee, Caliban, Friday, Jewel' (1995: 81).

21. 1993: 81. Spurr's texts are *Journal of Researches into the Geology and Natural History of the Various Countries Visited by H.M.S. Beagle*, London: 1839, esp. 118; and *Origin of Species and the Descent of Man in Relation to Sex*, New York: 1936, esp. 489. The drunken Indians appear in the journal.

22. Spurr 1993: 82, quoting from *Young Winston's Wars: The Original Despatches of Winston S. Churchill, War Correspondent, 1897-1900*, ed. Fredrick Woods, London: 1972, 33-9.

23. Spurr 1993: 172, quoting from Kipling's 'The Riddle of Empire', in *Collected Works*, vol. 19: *Letters of Travel*, 1892-1927, New York: 1970, 303.

24. For a similar backhanded idealizing gesture, see Juv. 2.108-9: the emperor Otho is more effeminate than the 'barbarian queens' Sameramis and Cleopatra.

25. Spurr discusses the shifting meaning of 'nature' in colonial discourse under the trope of 'naturalization' (1993: ch. 10).

26. Spurr 1933: 134, quoting *Of Grammatology*, trans. G.C. Spivak, Baltimore: 1976, 116. On the alternation between debasement and idealization, sometimes in the same text (as in Tacitus), see also e.g. Mills 1991: 51-2: 'Sometimes countries, such as India, slipped in and out of such categories at various times during the colonial period. Hulme analyses Christopher Columbus's diaries in order to show the way that the narratorial position vacillates between the discourse of the savage and that of the civilised

Orient: the barbarous and the riches of Cathay. Africans can be portrayed as noble savages or savage cannibals depending on the colonial situation.'

27. Spurr 1993: 85-6. His Kipling text is 'City of Dreadful Night', about colonial life in Calcutta, in *Collected Works*, vol. 18: *From Sea to Sea and Other Sketches*, New York: 1970, esp. 186 and 221.

28. Boehmer sees this insistence on boundaries and its inconsistency with other premises of the discourse as its fatal flaw: 'This basic distinction [between colonizer and colonized and the values they were thought to represent] ... undermined the arguments of those who defended empire as 'uplifting' natives. Progress in the image of Europe might be advised, but the divide between Europeans and colonized peoples had to stay in place. Till the end of the British Empire all rationales based on 'civilizing the natives' remained hobbled by this basic paradox' (1995: 82).

29. Woolf 1998: 58-9: 'Greeks ... distinguished themselves from barbarians in terms of a barrier, clear-cut and difficult to cross, while Romans conceived of a continuum along which it was relatively easy to progress ... . [T]he disengaging of civilization from ethnicity was a commonplace among Roman writers.' The idea of *humanitas* and its acquisition has generated a large bibliography. One might start with Woolf 1998: 48-76 (ch. 3, 'The Civilizing Ethos'); Veyne 1993; and Braund 1997, and works cited therein. As its title indicates, the subject of Woolf's entire book is the process through which provincials could, in fact, 'become Roman'.

30. See e.g. Cicero, *Pro Fonteio* 9, 19, 28-31, 33 (Gallic drunkenness, barbaric dress and language, perfidy, impiety, etc.). For discussion see Woolf 1998: 61-3 and works cited.

31. Another possibility, proposed by Walser 1951: 86-128, is that Tacitus deliberately barbarizes Civilis as part of a pro-Flavian strategy of making what was really a civil conflict look like a foreign war, which would redound more to Vespasian's glory when he prevailed. In short, Walser argues that there was no nationalist revolt at all. Brunt (1960) effectively refutes this theory, though he is non-committal on the authenticity of Civilis' barbarian practices (507).

32. For concise accounts of the modern rhetoric of imperial justification, see Spurr 1993: ch. 7 ('Affirmation') and Boehmer 1995: 36-44, to which my overview is indebted.

33. Cf. most recently President George W. Bush's characterization of the American invasion and occupation of Iraq, arguably a neo-colonial exercise, and the resistance encountered there from disparate groups of insurgents: 'No free nation can be neutral in the fight between civilization and chaos. Terrorists in Iraq have attacked representatives of the civilized world and opposing them and defeating them must be the cause of the civilized world' ('Bush Urges Allies to Help Fight Chaos in Iraq', *The Washington Post*, 12 September 2003). On his blanket designation of all who resist American power as 'terrorists', see below.

34. See Spurr 1993: ch. 2 ('Appropriation'), with textual support, including the writings of Henry Morton Stanley, who was especially inclined to 'speak for the African', as Spurr notes. Spurr reads Stanley's satisfaction at the growth of native markets at river stations, for example, as a sign of the explorer's conviction that 'native peoples are gathered into the fold, and ... are ... embracing the institutions of their conquerors' (34, commenting on Stanley's *The Congo and the Founding of its Free State*, vol. 1, New York: 1885, 500-1).

35. For surveys of how Romans talked about imperial conquest and expansion in the late Republic and the early Augustan period, see Brunt 1978 (his focus is on Cicero and Caesar); also Gruen 1984: 273-87.

36. H. Mattingly, trans. (rev. S.A. Handford), *Tacitus: The Agricola and the Germania*, London and New York: 1970, 84.

37. 'Fortune can offer nothing greater than discord among our enemies as the destiny of empire presses toward its end' (*urgentibus imperii fatis nihil iam praestare fortuna maius potest quam hostium discordiam*). But see Benario 1991: 3344-47 and works cited for more 'pessimistic' readings of the phrase *urgentibus imperii fatis*.

38. E.g., *Ann.* 3.40, the Gauls plot sedition relying on those prone to violence and crime; *H.* 4.37, by rebelling the Treviri sully their distinguished service to Rome; *H.* 4.67, revolting Gauls begin to 'return to reason' (*resipiscere*) and find renewed respect for 'treaties and what is right' (*fasque et foedera*). Compare George W. Bush's characterization of any violent resistance to American power in Iraq as the work of 'thugs and assassins' and 'terrorists', a simplification that obliterates crucial distinctions between criminal and political agents, Iraqi nationalists and Islamic fundamentalists, etc., while shutting down any discussion of American motives.

39. *protulit enim magnitudo populi Romani ultra Rhenum ultraque veteres terminos imperii reverentiam. ita sede finibusque in sua ripa, mente animoque nobiscum agunt.*

40. 'What else would there be here but warfare among all the peoples if the Romans were driven out – may the gods forbid it. This imperial structure has taken shape over 800 years of good fortune and hard work, and it cannot be destroyed without the ruin of those destroying it' (*H.* 4.74: *pulsis, quod di prohibeant, Romanis quid aliud quam bella omnium inter se gentium existent? octingentorum annorum fortuna disciplinaque compages haec coaluit, quae convelli sine exitio convellentium non potest*).

41. Bastomsky 1988: 414; see Keitel 1993: 51-7 for a more nuanced view. Haynes observes that whatever the reader's verdict on the question of authorial tone, 'these speeches are sure statements of contemporary Roman ideology' (2004: 164).

42. Spurr 1993: 115-16; he quotes from Blixen (Isak Dineson), *Out of Africa*, New York: 1937, repr. 1983, 213 and Waugh, *Remote People*, London: 1931, 182-3. Waugh's picture of this type is, of course, often satiric, but this does not cancel out his basic sympathy with their complaints about the modern world.

43. To some extent Germanicus, on the German frontier and later in the East, fits this mould as well (*Ann.* 1-2, *passim*).

4. 'Crazy Egypt' and Colonial Discourse in Juvenal's Fifteenth Satire

1. On the social history of Hellenistic and Roman Egypt, see Bowman 1986; Lewis 1983. Both note that for administrative purposes the Romans lumped together as 'Egyptians' all inhabitants of the province outside of Roman citizens and citizens of the four Greek cities of Alexandria, Naukratis, Ptolemais, and after AD 130, Antinoöpolis; the category 'Egyptians' thus included descendents of Greek settlers in the nome capitals and country towns. So the generalizing rhetorical moves in Tacitus and Juvenal have a correspondent in Roman legal if not social practice.

2. See also (e.g.) Loomba 1998: 108-9: ' "New World natives" have been projected as [brought into being] by the European encounter with them; accordingly, a discourse of primitivism surrounds them. On the other hand, the "East" is constructed as ... degenerate ... [in] an alternate version of savagery understood not as lack of civilisation but as an excess of it, as decadence rather than primitivism.'

3. See De Decker 1913; Anderson 1961; Kenney 1963.

4. It really happened: Moreau 1940, Highet 1949-50; religious misunderstanding: Powell 1979; declamatory *topos*: Courtney 1980: 591, 603 (though he himself seems to accept the event as fact); satiric *topos*: Rankin 1969. Singleton 1983: 200 points out that the cannibal motif persisted in modern satire, citing Swift's *A Modest Proposal* and Waugh's *Black Mischief*. Both put Juvenal 15 in good colonialist company.

5. Not a unique sentiment in Roman antiquity, as Courtney 1980 notes ad loc.; see also Smelik and Hemelrijk 1984. Here Juvenal may even be imitating Cicero, *Tusculan Disputations* 5.78: 'Who is not familiar with the custom of the Egyptians, who with their superstition-steeped minds would undergo any torture before they would harm a water-bird or a snake or a cat or a dog or a crocodile?' (*Aegyptiorum morem quis ignorat, quorum imbutae mentes pravitatis erroribus quamvis carnificinam prius subierint quam ibim aut aspidem aut faelem aut canem aut crocodilum violent?*)

6. Courtney 1980 ad loc. can find no other evidence of Egyptian abstention from leeks, for example, and in general dietary taboos seem to have been regional rather than national, as the speaker implies.

7. Juvenal's introduction of an epic hero for comparative purposes and his assimilation of events in Egypt to tragedy could be viewed as a harbinger of the later colonialist practice of referring 'metaphorically to established art forms in order to provide a context for the understanding of foreign reality', as Spurr puts it (1993: 54). He calls this trope 'aestheticization'.

8. On climate and culture, cf. e.g. the Victorian explorer Richard Burton's association of 'tropical geography, the ascendency of female sexual desire, and corruption in the social sphere' (Spurr 1993: 180). Like many devices now widely identified as typical of modern colonial discourse, this one has roots in ancient ethnography and was not uncommon in other genres; see e.g. Lucan, *Civil War* 8.363-8, where hot Eastern climates, in this case in Parthia, are connected with effeminacy and related failings.

9. Cf. Lucan, who castigates both the 'barbarous' Egyptians of Memphis and the 'soft' Egyptians of a more cosmopolitan Canopus for their treachery in murdering Pompey, leaving aside the fact that the main connivers were members of the Greek court and that it was a Roman soldier who wielded the knife (*Civil War* 8.542-3: *o superi, Nilusne et barbara Memphis / et Pelusiaci tam mollis turba Canopi / hos animos?*).

10. E.g. 52, *haec tuba rixae*, 'this was the trumpet-call to battle'; 67-71, a variation on the epic 'he wielded a rock, such as men nowadays would not be able to lift' motif; 76, the epic-sounding epithet in *qui vicina colunt umbrosae Tentura palmae*, 'who inhabit neighbouring Tentyra of the shady palm-tree'.

11. Lewis 1983: 67. See van Minnen 1998 for a thorough discussion of the question of Greek learning among non-urban Egyptians.

12. The distinction between humans and animals and the kinship of the former with the gods is conventional; see e.g. Sallust, *Catiline* 1.1-2. *Grex* is used again of Egyptians (this time, priests of Isis) by Juvenal at Satire 6.533, and famously by Horace (of Cleopatra's retinue of eunuchs) at *Odes* 1.37.9-10 ('a contaminated herd of men polluted by disease', *contaminato cum grege turpium / morbo virorum*). In both cases the dehumanizing gesture targets sexual deviance as much as foreignness.

13. One of the best-known narratives of progress in Latin literature is Lucretius, *De Rerum Natura* 5.925-1457, which shows all the conventional elements.

14. On cannibalism as a marker of alterity in the Greco-Roman world, see Alston 1996: 101 and references. As he points out, texts other than Juvenal's represented Egyptians as anthropophagous (or as practising human sacrifice, a related taboo; he cites Sextus Empiricus 3.24; Achilles Tatius 3.15; Dio Cassius 72.4), but on the other hand there is evidence that 'Pharaonic Egyptians also employed the charge of cannibalism to designate the Other'.

15. The Augustan poems are Horace, *Odes* 1.37, *Epodes* 9; Propertius 3.11 and 4.6; Virgil, *Aeneid* 8.675-728; on their Orientalizing dualism see especially Wyke 1992. Later versions of the Cleopatra narrative with a similar 'spin' include Velleius Paterculus 2.82-7; Dio Cassius books 42, 43, 47-51 *passim*; Lucan, *Civil War* 10, on Cleopatra and Caesar rather than Antony, stressing 'Egyptian' lasciviousness, *luxuria*, and duplicity; see esp. 10.60-81, 104-71, 332-98, 467-85. Lucan stresses the distinctive blend of *luxuria* and *saevitia* thought to typify 'Orientals', and his denunciation of Egyptian treachery and indifference to law and custom along with their capacity for unheard-of crimes (10.471-8) closely parallels the charges of Juvenal's speaker. To the strategic erasure of Egypt's Hellenization, cf. Ovid's barbarizing picture of Tomis in *Tristia* 3-5 *passim* (see Habinek 1998: 158-9).

16. On the Grecization of Egyptian religion in Plutarch's treatise, see Alston 1996: 103-4 and the commentary of Griffiths (1970). On Roman Egyptomania and Roman–Egyptian cultural syncretism, especially in religion, see Alston 1996: 100-1 and references to the main studies there. On Roman late Republican and early Imperial representations of Egypt in general, see Sonnabend 1986; on Greek discourses of Egypt up to the time of Alexander, see most recently Vasunia 2001.

17. Quoted in Spurr 1993: 82; see Chapter 3 n. 22 above for citation of the Churchill text.

18. Quoted in Spurr 1993: 91, from the translation of C. Farrington (New York: 1966, 34).

19. Spurr 1993: 88, quoting from a 1931 translation by J. Peile (repr. New York: 1970, 19).

20. On the cannibal sign in early modern colonial texts, see also Motohashi 1999; see Lestringant 1997 for a more general cultural history of cannibalism.

21. Boehmer makes the same connection between the representation of land and people: 'The insecurity surrounding colonial interpretation is ... reflected in imagery of the vastness or shapelessness of the other land ... and of the distressing opacity of native peoples to European understanding, usually represented as their ignorance, their black magic, and strange fetishism' (1995: 93).

22. Spurr 1993: 36; on the tropes of 'affirmation' and 'appropriation', see above Chapter 3, 114-17, and Spurr 1993: chs 2 and 7.

23. On the imperfectly assimilated native in modern colonial discourse, see Chapter 3, 107-9. On the acquisition of Romanness, see Chapter 3, 109-10 with n. 29 and references there.

24. (www.nationalreview.com/ledeen/ledeen200404070843.asp).

25. See Anderson 1987 and esp. McKim 1986 for complete analysis of the ironic strain and how it skewers the poem's speaker and his sentiments, often turning the critical spotlight on Roman culture instead. Tennant 1995 argues against an author/*persona* distinction: Juvenal is expressing his own views in this poem.

26. 'An Outpost of Progress', in *The Complete Short Fiction of Joseph Conrad*, vol. 1, ed. S. Hynes, New York: 1991, 40, 43-4.

27. Boehmer 1995: 158. See 138-79 on the British literature of late colonial disillusionment, including Waugh, about whom she writes: 'In the caricatures of ... Waugh late colonialist cynicism achieves what is perhaps its culminating expression. Waugh's tales ... transform the conventional motifs of empire into the stuff of mock-exotic and pseudo-epic. Slapstick and grotesque effects parody Boy's Own heroics. The trend is consistently towards deflation. The grand themes of the civilizing mission ... are converted into jokes. But Waugh's devices do not mask the underlying social and political structures of his world' (165).

Works Cited

Alcock, S. and K. Morrison (2001), 'Imperial Ideologies', in S. Alcock, T. D'Altroy, K. Morrison, and C. Sinopoli, eds, *Empires: Perspectives from Archaeology and History*, Cambridge: 279-82.

Alston, R. (1996), 'Conquest by Text: Juvenal and Plutarch on Egypt', in Webster and Cooper 1996: 99-109.

Anderson, B. (1983), *Imagined Communities: Reflections on the Origins and Spread of Nationalism*, London.

Anderson, W. (1961), 'Juvenal and Quintilian', *Yale Classical Studies* 17: 1-91. Reprinted in W. Anderson 1982: 396-486.

—— (1964), 'Roman Satirists and Literary Criticism', *Bucknell Review* 12: 106-13. Reprinted in W. Anderson 1982: 3-10.

—— (1970), '*Lascivia* vs. *Ira*: Martial and Juvenal', *California Studies in Classical Antiquity* 3: 1-34. Reprinted in W. Anderson 1982: 362-95.

—— (1982), *Essays on Roman Satire*, Princeton.

—— (1987), 'Juvenal *Satire* 15: Cannibals and Culture', *Ramus* 16: 203-14.

Ando, C. (2000), *Imperial Ideology and Provincial Loyalty in the Roman Empire*, Berkeley.

Arieti, J. (1990), 'Horatian Philosophy and the Regulus Ode (3.5)', *Transactions of the American Philological Association* 120: 209-20.

Armstrong, J. (1982), *Nations before Nationalism*, Chapel Hill.

Ashcroft, B., G. Griffiths and H. Tiffin (2000), *Post-Colonial Studies: The Key Concepts*, London and New York.

Baldwin, B. (1990), 'Tacitus *Agricola* 21: An Explanation', *Mnemosyne* 43: 455-6.

Baruma, I. and A. Margalit (2002), 'Occidentalism', *New York Review of Books* 49.1 (17 January 2002): 4-7.

—— (2004), *Occidentalism: The West in the Eyes of its Enemies*, New York.

Bastomsky, S. (1988), 'Tacitus *Histories* 4.73-4: A Unique View of Roman Rule?', *Latomus* 47: 413-16.

Bellandi, F. (1991), 'Mito e ideologia: età dell'oro e *mos maiorum* in Giovenale', *Materiali e discussioni per l'analisi dei testi classici* 27: 89-128.

Benario, H. (1991), 'Tacitus' View of the Empire and the *Pax Romana*', *Aufstieg und Niedergang der römischen Welt* 33.5: 3332-53.

Bernstein, H., T. Hewitt and A. Thomas (1992), 'Capitalism and the Expansion of Europe', in T. Allen and A. Thomas, eds, *Poverty and Development in the 1990s*, Oxford: 168-84.

Blundell, S. (1986), *The Origins of Civilization in Greek and Roman Thought*, London and Sydney.

Boehmer, E. (1995), *Colonial and Postcolonial Literature*, Oxford.

Bond, R. (2001), '*Urbs Satirica*: The City in Roman Satire', *Scholia* 10: 77-91.

Bonjour, M. (1975), *Terre Natale: étude sur une composante affective du patriotisme romaine*, Paris.

Borzsák, S., ed. (1992), *Cornelius Tacitus I.1: Annales I-VI*, Stuttgart and Leipzig.

Bowersock, G.W. (1986), 'The Mechanics of Subversion in the Roman Provinces', in A. Giovannini, ed., *Opposition et résistance à l'empire d'Auguste à Trajan*, Geneva: 291-320.

Bowman, A.K. (1986), *Egypt after the Pharaohs*, Berkeley.

Braund, S.H. (1989), 'City and Country in Roman Satire', in S.H. Braund, ed., *Satire and Society in Ancient Rome*, Exeter: 23-47.

Braund, S.M. (1996a), *The Roman Satirists and Their Masks*, London.

————, ed. (1996b), *Juvenal: Satires, Book I*, Cambridge.

———— (1997), 'Roman Assimilations of the Other: *Humanitas* at Rome', *Acta Classica* 40: 5-32.

Brunt, P.A. (1960), 'Tacitus on the Batavian Revolt', *Latomus* 19: 494-517. Reprinted in Brunt 1990: 33-52.

———— (1978), '*Laus Imperii*', in P. Garnsey and C. Whittaker, eds, *Imperialism and the Ancient World*, Cambridge: 159-91. Reprinted in Brunt 1990: 288-323.

———— (1990), *Roman Imperial Themes*, Oxford.

Cannadine, D. (2001), *Ornamentalism: How the British Saw Their Empire*, Oxford.

Cartledge, P. (1993), *The Greeks: A Portrait of Self and Others*, Oxford and New York.

Clausen, W. (1959, rev. 1992), *A. Persi Flacci et D. Iuni Iuvenalis Saturae*, Oxford.

Courtney, E., ed. (1980), *A Commentary on the Satires of Juvenal*, London.

Dauge, Y. (1981), *Le barbare: recherches sur la conception romaine de la barbarie et de la civilization*, Brussels.

Davis, G. (1983), 'Silence and Decorum: Encomiastic Convention and the Epilogue of Horace *Carmen* 3.2', *Classical Antiquity* 2: 9-26.

De Decker, J. (1913), *Juvenalis declamans. Étude sur la rhétorique déclamatoire dans les* Satires *de Juvénal*, Ghent.

DeGrazia, V. (1992), *How Fascism Ruled Women: Italy, 1922-1945*, Berkeley.

Derné, S. (2000), 'Men's Sexuality and Women's Subordination in Indian Nationalisms', in Mayer 2000: 237-58.

Dupont, F. (1995), 'En Germanie, c'est-à-dire nulle part: rhétorique de l'altérité et rhétorique de l'identité: l'aporie descriptive d'un territoire barbare dans la *Germanie* de Tacite', in A. Rousselle, ed., *Frontières terrestres, frontières célestes dans l'Antiquité*, Perpignan: 189-219.

Dyson, S. (1971), 'Native Revolts in the Roman Empire', *Historia* 20: 239-74.

Edelman, L. (1992), 'Tearooms and Sympathy, or The Epistemology of the Water Closet', in Parker, Russo, Sommer and Yaeger 1992: 263-84.

Edwards, C. (1993), *The Politics of Immorality in Ancient Rome*, Cambridge.

Feminist Review (1993), Special issue: 'Nationalisms and National Identities'.

Ferguson, J., ed. (1979), *Juvenal: The Satires*, New York.

Freeman, P. (1996), 'British Imperialism and the Roman Empire', in Webster and Cooper 1996: 19-34.

Gaisser, J.H. (1994), 'The Roman Odes at School: The Rise of the Imperial Horace', *Classical World* 87: 443-56.

Galinsky, K. (1988), 'The Anger of Aeneas', *American Journal of Philology* 109: 321-48.

Gellner, E. (1983), *Nations and Nationalism*, Oxford.

Gilman, S. (1985), *Difference and Pathology: Stereotypes of Sexuality, Race, and Madness*, Ithaca.

—— (1991), *Inscribing the Other*, Lincoln, Nebraska.

Goff, B., ed. (2005), *Classics and Colonialism*, London.

Griffiths, J.G., ed. (1970), *Plutarch's* de Iside et Osiride, Cardiff.

Gruen, E. (1984), *The Hellenistic World and the Coming of Rome*, Berkeley.

—— (1995), *Culture and National Identity in Republican Rome*, Ithaca.

Habinek, T. (1995), 'Ideology for an Empire in the Prefaces to Cicero's Dialogues', in A.J. Boyle, ed., *Roman Literature and Ideology: Ramus Essays for J.P. Sullivan*, Bendigo, Vic., Australia: 55-67.

—— (1998), *The Politics of Latin Literature: Writing, Identity, and Empire in Ancient Rome*, Princeton.

Hall, E. (1989), *Inventing the Barbarian: Greek Self-Definition through Tragedy*, Oxford.

Hardie, P. (1986), *Virgil's* Aeneid: *Cosmos and Imperium*, Oxford.

Harris, W. (1979), *War and Imperialism in Republican Rome, 327-70 BC*, Oxford.

Harrowitz, N. and B. Hyams, eds (1995), *Jews and Gender: Responses to Otto Weininger*, Philadelphia.

Hartog, F. (1988), *The Mirror of Herodotus: The Representation of the Other in the Writing of History*, trans. J. Lloyd, Berkeley.

Haynes, H. (2004), *The History of Make-Believe. Tacitus on Imperial Rome*, Berkeley.

Helsinger, E. (1997), *Rural Scenes and National Representation: Britain, 1815-1850*, Princeton.

Herman, A. (1997), *The Idea of Decline in Western History*, New York.

Hermand, J. (1992), *Old Dreams of a New Reich: Volkish Utopias and National Socialism*, trans. P. Levesque and S. Soldovieri, Bloomington.

Hermann, H.P., H.-M. Blitz and S. Mossman (1996), *Machtphantasie Deutschland: Nationalismus, Männlichkeit und Fremdenhass im*

Vaterlandsdiskurs deutscher Schriftsteller des 18. Jahrhunderts, Frankfurt am Main.

Highet, G. (1949-50), 'A Fight in the Desert: Juvenal 15 and a Modern Parallel', *Classical Journal* 45: 94-6.

Hoberman, J. (1995), 'Otto Weininger and the Critique of Jewish Masculinity', in Harrowitz and Hyams 1995: 141-53.

Hobsbawn, E. (1990), *Nations and Nationalism since 1780: Programme, Myth, Reality*, Cambridge.

——— (1994), 'The Nation as Invented Tradition', in J. Hutchinson and A. Smith, eds, *Nationalism*, Oxford: 76-83. (Reprinted from E. Hobsbawm and T. Ranger, *The Invention of Tradition* [Cambridge 1983] 13-14, 264-5, 271-8.)

Hodgart, M. (1969), *Satire*, London.

Howkins, A. (1986), 'The Discovery of Rural England', in R. Colls and P. Dodd, eds, *Englishness: Politics and Culture, 1880-1920*, London: 62-88.

Hulme, P. (1986), *Colonial Encounters: Europe and the Native Caribbean, 1492-1797*, London.

Hurst, H. and S. Owen, eds (2005), *Ancient Colonizations: Analogy, Similarity and Difference*, London.

Hutchinson, J. (1994), 'Cultural Nationalism and Moral Regeneration', in J. Hutchinson and A. Smith, eds, *Nationalism*, Oxford: 122-31. (Reprinted from J. Hutchinson, *The Dynamics of Cultural Nationalism: The Gaelic Revival and the Creation of the Irish National State* [London 1987] 12-19, 30-6.)

Innes, C.L. (1993), *Women and Nation in Irish Literature and Society, 1880-1935*, Athens, GA.

Isaac, B. (2004), *The Invention of Racism in Classical Antiquity*, Princeton.

Jameson, V. (1984), '*Virtus* Reformed: An 'Aesthetic Response' Reading of Horace *Odes* 3.2', *Transactions of the American Philological Association* 114: 219-40.

Jens, W. (1956), '*Libertas* bei Tacitus', *Hermes* 84: 331-52.

Johnson, W.R. (1987), *Momentary Monsters: Lucan and His Heroes*, Ithaca.

——— (1996), 'Male Victimology in Juvenal 6', *Ramus* 25: 170-86.

Jones, G. Stedman (1971), *Outcast London: A Study in the Relationship Between Classes in Victorian Society*, Oxford.

Joplin, P. (1990), 'Ritual Work on Human Flesh: Livy's Lucretia and the Rape of the Body Politic', *Helios* 17: 51-70.

Joshel, S. (1992), 'The Body Female and the Body Politic: Livy's Lucretia and Verginia', in A. Richlin, ed., *Pornography and Representation in Greece and Rome*, New York and Oxford: 112-30.

Journal of Gender Studies (1992), Special Issue: 'Feminism and Nationalism'.

Just, R. (1989), *Women in Athenian Law and Life*, London and New York.

Works Cited

Kandiyoti, D. (1991), 'Identity and its Discontents: Women and the Nation', *Millennium: Journal of International Studies* 20: 429-44.

Keitel, E. (1993), 'Speech and Narrative in *Histories* 4', in T.J. Luce and A.J. Woodman, eds, *Tacitus and the Tacitean Tradition*, Princeton: 39-58.

Kenney, E. (1963), 'Juvenal: Satirist or Rhetorician?', *Latomus* 22: 704-20.

Kernan, A. (1959), *The Cankered Muse: Satire in the English Renaissance*, New Haven.

Ketelsen, U.-K. (1976), *Völkisch-nationale und nationalsozialistische Literatur in Deutschland, 1890-1945*, Stuttgart.

Koestermann, E., ed. (1970), *Cornelius Tacitus II.2: Germania, Agricola, Dialogus de Oratoribus*, Leipzig.

Konstan, D. (1993), 'Sexuality and Power in Juvenal's Second Satire', *Liverpool Classical Monthly* 18: 12-14.

Koonz, C. (1987), *Mothers in the Fatherland: Women, Family, and Nazi Politics*, New York.

Kraggerud, E. (1995), 'The Sixth Roman Ode of Horace: Its Date and Function', *Symbolae Osloenses* 70: 54-67.

Leach, E.W. (1974), *Vergil's Eclogues: Landscapes of Experience*, Ithaca.

Lestringant, F. (1997), *Cannibals: The Discovery and Representation of the Cannibal from Columbus to Jules Verne*, trans. R. Morris, Berkeley.

Lewis, N. (1983), *Life in Egypt under Roman Rule*, Oxford.

Link, J. (1991), 'Fanatics, Fundamentalists, Lunatics, and Drug Traffickers – the New Southern Enemy Image', trans. L. Schulte-Sasse, *Cultural Critique* 19: 33-53.

Lohmann, D. (1991), 'Horaz *Carmen* 3. 2 und der Zyklus der Römer-Oden', *Der altsprachliche Unterricht* 34: 62-75.

Loomba, A. (1998), *Colonialism/Postcolonialism*, London and New York.

Lovejoy, A. and G. Boas. (1935), *Primitivism and Related Ideas in Antiquity*, Baltimore.

Lund, A. (1990), *Zum Germanenbild der Römer: Eine Einführung in die antike Ethnographie*, Heidelberg.

McClintock, A. (1995), *Imperial Leather: Race, Gender, and Sexuality in the Colonial Contest*, New York.

——— (1996), ' "No Longer in a Future Heaven": Nationalism, Gender, and Race', in G. Eley and R.G. Suny, eds, *Becoming National: A Reader*, Oxford: 260-84.

McKim, R. (1986), 'Philosophers and Cannibals: Juvenal's Fifteenth Satire', *Phoenix* 40: 58-71.

MacMullen, R. (1966), *Enemies of the Roman Order: Treason, Unrest, and Alienation in the Empire*, Cambridge, MA.

——— (2000), *Romanization in the Time of Augustus*, New Haven.

Maleuvre, J.-Y. (1995), 'Les Odes Romaines d'Horace, ou un chef-d'oeuvre ignoré de la cacozélie (presque) invisible', *Revue belge de philologie et d'histoire* 73: 53-72.

Martindale, C. (1993), *Redeeming the Text: Latin Poetry and the Hermeneutics of Reception*, Cambridge.

Mayer, T., ed. (2000), *Gender Ironies of Nationalism: Sexing the Nation*, London and New York.

Miles, G. (1997), *Livy: Reconstructing Early Rome*, Ithaca.

Millett, M. (1990), *The Romanization of Britain: An Essay in Archaeological Interpretation*, Cambridge.

Mills, S. (1991), *Discourses of Difference: An Analysis of Women's Travel Writing and Colonialism*, London.

Moghadam, V. (1994), *Gender and National Identity: Women and Politics in Muslim Society*, London.

Moreau, J. (1940), 'Une scène d'anthropophagie en Égypte en l'an 127 de nôtre ère (*Sat.* XV de Juvénal)', *Chronique d'Égypte* 15: 279-85.

Morford, M. (1991), 'How Tacitus Defined Liberty', *Aufstieg und Niedergang der römischen Welt* 33.5: 3420-50.

Mosse, G. (1985), *Nationalism and Sexuality: Middle-Class Morality and Sexual Norms in Modern Europe*, Madison.

Motohashi, T. (1999), 'The Discourse of Cannibalism in Early Modern Travel Writing', in S. Clark, ed., *Travel Writing and Empire: Postcolonial Theory in Transit*, New York and London: 83-99.

Nappa, C. (1998), '*Praetextati Mores*: Juvenal's Second Satire', *Hermes* 126: 90-108.

O'Gorman, E. (1993), 'No Place Like Rome: Identity and Difference in the *Germania* of Tacitus', *Ramus* 22: 135-54.

Parker, A., M. Russo, D. Sommer and P. Yaeger, eds (1992), *Nationalisms and Sexualities*, New York.

Parry, A. (1963), 'The Two Voices of Virgil's *Aeneid*', *Arion* 2: 66-80.

Pickering, J. and S. Kehde, eds (1997), *Narratives of Nostalgia, Gender, and Nationalism*, New York.

Pickering-Iazzi, R., ed. (1995), *Mothers of Invention: Women, Italian Fascism, and Culture*, Minneapolis.

Porter, D. (1987), *Horace's Poetic Journey: A Reading of Odes 1-3*, Princeton.

Powell, B. (1979), 'What Juvenal Saw: Egyptian Religion and Anthropology in Satire XV', *Rheinisches Museum* 122: 185-9.

Quinn, K., ed. (1980), *Horace: The Odes*, New York.

Rankin, H. (1969.), 'Eating People is Right: Petronius 141 and a Topos', *Hermes* 97: 381-4.

Richlin, A. (1984), 'Invective Against Women in Roman Satire', *Arethusa* 17: 67-80.

———— (1992), *The Garden of Priapus: Sexuality and Aggression in Roman Humor*, 2nd edn, Oxford.

———— (1993), 'Not Before Homosexuality: The Materiality of the *Cinaedus* and the Roman Law against Love between Men', *Journal of the History of Sexuality* 3: 523-73.

Rives, J.B. (1999), *Tacitus: Germania*, Oxford.

Roberts, M. (1988), 'The Revolt of Boudicca (Tacitus *Annals* 14.29-39) and the Assertion of *libertas* in Neronian Rome', *American Journal of Philology* 109: 118-32.

Rudd, N. (1986), 'The Idea of Empire in the *Aeneid*', in R. Cardwell and J. Hamilton, eds, *Virgil in a Cultural Tradition. Essays to Celebrate the Bimillennium*, Nottingham: 25-42.

Rutledge, S. (2000), 'Tacitus in Tartan: Textual Colonization and Expansionist Discourse in the *Agricola*', *Helios* 27: 75-95.

Said, E. (1979), *Orientalism*, New York.

Ste Croix, G.E.M. de (1981), *The Class Struggle in the Ancient Greek World*, London and Ithaca.

Sanborn, G., ed. (2004), Herman Melville: *Typee*, Boston and New York.

Santirocco, M. (1995), 'Horace and Augustan Ideology', *Arethusa* 28: 225-43.

Schulte-Sasse, L. (1996), *Entertaining the Third Reich: Illusions of Wholeness in Nazi Cinema*, Durham, NC.

Schumpeter, J.A. (1951), *Imperialism and Social Classes*, trans. H. Norden, New York.

Seager, R. (1993), 'Horace and Augustus: Poetry and Policy', in N. Rudd, ed., *Horace 2000: A Celebration: Essays for the Bimillennium*, London and Ann Arbor: 23-40.

Sedgewick, E.K. (1992), 'Nationalisms and Sexualities in the Age of Wilde', in Parker, Russo, Sommer and Yaeger 1992: 235-45.

Sengoopta, C. (2000), *Otto Weininger: Sex, Science and Self in Imperial Vienna*, Chicago.

Shackleton Bailey, D.R. (1985), *Horatius: Opera*. Stuttgart.

Shotter, D. (1978), '*Principatus ac libertas*', *Ancient Society* 9: 235-55.

Shumate, N. (1997), 'Compulsory Pretence and the 'Theatricalization of Experience' in Tacitus', in C. Deroux, ed., *Studies in Latin Literature and Roman History* 8, Brussels: 364-403.

Singleton, D. (1972), 'Juvenal 6.1-20 and Some Ancient Attitudes to the Golden Age', *Greece and Rome* 19: 151-64.

―――― (1983), 'Juvenal's Fifteenth Satire: A Reading', *Greece and Rome* 30: 198-207.

Smelik, K. and E. Hemelrijk (1984), ' "Who knows not what monsters demented Egypt worships?" Opinions on Egyptian Animal Worship in Antiquity as Part of the Ancient Conception of Egypt', *Aufstieg und Niedergang der römischen Welt* 2.17.4: 1852-2000.

Smith, A. (1997), 'The "Golden Age" and National Renewal', in G. Hosking and G. Schöpflin, eds, *Myths and Nationhood*, New York: 36-59.

―――― (2000), *The Nation in History: Historiographical Debates about Ethnicity and Nationalism*, Hanover, NH.

Smyth, G. (1997), *The Novel and the Nation: Studies in the New Irish Fiction*, London.

Sonnabend, H. (1986), *Fremdenbild und Politik. Vorstellungen der Römer von Ägypten und dem Partherreich in der späten Republik und der frühen Kaiserzeit*, Frankfurt.

Souza, P. de. (1996), ' "They are the Enemies of All Mankind": Justifying Roman Imperialism in the Late Republic', in Webster and Cooper 1996: 125-33.

Spackman, B. (1995), 'Fascist Women and the Rhetoric of Virility', in Pickering-Iazzi 1995: 100-20.

Spurr, D. (1993), *The Rhetoric of Empire: Colonial Discourse in Journalism, Travel Writing, and Imperial Administration*, Durham, NC

Steel, C. (2001), *Cicero, Rhetoric, and Empire*, Oxford.

Straub, J. (1977), '*Imperium-Pax-Libertas*', *Gymnasium* 84: 136-48.

Syed, Y. (2004), *Vergil's* Aeneid *and the Roman Self: Subject and Nation in Literary Discourse*, Ann Arbor.

Tennant, P. (1995), 'Biting Off More than One Can Chew: A Recent Trend in the Interpretation of Juvenal's Fifteenth Satire', *Akroterion* 40: 120-34.

Toll, K. (1991), 'The *Aeneid* as an Epic of National Identity: *Italiam laeto socii clamore salutant*', *Helios* 18: 3-14.

——— (1997), 'Making Roman-ness and the *Aeneid*', *Classical Antiquity* 16: 34-56.

Travers, M. (2001), *Critics of Modernity: The Literature of the Conservative Revolution in Germany, 1890-1933*, New York.

Trevor, W. (1995), *Felicia's Journey*, London.

Trzaska-Richter, C. (1991), *Furor Teutonicus: das römische Germanenbild in Politik und Propaganda von den Anfängen bis zum 2. Jahrhundert nach Christus*, Trier.

Vance, N. (1985), *The Sinews of the Spirit: The Ideal of Christian Manliness in Victorian Literature and Religious Thought*, Cambridge.

van Minnen, P. (1998), 'Boorish or Bookish? Literature in Egyptian Villages in the Fayum in the Greco-Roman Period', *Journal of Juristic Papyrology* 28: 99-184.

Vasunia, P. (2001), *The Gift of the Nile: Hellenizing Egypt from Aeschylus to Alexander*, Berkeley.

Veyne, P. (1993), '*Humanitas*: Romans and non-Romans', in A. Giardina, ed., *The Romans*, trans. L. Cochrane, Chicago: 342-69.

Wallace-Hadrill, A. (1982), 'The Golden Age and Sin in Augustan Ideology', *Past and Present* 95: 19-36.

Walser, G. (1951), *Rom, das Reich, und die fremden Völker in der Geschichtschreibung der frühen Kaiserzeit. Studien zur Glaubwürdigkeit des Tacitus*, Baden-Baden.

Webster, J. (1996a), 'Roman Imperialism and the "Post-Imperial" Age', in Webster and Cooper 1996: 1-17.

——— (1996b), 'Ethnographic Barbarity: Colonial Discourse and "Celtic Warrior Societies" ', in Webster and Cooper 1996: 111-23.

———— and N. Cooper, eds (1996), *Roman Imperialism. Post-Colonial Perspectives*, Leicester.

Wellesley, K., ed. (1986), *Cornelius Tacitus I.2: Annales XI-XVI*, Leipzig.

————, ed. (1989), *Cornelius Tacitus II.2: Historiae*, Leipzig.

Welwei, K.-W. and M. Meier (1997), 'Der Topos des ruhmvollen Todes in der zweiten Römerode des Horaz', *Klio* 79: 107-16.

Williams, C. (1999), *Roman Homosexuality: Ideologies of Masculinity in Classical Antiquity*, New York and Oxford.

Williams, G., ed. (1969), *The Third Book of Horace's* Odes, Oxford.

Winkler, M. (1983), *The Persona in Three Satires of Juvenal*, Hildesheim and New York.

Woolf, G. (1990), 'World Systems Analysis and the Roman Empire', *Journal of Roman Archaeology* 12: 223-34.

———— (1998), *Becoming Roman: The Origins of Provincial Civilization in Gaul*, Cambridge.

Wyke, M. (1992), 'Augustan Cleopatras: Feminine Power and Poetic Authority', in A. Powell, ed., *Roman Poetry and Propaganda in the Age of Augustus*, London: 98-140.

Yuval-Davis, N. (1997), *Gender and Nation*, London.

———— and F. Anthias (1989), *Woman-Nation-State*, London.

Zanker, P. (1988), *The Power of Images in the Age of Augustus*, trans. A. Shapiro, Ann Arbor.

Index

Alcock, Susan, 15-16
Alston, Richard, 151
Anderson, Benedict, 8-9
Anthias, Floya, 61-2
anti-Semitism: compared to Roman view of Greeks, 32, 162n.19, 163n.26; feminization of Jews, 26, 35-6; in Juvenal, 32, 42; in modern nationalist discourse, 26, 36-9, 162n.19; and Nazism, 48-50, 163n.26
Antony, 145, 174-5n.15
Armstrong, John, 10
artifice, 27-8, 43-4, 47, 59, 95, 113
artists, 58-9
Ashcroft, Bill, 9, 12, 82
Augustus, 26, 50, 56-7, 64, 67-8, 77-8, 145

barbarians: assimilated, 105-14, 121; Darwin's view of, 100-1; and depictions of Egypt, 145; and modern political discourse, 155-7; as Other, 96-105, 114; as reverse of Noble Savage, 96, 99, 143, 146; and Roman imperialism, 100, 114, 117-18; in Tacitus, 96-127, 130, 143; and women, 99
Baruma, Ian, 53-4
Bastomsky, Saul, 121
Bernstein, Henry, 159n.1
Blixen, Karen (Isak Dineson), 122-3
Boas, George, 81-2
Boehmer, Elleke, 58, 63, 88, 96-102 passim, 147, 150, 157-8, 168n.4, 170n.20, 171n.28

Braund, Susanna, 21, 47, 140-1, 164n.35
Brunt, Peter, 113

Caesar, 16, 83, 93, 168n.8, 174n.15
Cannadine, David, 123
cannibalism, 130-4, 136-7, 145-6, 151-2, 157, 173n.4
capitalism 7-11, 54
ceremonies, public. *See* rituals
Churchill, Winston, 101-2, 148-9
cinaedus, 20, 24
city and country: in anti-colonial discourse, 58-9; in English nationalist discourse, 50-3, 59-61; in German nationalist discourse, 35-6, 46-50, 52-3, 59; in Horace, 68, 72, 75-7; in Irish nationalist discourse, 59, 76-7; in Juvenal, 31, 41-6, 47-8, 51-3, 135; in Tacitus, 93, 126
Cleopatra, 26, 56, 145, 170n.24, 174-5n.5
coinage, 77
colonialism: anti-colonial movements, 58-9, 63-4; British, 100-3, 116-17; French, 30, 131; and gender, 99-104, 150-2; and natives, 107-9; and rhetoric, 15-16, 131, 146-9; study of, 12-14
Conrad, Joseph, 157
Courtney, Edward, 144-5
Curtius Rufus, Quintus, 81

Darwin, Charles, 100-1, 147-8
decline, topos of, 7, 46, 52, 57-8, 142-5

Dennery, Etienne, 149-50
Derné, Steve, 63
De Valera, Eamon, 76-7
Dineson, Isak. *See* Karen Blixen
disease, imagery of, 29, 38-9, 162
Domitian, 95, 126

Edelman, Lee, 40
Egypt, 26, 56, 129-54
enemies, national, 19, 21-3, 26, 28-
    9, 32, 37, 56, 144-5, 149-51

Fanon, Frantz, 149
film, 47-50, 161n.14
foreigners: in British nationalist
    discourse, 52-3; in Horace, 68,
    72; in Juvenal, 19, 21-3, 26-8, 31-
    2, 37-9, 41, 43, 45; in nationalist
    discourse, 35, 38-9, 48, 59; in
    Nazi ideology, 47-8; in Tacitus,
    95, 113-14; and US Cold War
    purges, 40
foundation myth, 57, 58

Gaisser, Julia, 78
gender: in anti-colonial movements,
    63-4; in colonial discourse, 99-
    104, 150-2; in Horace, 68-9, 71-4,
    78-9; and imperialism, 78-9; in
    Juvenal, 21-2, 27, 40; in nation-
    alist discourse, 34-5, 55, 61-7; in
    Tacitus, 89-92, 95
German Youth Movement, 36, 60
Gibbon, Edward, 52
Golden Age: in Horace, 75-6; in
    Juvenal, 44-6, 143, 164n.34; in
    nationalist discourse, 57, 68,
    165n.2; in Tacitus, 90, 97. *See
    also* past
Greece and Greeks: Augustan view
    of, 145-6, 174-5n.15; and depic-
    tions of Egypt, 144-6, 173n.1;
    and imperialism, 16; in Juvenal,
    26-9, 31, 32, 43, 45, 138, 162n.19,

163n.27; and modern anti-
    Semitism, 32, 162n.19, 163n.26;
    view of homosexuals, 65-6; view
    of race (*ethnos*), 109
Griffiths, J. Gwyn, 82

Harris, William, 11, 12
Haynes, Holly, 111
Helsinger, Elizabeth, 51
Hesiod, 22
Heyck, Hans, 36
Hobsbawm, Eric, 16, 55-7, 77
Hobson, John, 8
Homer: *Iliad*, 69-70, 125; *Odyssey*,
    133-4
homosexuals, 160n.4; Athenian view
    of, 65-6; *cinaedus*, 20, 24; in
    Juvenal, 21-3, 25-8, 40, 140,
    161nn.11-12; in nationalist
    discourse, 35-6, 37, 47, 64-5; and
    US Cold War purges, 40, 164n.30
Horace, 67-79; city and country in,
    68, 72, 75-7; foreigners in, 68, 72;
    gender in, 68-9, 71-4, 78-9; and
    rhetoric, 78-9; Roman past in,
    68, 75-6; and topos of decline, 57-
    8; women in, 73-5
  Works: 'Roman' Odes, 55, 61, 67-8,
    78; *Odes* 3.2, 68-70; *Odes* 3.5, 68-
    9, 70-3; *Odes* 3.6, 68-9, 73-7
Howkins, Alun, 50, 51-2, 60-1
Hulme, Peter, 130
humanitas, 109, 140-1, 171n.29
Hurst, Henry, 10
Hutchinson, John, 57-8, 75

imperialism: and Athens, 16;
    British, 11, 122-4, 159n.3; and
    capitalism, 9-11; and gender, 78-
    9; justifications of, 114-15,
    118-19, 122-4; and nostalgia,
    122-6; and rhetoric, 7, 15, 58, 84-
    8, 100-3, 113, 115-17, 131-2;
    Roman, 8-9, 11, 13, 16, 100, 109-

10, 114, 117-18, 130; study of, 8-14, 159n.1

Iraq, 155-7

Jews. *See* anti-Semitism

Juvenal, 19-54, 129-54; anti-Semitism in, 32, 42; artifice in, 43; and Cicero, 173n.5; city and country in, 31, 41-6, 47-8, 51-3, 135; on Egypt, 130-54; foreigners in, 19, 21-3, 26-8, 31-2, 37-9, 41, 43, 45; gender in, 21-2, 27, 40; Golden Age in, 44-6, 143, 164n.34; Greeks in, 26-9, 31, 32, 43, 45, 138, 162n.19, 163n.27; homosexuals in, 21-3, 25-8, 40, 140, 161nn.11-12; immigrants in, 26-8, 31, 38; Noble Savage in, 139-40; Orientalism in, 135, 137, 139; Other in, 29-30, 33, 130-7, 148-9; poetic persona, 19-22, 55, 132, 157-8, 160n.9, 175n.25; and rhetoric, 19-21, 26, 33-4, 38-9, 43, 46, 137-8; and topos of decline, 46, 52, 142-4; women in, 21-4, 27, 40

Works: Satire 1, 21, 26, 28, 30, 37-8, 39, 41-2, 47, 136; Satire 2, 21, 24-5, 29, 42, 140, 161n.11; Satire 3, 21, 26, 28-9, 30-1, 37-8, 41-7, 136; Satire 6, 21-7, 42, 45; Satire 9, 25; Satire 15, 129-55

Kipling, Rudyard, 102, 108, 115-17, 150-1

lascivia, 129-30

Le Bon, Gustave, 48

Ledeen, Michael, 155-7

Lenin, Vladimir, 8

libertas, 96-7, 107, 120, 169n.11

Link, Jürgen, 141

Livy, 63, 161n.10

Loomba, Ania, 15

Lovejoy, Arthur O., 81-2

luxuria, 45, 64, 68-9, 81, 92-3, 94, 98, 130, 174n.15

McClintock, Anne, 39-40, 57, 61-3, 67, 77, 151-2

Margalit, Avishai, 53-4

Martindale, Charles, 14

Marxism, 8-10, 159n.2

Melville, Herman, 85, 87, 168n.6

Miles, Gary, 58-9

monuments, public, 56, 77

Morrison, Kathleen, 15-16

Mosse, George, 20, 34, 35-9, 46-7, 62, 64-6

nationalism: African, 63; Afrikaner, 57, 67; and anti-Semitism, 26, 36-9, 162n.19; and artists, 58-9; British, 39, 52-3, 56, 64-5; and capitalism, 7-11; and construction of the Other, 33, 37, 39-41, 131, 161-2n.15, 163-4n.29; and fascism, 67; and foreigners, 35, 38-9, 48, 52-3, 59; and foundation myths, 57, 58; French, 131; and gender, 34-5, 55, 61-7; German, 35-7, 46-50, 52-3, 56-7, 59, 64-5; and homosexuals, 35-6, 37, 47, 64-5; Indian, 63; Irish, 59, 63-4, 76-7; and mass media, 77; and modernity, 7-10, 32-4, 64-6; and perennialism, 10; and race, 28-9, 32; and rhetoric, 7, 12-16, 32-4, 37-41, 59-62, 79, 131; study of, 7-14, 32-4, 79; and women, 22-3, 54, 61-7

nature, 36, 47, 85-6, 99, 104-5, 138-41, 168n.6

Nazism, 33-4, 46-50; and anti-Semitism, 48-50, 163n.26; and film, 47-50, 161n.14; and foreigners, 47-8

Nero, 95, 106, 126, 170n.19

Nietzsche, Friedrich, 66
Noble Savage: in classical literature, 81-2; in colonial discourse, 82-8, 92, 123-4; in Juvenal, 139-40; as reverse of barbarian, 96, 99, 143, 146; in Seneca, 81-2; in Tacitus, 88-96, 114, 120, 143; Tasaday as, 86-7, 168n.5
Nordau, Max, 46

Occidentalism, 53-4
O'Gorman, Ellen, 83, 95-6
Orientalism: and Augustan view of Greek culture, 145-6, 174-5n.15; and construction of national enemies, 26, 149-51; and feminized colonial Other, 102, 139; in Horace, 72, 76; in Juvenal, 135, 137, 139; and Occidentalism, 53; and Edward Said, 15, 20; and study of colonialism, 15, 102; in Tacitus, 99
'Other', othering, 163-4n.29; barbarians as, 96-105, 114; and cannibalism, 132, 150-1; and European colonialism, 108-9; feminization of, 20, 22, 26-7, 36, 63-4, 99-100, 102-4, 130-2, 150-1, 161-2n.15, 170n.20; in Juvenal, 29-30, 33, 130-7, 148-9; and nationalism, 33, 37, 39-41, 131, 161-2n.15, 163-4n.29; and Noble Savage, 92; and Orientalism, 102, 139; and Roman imperialism, 109-10, 130; study of, 20-1
Ovid, 160n.6
Owen, Sara, 10

past, idealization of, 55-67, 68. *See also* Golden Age
pastoral. *See* city and country
perennialism, 10
Plutarch, 146
Porter, David, 69-70

race and racism, 28-9, 32, 34, 40, 63-4, 109, 162n.19
religion, 25, 78, 101, 132-5, 146, 148, 175n.16
rhetoric: and colonialism, 15-16, 131, 146-9; in Horace, 78-9; and imperialism, 7, 15, 58, 84-8, 100-3, 113, 115-17, 131-2; in Juvenal, 19-21, 26, 33-4, 38-9, 43, 46, 137-8; and nationalism, 7, 12-16, 32-4, 37-41, 59-62, 79, 131; in Tacitus, 82, 90-1, 93-6, 103-4, 117-22
Richlin, Amy, 140
rituals, public, 56-7, 115, 123
Rousseau, Jean-Jacques, 85, 104
Rutledge, Steven, 83, 167-8n.2, 170n.18

Said, Edward, 15, 20
Sallust, 68, 90-1
satire, 34, 46, 132, 164n.35, 165n.39
Schulte-Sasse, Linda, 33, 39, 47-50, 141, 161n.14
Schumpeter, Joseph, 11
Scythians, 81
Seneca, 81-2
slavery, 91-2, 107, 121
Smith, Anthony, 7-8
Smyth, Gerry, 59, 63
Souza, Philip de, 159n.5
Spurr, David, 30, 82-7, 96-7, 100-5, 108-9, 114-19 passim, 123, 147-54 passim, 167-8n.2
Strabo, 81
Suetonius, 57
superstitio, 99, 129-30
Swift, Jonathan, 157, 173n.4

Tacitus, 81-127; authorial views, 93-4, 107, 109-10, 112-13, 118-22, 168n.3, 169n.14; barbarians in, 96-127, 130, 143; city and country in, 93, 126; Egypt in,

190

129-30; foreigners in, 95, 113-14; gender roles in, 89-92, 95; Golden Age in, 90, 97; and justifications of imperialism, 117-19; nature in, 105; Noble Savage in, 88-96, 114, 120, 143; Orientalism in, 99; post-colonial readings of, 83-4; and rhetoric, 82, 90-1, 93-6, 103-4, 117-22

Works: *Agricola*, 83, 92, 93-4, 95, 98, 118, 124-7, 167-8n.2; *Annals*, 84, 88-9, 91-2, 95, 96-9, 102, 103, 106-7, 118-19, 124-7; *Dialogue on Orators*, 89, 168-9n.9; *Germania*, 84, 88-91, 95-6, 97-8, 118-19, 168n.7; *Histories*, 84, 97, 99, 106, 110-14, 119-20, 129-30

theatre, 22-4, 26-7, 35-6, 57, 89, 160n.6

Tiffin, Helen, 82

Toll, Katharine, 9

Trajan, 109

Travers, Martin, 47, 162n.19

Virgil, *Aeneid*, 9, 14, 16, 56-7, 69-71
virtus, 69-70, 72-3, 90-2

Walser, Gerold, 171n.31

Waugh, Evelyn, 122, 172n.42, 173n.4, 175-6n.27

Webster, Jane, 8, 9-10, 12, 100

Weininger, Otto, 34-6

Winkler, Martin, 45, 160n.9

women: and barbarians, 99; and construction of the Other, 20, 22, 26-7, 36, 63-4, 99-100, 102-4, 130-2, 150-1, 161-2n.15, 170n.20; and fascism, 67; in Horace, 73-5; in Juvenal, 21-4, 27, 40; in nationalist discourse, 22-3, 54, 61-7; in Tacitus, 89-91, 95; and theatre, 22-4

World War I, 48-50, 60-1, 66

Yuval-Davis, Nira, 61-2